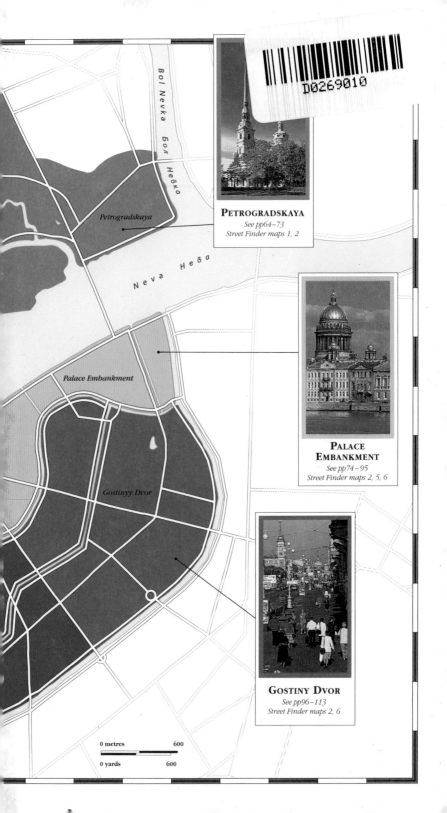

Bol Nevka Бол Невка

Petrogradskaya

PETROGRADSKAYA
See pp64–73
Street Finder maps 1, 2

Neva Нева

Palace Embankment

PALACE EMBANKMENT
See pp74–95
Street Finder maps 2, 5, 6

Gostinyy Dvor

GOSTINY DVOR
See pp96–113
Street Finder maps 2, 6

| 0 metres | 600 |
| 0 yards | 600 |

EYEWITNESS TRAVEL GUIDES

ST PETERSBURG

EYEWITNESS TRAVEL GUIDES

ST PETERSBURG

Main contributors:
CATHERINE PHILLIPS
CHRISTOPHER AND MELANIE RICE

DK

LONDON, NEW YORK,
MELBOURNE, MUNICH AND DELHI
www.dk.com

PROJECT EDITOR Anna Streiffert
ART EDITOR Marisa Renzullo
EDITOR Ella Milroy
DESIGNERS Gillian Andrews, Carolyn Hewitson,
Paul Jackson, Elly King, Nicola Rodway
VISUALIZER Joy Fitzsimmons
MAP CO-ORDINATORS Emily Green, David Pugh
PICTURE RESEARCH Brigitte Arora
DTP DESIGNERS Samantha Borland, Sarah Martin, Pamela Shiels

MAIN CONTRIBUTORS

Catherine Phillips, Christopher and Melanie Rice

PHOTOGRAPHERS

Demetrio Carrasco, John Heseltine

ILLUSTRATORS

Stephen Conlin, Maltings Partnership, Chris Orr & Associates,
Paul Weston

Reproduced by Colourscan, Singapore
Printed and bound by South China Printing Co. Ltd., China
First published in Great Britain in 1998
by Dorling Kindersley Limited, 80 Strand, London WC2R 0RL
Reprinted with revisions 2000, 2001, 2004

Copyright 1998, 2004 © Dorling Kindersley Limited, London
A Penguin Company

ISBN 0 7513 6883 0
FLOORS ARE REFERRED TO THROUGHOUT IN ACCORDANCE WITH EUROPEAN
USAGE; IE THE "FIRST FLOOR" IS THE FLOOR ABOVE GROUND LEVEL.

**The information in this
Dorling Kindersley Travel Guide is checked regularly.**
Every effort has been made to ensure that this book is as up-to-date as
possible at the time of going to press. Some details, however, such as
telephone numbers, opening hours, prices, gallery hanging
arrangements and travel information are liable to change. The
publishers cannot accept responsibility for any consequences arising
from the use of this book, nor for any material on third party websites,
and cannot guarantee that any website address in this book will be a
suitable source of travel information. We value the views and
suggestions of our readers very highly. Please write to: Publisher,
DK Eyewitness Travel Guides, Dorling Kindersley, 80 Strand,
London WC2R 0RL, Great Britain.

CONTENTS

HOW TO USE
THIS GUIDE 6

**Bronze model of ship, a symbol
of St Petersburg**

INTRODUCING
ST PETERSBURG

PUTTING
ST PETERSBURG
ON THE MAP 10

THE HISTORY OF
ST PETERSBURG 16

ST PETERSBURG
AT A GLANCE 32

ST PETERSBURG
THROUGH THE YEAR 50

**Petersburgers enjoying the snow
outside the Admiralty**

ST PETERSBURG
AREA BY AREA

VASILEVSKIY ISLAND 56

PETROGRADSKAYA 64

PALACE EMBANKMENT
74

Little Stable Bridge crossing the Moyka river

Pelmeny, **a meat or fish dumpling
dish originally from Siberia**

**15th-century icon of St George
and the Dragon, Russian Museum**

SURVIVAL GUIDE

**Golden statues of the Grand
Cascade at Peterhof**

TRAVELLERS'
NEEDS

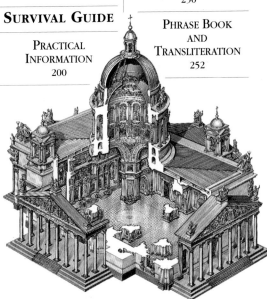
**St Isaac's Cathedral, lavishly decorated inside with more than
40 different stones and minerals**

HOW TO USE THIS GUIDE

THIS GUIDE WILL HELP you to get the most from your visit to St Petersburg, providing expert recommendations as well as detailed practical information. *Introducing St Petersburg* maps the city and sets it in its geographical, historical and cultural context, with a quick-reference timeline on the history pages giving the dates of Russia's rulers and significant events. *St Petersburg at a Glance* is an overview of the city's main attractions. *St Petersburg Area by Area* starts on page 54 and describes all the important

sights, using maps, photographs and illustrations. The sights are arranged in two groups: those in St Petersburg's central districts and those a little further afield. The guided walks reveals two characteristics of the city – its canals and its islands. *Beyond St Petersburg* describes sights requiring one- or two-day excursions. Hotel, restaurant, shopping and entertainment recommendations can be found in *Travellers' Needs*, while the *Survival Guide* includes tips on everything from transport and telephones to personal safety.

FINDING YOUR WAY AROUND THE SIGHTSEEING SECTION

Each of the seven sightseeing areas is colour-coded for easy reference. Every chapter opens with an introduction to the area it covers, describing its history and character. For central districts, this is followed by a Street-

by-Street map illustrating a particularly interesting part of the area; for sights beyond the city limits, by a regional map. A simple numbering system relates sights to the maps. Important sights are covered by several pages.

1 Introduction to the area
For easy reference, the sights are numbered and plotted on an area map, with metro stations shown where helpful. The key sights (great buildings, museums and open-air sights) are listed by category.

A locator map shows where you are in relation to other areas of the city centre.

Each area has colour-coded thumb tabs.

Locator map

The area shaded in pink is shown in greater detail on the Street-by-Street map.

2 Street-by-Street map
This gives a bird's eye view of interesting and important parts of each sightseeing area, with accurate drawings of all the buildings within them. The numbering of the sights ties in with the preceding area map and with the fuller descriptions on the pages that follow.

A suggested route for a walk is shown in red.

St Petersburg Area Map

The coloured areas shown on this map *(see pp14–15)* are the five main sightseeing areas into which central St Petersburg has been divided for this guide. Each is covered in a full chapter in the *St Petersburg Area by Area* section *(pp54–131)*. They are also shown on other maps throughout the book. In *St Petersburg at a Glance (pp32–49)*, for example, they help you locate the most interesting museums and palaces or where to see the city's many delightfully designed bridges. The maps' coloured borders match the coloured thumb tabs on each page of the section.

Numbers refer to each sight's position on the area map and its place in the chapter.

Practical information lists all the information you need to visit every sight, including a map reference to the *Street Finder* maps *(pp230–37)*.

3 Detailed information on each sight

All the important sights are described individually. They are listed to follow the numbering on the area map at the start of the section. The key to the symbols summarizing practical information is on the back flap.

A Visitors' Checklist provides the practical information you will need to plan your visit.

Story boxes highlight unique aspects or historical connections of a particular sight.

4 St Petersburg's major sights

These are given two or more full pages in the sightseeing area in which they are found. Buildings of interesting architecture are dissected to reveal their interiors; museums and galleries have colour-coded floorplans to help you find important exhibits.

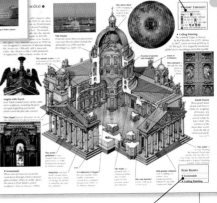

Stars indicate the best features or works of art.

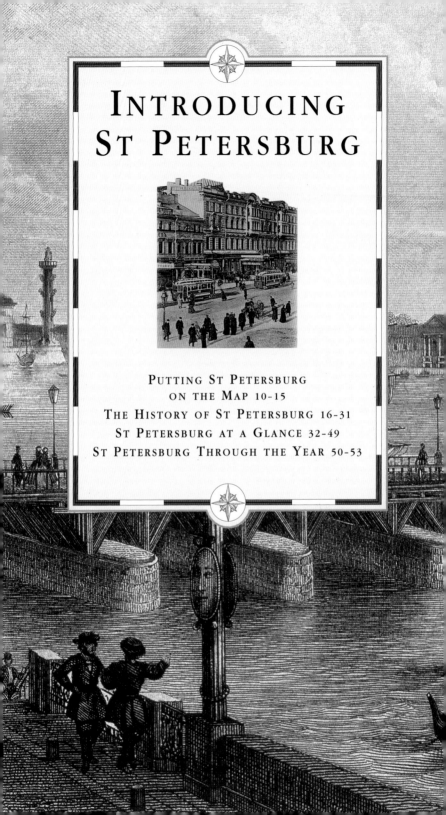

INTRODUCING
ST PETERSBURG

Putting St Petersburg on the Map

T HE RUSSIAN FEDERATION, or Russia as it is usually known, is the world's largest country, covering an area of 17.4 million sq km (6.7 million sq miles). Situated in its north-west corner, St Petersburg is Russia's second city, with a population of just under five million. Once Russia's capital and known as its "Window on the West" *(see pp20–21)*, the city was built on the marshy lands where the Neva joins the Gulf of Finland. Of the 13 countries bordering Russia, Estonia and Finland are St Petersburg's closest neighbours.

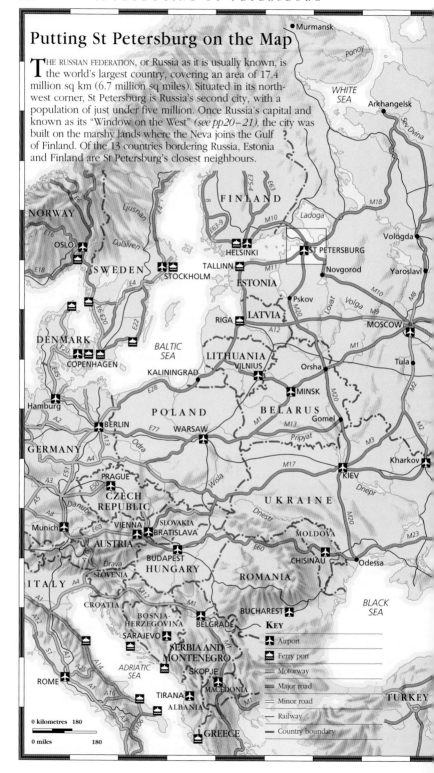

KEY

✈	Airport
⛴	Ferry port
—	Motorway
—	Major road
—	Minor road
—	Railway
—	Country boundary

0 kilometres   180

0 miles   180

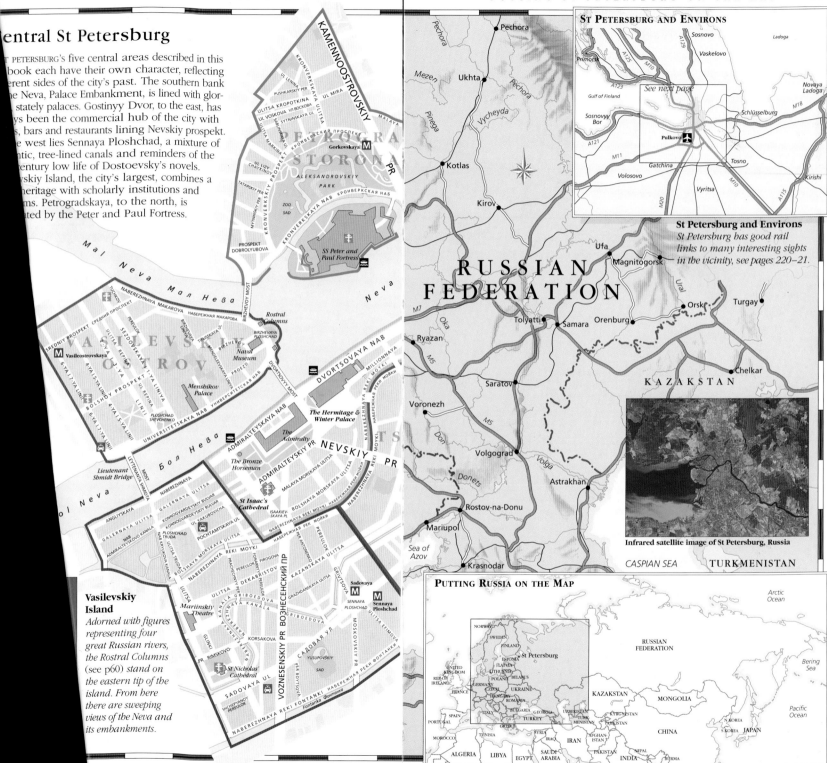

Central St Petersburg

ST PETERSBURG's five central areas described in this book each have their own character, reflecting different sides of the city's past. The southern bank of the Neva, Palace Embankment, is lined with glorious stately palaces. Gostinyy Dvor, to the east, has always been the commercial hub of the city with shops, bars and restaurants lining Nevskiy prospekt. To the west lies Sennaya Ploshchad, a mixture of romantic, tree-lined canals and reminders of the 19th-century low life of Dostoevsky's novels. Vasilevskiy Island, the city's largest, combines a naval heritage with scholarly institutions and museums. Petrogradskaya, to the north, is dominated by the Peter and Paul Fortress.

Vasilevskiy Island

Adorned with figures representing four great Russian rivers, the Rostral Columns (see p60) stand on the eastern tip of the island. From here there are sweeping views of the Neva and its embankments.

St Petersburg and Environs

St Petersburg has good rail links to many interesting sights in the vicinity, see pages 220–21.

Infrared satellite image of St Petersburg, Russia

PUTTING RUSSIA ON THE MAP

Greater St Petersburg

St Petersburg's first buildings were situated on islands on the north side of the Neva but, as the city started to grow, the centre moved south of the river. Today St Petersburg spreads out over more than 40 islands, with high-rise suburbs sprawling almost all the way out to the imperial country palaces (see pp146–59). The metro and suburban trains offer easy transport to sights situated further away from the city centre (see pp220–21).

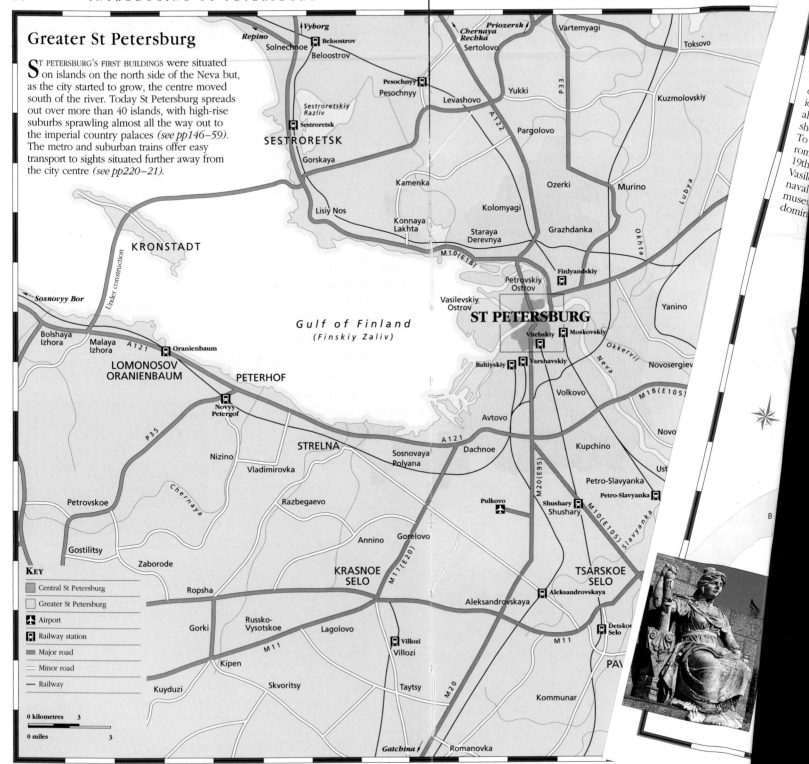

Gulf of Finland
(Finskiy Zaliv)

KRONSTADT

Sosnovyy Bor

Vyborg
Repino
Solnechnoe
Beloostrov
Beloostrov
Sestroretskiy Razliv
Pesochnyy
Pesochnyy
SESTRORETSK
Sestroretsk
Gorskaya
Lisiy Nos
Kamenka
Konnaya Lakhta
Kolomyagi
Staraya Derevnya

Priozersk
Chernaya Rechka
Sertolovo
Levashovo
Yukki
Pargolovo
Ozerki
Murino
Grazhdanka

Vartemyagi
Toksovo
Kuzmolovskiy

Petrovskiy Ostrov
Vasilevskiy Ostrov
ST PETERSBURG
Vitebskiy   Moskovskiy
Baltiyskiy   Yarshavskiy

Finlyandskiy
Yanino
Novosergiev
Volkovo
Avtovo
Kupchino
Ust
Novo
Petro-Slavyanka
Petro-Slavyanka

Bolshaya Izhora
Malaya Izhora
Oranienbaum
LOMONOSOV ORANIENBAUM
PETERHOF
Novyy Petergof
STRELNA
Nizino
Vladimirovka
Sosnovaya Polyana
Dachnoe

Petrovskoe
Razbegaevo
Annino
Gorelovo
Gostilitsy
Zaborode
KRASNOE SELO
Ropsha
Aleksandrovskaya
Aleksandrovskaya
TSARSKOE SELO
Gorki
Russko-Vysotskoe
Lagolovo
Villozi
Villozi
Detskoe Selo
Kipen
Kuyduzi
Skvoritsy
Taytsy
Kommunar
PAV
Gatchina
Romanovka
Pulkovo
Shushary
Shushary

KEY

- ▉ Central St Petersburg
- ▢ Greater St Petersburg
- ✈ Airport
- 🚉 Railway station
- ▬ Major road
- Minor road
- Railway

0 kilometres   3

0 miles   3

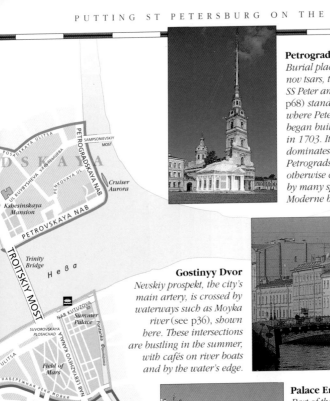

Petrogradskaya

Burial place of the Romanov tsars, the Cathedral of SS Peter and Paul (see p68) stands in the fortress where Peter the Great began building the city in 1703. Its gilded spire dominates the skyline of Petrogradskaya, an area otherwise characterized by many splendid Style-Moderne buildings.

Gostinyy Dvor

Nevskiy prospekt, the city's main artery, is crossed by waterways such as Moyka river (see p36), shown here. These intersections are bustling in the summer, with cafés on river boats and by the water's edge.

Palace Embankment

Part of the Hermitage, the former imperial Winter Palace (see pp92–3), dominates this grand waterfront with a burst of Baroque splendour. The embankment is lined with monuments from the famous Bronze Horseman (p78) to Peter the Great's modest Summer Palace (p95).

0 metres   600

0 yards   600

KEY

	Major sight
	Main sight
M	Metro station
	River boat pier
	Police station
	Orthodox church

Sennaya Ploshchad

St Petersburg's most famous theatre, the Mariinskiy (see p119), is best known for its classical ballet. The surrounding area, with quiet streets lining its canals, is perfect for walks during the atmospheric White Nights.

THE HISTORY OF
ST PETERSBURG

FOUNDED IN 1703, *within ten years St Petersburg had become capital of the vast Russian empire and quickly gained a reputation as one of Europe's most beautiful cities. In the 20th century it underwent three name changes, three revolutions and a 900-day siege. For a city less than 300 years old, it has an amazing history.*

Some 850 years before St Petersburg became capital of Russia, local Slavic tribes invited the Viking chieftain Rurik to rule them. His successor founded Kiev, which grew into a great princedom. In 988 Grand Prince Vladimir adopted Orthodox Christianity with profound consequences; Orthodoxy was to become a cornerstone of Russian identity. Paradoxically, Russia only emerged as a united entity during the 250-year domination of the Muslim Mongols. In 1237 these fierce tribes conquered all the principalities except Novgorod. In the 14th century the Mongols chose Moscow's power-hungry grand prince, Ivan I (1325–40), to collect tribute from other subjugated principalities. This sealed the fate of the Mongols for, as Moscow thrived under their benevolence, she also became a real threat.

Ivan IV "the Terrible"

Mongol warriors in a 14th-century manuscript illustration

Within 50 years, an army led by Moscow's Grand Prince Dmitriy Donskoy won a first victory over the Mongols, and the idea of a Russian nation was born.

During the long reign of Ivan III (1462–1505) the Mongols were finally vanquished and Moscow's prestige increased. Ivan the Terrible (1533–84) was the first to be called "Tsar of All the Russias". Yet his reign, which began in glory, ended in disaster. Ivan killed his only heir, and the so-called Time of Troubles followed as Russia came under a succession of weak rulers and Polish usurpers invaded Moscow.

THE FIRST ROMANOVS

To end this strife, in 1613 the leading citizens chose Mikhail Romanov to be tsar, thus initiating the 300-year Romanov rule. Under Mikhail, Russia recovered from her upheavals, but his greatest legacy was his son Alexis. Intelligent and pious, Alexis modernized the state, encouraging an influx of foreign architects, codifying laws and asserting the power of the state over the church.

TIMELINE

862 Rurik establishes Viking stronghold at Novgorod	**1147** Moscow is founded	**1480** Ivan III stops paying tribute to Mongols	**1605–13** Time of Troubles	*Boris Godunov*
863 Cyril and Methodius create early version of Cyrillic	**1462–1505** Reign of Ivan III			

800	1000	1200	1400	1600
	1108 Town of Vladimir is founded	**1223** First Mongol raid	**1242** Alexander Nevsky defeats the Teutonic Knights	**1533–84** Reign of Ivan IV the Terrible	**1613** Mikhail Romanov becomes first tsar of the Romanov dynasty
988 Prince Vladimir converts to Orthodox Christianity		**1240** Mongol rule established in Rus	**1598** Boris Godunov claims title of tsar after 12 years as regent	

◁ **Peter the Great instructing his workers during the building of St Petersburg (Alexander von Kotzebue, 1862)**

PETER THE GREAT

In the atmosphere of transition from a medieval to a more modern state, the future Peter the Great, founder of St Petersburg, was born. After his father Alexis' death, Peter's childhood was overshadowed by severe rivalry between his mother's family, the Naryshkins, and that of his father's first wife, the Miloslavskiys. At the age of ten Peter ascended the throne, but the Streltsy Guards, influenced by the Miloslavskiys, started a bloody revolt. As a result his sickly half-brother Ivan became his co-tsar, and Ivan's sister Sophia their regent. The memory of seeing his family brutally killed caused his hatred of Moscow and distrust of its conservative, scheming society.

Peter the Great (1682–1725)

When Ivan died in 1696, the 24-year-old Peter had grown to a giant of a man with a tempestuous combination of willpower and energy. Long hours spent drilling toy soldiers as a child developed into a full-scale reform of the Russian army. But Peter's dream was of a Russian navy. In 1697, he went on a European tour to study shipbuilding and other wondrous achievements. To everyone's dismay the young tsar spent more hours working at the docks than socializing at court. On his return to Russia he lost no time in enforcing westernizing reforms.

A NEW CAPITAL

It was Peter's determination to found a northern port with an unrestricted passage to the Baltic that led to war with Sweden, at the time one of the strongest countries in Europe. By May 1703 Peter had secured the Neva river and began to build the Peter and Paul Fortress and a shipyard opposite *(see pp20–21)*. Only an autocrat with Peter's drive could have succeeded in building a

View of St Petersburg in the early 17th century, with the Admiralty shipyard to the left

TIMELINE

Sophia, regent 1682–9

1672 Birth of Peter the Great at Kolomenskoe Palace, Moscow	**1689** Peter banishes Sophia to Novodevichy Monastery, Moscow	**1697–8** Peter tours western Europe	**1698** Peter destroys the Streltsy Guards *(see p20)*.	**1703** St Petersburg is founded
				1712 Seat of government moves to St Petersburg
1680		**1690**	**1700**	**1710**
1682 The Streltsy rebellion. Peter becomes co-tsar with half-brother Ivan V, under regency of his half-sister Sophia		**1696** Ivan V dies; Peter becomes sole ruler.	**1700** Start of Northern War against Sweden	**1714** Peter forbids the use of stone in buildings, except in St Petersburg
			1709 Victory over Charles XII of Sweden at Battle of Poltava	

LIFE AT ELIZABETH'S COURT

When Elizabeth was not busy looking over architectural plans, she would lie around on her bed, gossiping with a group of ladies whose chief task it was to tickle her feet. Her restless nature meant that her courtiers had to endure endless hunts and skating parties, and were required to keep her company at all hours. Her riotous cross-dressing masquerades were notorious, as was her vast wardrobe, allegedly containing over 15,000 dresses.

Tsarina Elizabeth going for a stroll at Tsarskoe Selo, surrounded by eager courtiers

THE PETTICOAT PERIOD

For most of the rest of the 18th century Russia was ruled by women, whose taste did much to set the celebrated architectural tone of St Petersburg.

During the brief reigns of Peter's wife Catherine I (1725–27) and his grandson Peter II (1727–30), the court abandoned this frontier city for the more comfortable life in Moscow. But when the throne passed to Anna, daughter of Peter's co-tsar Ivan, she decided to create a recognizably European court in St Petersburg. Anna was 37 at the time, and had spent most of her life in Germany. This was obvious in her choice of ministers and favourites, of whom many were German. Fashion and style, however, were imported from France and opera from Italy. Though she herself was serious, plain and somewhat cruel, Anna did much to put the court on a footing with the most frivolous in Europe, as well as encouraging a flowering of civilization.

Tsarina Elizabeth, daughter of Peter the Great, was the ideal successor to this twittering court. Elizabeth was attractive, energetic and cheerful, a combination that endeared her to almost everyone, especially the Guards who helped secure her place on the throne. She left the affairs of state to a series of well chosen advisors. The only element of seriousness lay in Elizabeth's perhaps surprising piety, which at times led her to retire temporarily into a convent. Her chief legacy is the splendid Baroque architecture she commissioned, mainly designed by her favourite architect Rastrelli (see p93).

city on this fetid bogland, where daylight and building materials were in short supply and disastrous floodings regular. More than 40,000 Swedish prisoners-of-war and peasants laboured and perished here, their bones contributing to the city's foundations.

Whether or not it was always Peter's intention to make this his new capital, it only became possible after his decisive victory at Poltava in 1709 put an end to the Swedish threat. St Petersburg was named capital of Russia in 1712 and, by Peter's death in 1725, there were 40,000 inhabitants in the city and many more in the surrounding labour encampments.

Elizabeth (1741–61)

1721 Peace of Nystad ends war with Sweden

1733 Cathedral of SS Peter and Paul is finished after 12 years' work

1738 Russia's first ballet school is founded in St Petersburg

1745 Tsarevich Peter marries the future Catherine the Great

1757 St Petersburg Academy of Arts is founded

1720 **1730** **1740** **1750**

1717 Peter travels to Holland and France

1725 Catherine I is empress after death of Peter the Great

1730–40 Reign of Anna

1727–30 Reign of Peter II

Anna Ivanovna, daughter of Ivan V

1741 Anna's successor Ivan VI is deposed; Elizabeth takes power, supported by Guards' officers

1754 Rastrelli's Winter Palace is begun

A Window on the West

DETERMINED TO drag his country out of the medieval period, and inspired by the few westerners he met in Moscow, Peter the Great was the first tsar to travel to Europe. He returned with many ideas for reforms and architectural novelties which he put into practice in his new city. In 1710, when the Swedish threat was over, the reluctant imperial family and government were moved to this chilly, damp outland. But Peter was adamant and soon a rational street plan, stone buildings and academies made St Petersburg a thriving capital in which fashions and discoveries from Europe were tried out before filtering through to the rest of Russia.

EXTENT OF THE CITY

■ 1712   □ Today

PLAN OF THE NEW CITY

This map of 1712 shows Peter's original plan for his capital, with Vasilevskiy Island as centre. This was abandoned due to the hazards of crossing the Neva, and the city spread out around the Admiralty instead.

The Carpenter Tsar
During his 1697–8 tour of Europe, Peter (to the left in this picture) spent months at the Deptford Docks, labouring with his men to learn the basics of ship building.

Based on Amsterdam, the original city grid was meant to follow a strict network of canals but this had to change (see p57).

Menshikov palace

New Fashions
Peter's desire to westernize Russia led to a rule forcing his courtiers to have their bushy beards shaved off.

THE STRELTSY REBELLION

As a result of a malicious rumour that Peter's relatives planned the murder of his half-brother Ivan, in 1682 the Streltsy Guard regiments invaded the Kremlin. A horrifying massacre took place in front of the 10-year old Peter who saw his adviser and members of his family murdered. This traumatic event is probably what caused Peter's facial tic and certainly his wish to build another capital city. In 1698 he took a terrible revenge by torturing over a thousand Streltsy Guards to death.

Brutal murders in the Kremlin, 1682

The Battle of Poltava

The struggle with Sweden for control over the Baltic led to the Great Northern War. Nine years after the embarassing defeat at Narva, Peter the Great's army reforms bore fruit. In 1709 he won a decisive battle over Charles XII at Poltava, and thereby Russia's first victory over a major European power.

WHERE TO SEE PETER THE GREAT'S CITY

Some of the buildings from the early St Petersburg still exist in the city centre, including the rustic Peter the Great's Cabin *(p73)*, the Summer Palace *(p95)* and the Baroque Menshikov Palace *(p62)*. Much of Peter and Paul Fortress *(pp66–7)* also dates from this time. It is also well worth visiting Monplaisir, Peter's first home at Peterhof *(pp148)*.

Peter the Great's workshop, the Summer Palace

Kronwerk (outer defense walls)

Peter and Paul Fortress

The port was here until the 1880s.

Admiralty

Summer Palace

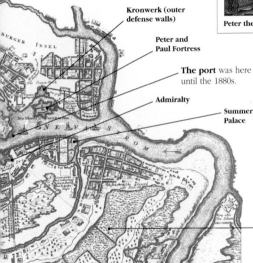

Wine Goblet

The tsar, who could hold his drink, enjoyed pressing alcohol on his guests until they passed out. This elegant crystal goblet belonged to his close friend Aleksandr Menshikov and is engraved with his coat of arms.

Marshy soil and a lack of local stone made construction difficult. Thousands of labourers died during the first stages.

Catherine I

After an unsuccessful first marriage, Peter was drawn to a Lithuanian girl who had followed the army back from the wars in 1704. Her healthy good looks were brought to the tsar's attention by Aleksandr Menshikov (see p62). Although only two daughters survived, their marriage was happy and Catherine succeeded Peter as the first woman on Russia's throne.

Mice Bury the Cat

Coloured woodcuts, lubki, *served as political cartoons in Peter's day. The tsar was always portrayed as a cat on account of his moustache.*

CATHERINE THE GREAT

Catherine, a German princess, was chosen by Elizabeth as wife for her successor, the petty-minded Peter III. When Peter ascended the throne in 1761 Catherine had resided in Russia for 18 years and was fully fluent in Russian. She had made it her duty to steep herself in the Russian culture which she later came to adore. Six months into Peter's reign, Catherine and her allies in the Imperial Guard deposed the tsar. He was assassinated within days and she was crowned Catherine II.

Catherine the Great in 1762

By Catherine's death at the age of 67, her reputation as an enlightened leader (see p24) had been overshadowed by her illiberal reaction to the news of the French Revolution in 1789 and by scandalous rumours concerning her later love-affairs. However, she left a country vastly enlarged after successful campaigns against Turkey and Poland.

WAR AND PEACE

During the Napoleonic Wars, under Catherine's grandson Alexander I, Russia finally took her place alongside the other great European powers.

Despite his part in the murder of his father Paul, much was expected of the handsome new tsar who was infected by the ideals of enlightened government. Russia was by now desperately in need of reform. Of particular concern was the plight of the peasantry, who were tied to the land in serfdom.

However, the necessities of war subsumed everything, and no inroads were made against the Russian autocracy during Alexander I's reign.

Determined to harness the wave of Russian patriotism, Alexander joined Britain and marched against Napoleon in Austria in 1805. After the crushing defeat at the battle of Austerlitz, however, the inexperienced tsar retreated, his army having lost 11,000 men.

At the Peace of Tilsit, signed in 1807, Napoleon divided Europe into French and Russian spheres, lulling Alexander into a false sense of security. In 1812 the French emperor invaded Russia, but was defeated by its size and climate. The Russian army followed his forces to Paris, taking part in the allied campaign which led Napoleon to abdicate in 1814. In celebration, Alexander commissioned a series of imposing public edifices in a fitting Empire style.

Murder of Paul I, 1801. Despite all his precautions, Catherine's unstable, paranoid son was murdered in a coup in his own fortified palace (see p101)

TIMELINE

1762 Death of Elizabeth. Peter III becomes emperor but is murdered after six months. His wife takes the throne as Catherine II	1783 Annexation of the Crimea	1787–92 2nd Russo-Turkish War	1801 Paul I murdered. Alexander I becomes tsar	1805–1807 War with France ends with Treaty of Tilsit

1760	1780	1800

1763 Catherine II begins correspondence with Voltaire	1767 Catherine II publishes her Bolshoy Nakaz	1773–5 Pugachev Rebellion	1782 Falconet's statue, the Bronze Horseman, is completed	1796 Death of Catherine II; Paul I accedes	Alexander I (1801–25)	1812 Napoleon invades Russia
		1768–74 1st Russo-Turkish War				1816 Alexander I clamps down on reforms

Decembrist rebels defeated by tsarist troops, 1825

THE DECEMBRIST REBELLION

Officers of the Russian army who had witnessed the freedoms of democratic Europe were frustrated by Alexander's failure to consider constitutional reform. When his stern brother Nicholas was declared tsar in 1825, these liberals rallied their soldiers to support the older brother Constantine, who had given up his rights to the throne, in the hope that he would be more open-minded. They made a stand on 14th December on what is now Decembrists' Square *(see p 78)*. Troops loyal to the tsar were instructed to fire on the rebels, killing hundreds before the leaders surrendered. The new tsar, Nicholas I, treated them with the severity which was to become the hallmark of his reign. Five leading figures were hanged, and over a hundred exiled to Siberia.

A CITY OF RICH AND POOR

For much of the 19th century, a walk along Nevskiy prospekt offered a microcosm of an increasingly divided society. Striding past drunks, beggars and prostitutes, the city's courtiers, cocky young officers and leading citizens headed for shops selling imported fashionable accessories, or to the distinguished delicatessen Yeliseev's to buy caviar and champagne. They often lived above their means, mortgaging their serfs and lands to keep up with the astronomical costs of their luxurious lives. This was also a city in which the salary of a low ranking government clerk was never sufficient to feed a family. In the countryside, tension was growing among the serfs tied to the large estates of the aristocracy. With such blatant inequality, growing pressure for political reform was inevitable.

After the unrelenting autocracy of Nicholas I, the "Iron Tsar", liberals welcomed the reign of his fair-minded son Alexander II. In 1861, the tsar passed the Edict of Emancipation, abolishing serfdom, but requiring peasants to buy their land at far from advantageous terms. Thus industrialization finally took off as peasants flocked to the big cities to work in factories, only to be met by even worse living conditions.

THE NAPOLEONIC INVASION

Napoleon's Grand Army of 600,000 men reached Moscow in September 1812, after the victory at Borodino, but was defeated by the tactics of non-engagement devised by the great Russian hero General Kutuzov. Finding himself in a city abandoned by its rulers and set on fire by its people, and with the Russian winter ahead, Napoleon was forced into a retreat over the frozen countryside. He eventually reached the border, with only 30,000 men left alive.

French army retreating from Moscow 1812

1822 Abolition of Masonic and secret societies	**1833** Pushkin publishes *The Bronze Horseman*	**1855** Death of Nicholas I; Alexander II succeeds him **1853–6** Crimean War	*Leo Tolstoy*	**1865–9** Tolstoy writes *War and Peace*

1820		**1840**		**1860**	
	1825 The Decembrist Rebellion. Nicholas I becomes tsar			**1861** Emancipation of serfs	**1874** 3,000 Narodniki (Populists) take their ideals "to the people" in the countryside
1818 Construction of St Isaac's Cathedral starts		**1851** The "Nicholas Railway" opens between Moscow and St Petersburg		**1864** Reforms in local government, law and education	

The Enlightened Empress

BORN A MINOR GERMAN PRINCESS, Catherine II was a learned and energetic woman. She recognized the importance of the great Enlightenment philosophers Voltaire and Diderot, with whom she corresponded. She bought impressive collections of European art for the Hermitage *(see pp84–93)*, libraries for Russia's scholars and talked much about reducing the burden on Russia's serfs. However, a peasant uprising in the 1770s and news of the French Revolution in 1789 put paid to her liberal notions and, when she died, the majority of Russians were just as badly off as before.

EXTENT OF THE CITY

▨ *1790*   ☐ *Today*

Royal Guards Swear Allegiance
On 28 June 1762, Catherine usurped the throne of her unpopular husband Peter III in a palace coup. The guards regiments flocked to support her and the tsar was assassinated on 6 July.

The Temple alludes to Catherine's passion for Neo-Classical architecture.

The medal is presented to Count Orlov for his victory over the Turks at Chesma in 1770.

CATHERINE THE GREAT

Catherine II "the Great" (1762–96) pursued an expansionist foreign policy. Russia's first naval victory, leading to the annexation of the Crimea, is commemorated allegorically on this fabric.

Count Alexey Orlov, brother of Catherine's one-time lover Grigoriy, played an important role in her takeover of the throne.

Catherine's Instructions
In 1767 the 36-year-old Catherine published her 22-chapter Great Instruction (Bolshoy Nakaz). *The book is a collection of ideas on which a reform of Russia's legal system was to be based.*

Pretender Pugachev
The greatest threat to Catherine's reign was caused by the Cossack Pugachev who claimed to be Peter III. He was arrested, but escaped to lead a widespread peasant uprising which broke out in 1773 and only ended with his execution in 1775.

The New Academy of Sciences
Catherine, who founded over 25 major academic institutions in Russia, also commissioned new buildings for those already existing. Quarenghi built the Neo-Classical Academy of Sciences in 1783–5.

WHERE TO SEE THE NEO-CLASSICAL CITY

Catherine had the Marble Palace *(see p94)* and the Tauride Palace *(p128)* erected for two of her lovers, and added the Small and Large Hermitage and the theatre *(p84)* to the Winter Palace. Her architect Cameron designed the Cameron Gallery and the Agate Pavilion at Tsarskoe Selo *(p150)* and Pavlovsk Palace *(pp156–9).*

Grecian Hall at Pavlovsk, created by Charles Cameron in 1782–6

Catherine is portrayed as Pallas Athena, goddess of wisdom and warfare, with her attributes of a shield and helmet.

Empire-Style Vase (1790)
Porcelain was much prized at court. In 1744 the first Russian producer, the Imperial Porcelain Factory, opened in St Petersburg.

The fabric, used for a screen, was made by the Pernons factory, Lyons, in 1770.

Mikhail Lomonosov
A philosopher, historian, linguist and scientist, Lomonosov (1711–65) personified the intellectual enlightenment of 18th-century Russia (see p61). This sculpture of him as a boy by the seashore refers to his fisherman origins.

Grigoriy Potemkin (1739–91)
Of all her lovers, Catherine respected and admired Prince Potemkin the most. He was a successful general and an influential counsellor. They remained friends until his death.

Alexander II was murdered by a revolutionary group in 1881. Tragically, he is said to have had the plans for a Russian parliament in his pocket

THE DEATH OF TSARIST RUSSIA

Pressure for reform had built up such a head of steam that in 1881, when still no radical changes had taken place, a revolutionary group murdered Alexander II. The reign of Alexander III was one of rabid reaction. The press was under strict censorship and the secret police more active than ever. But workers began to get organized and opposition was growing. Nicholas II took over a country on the verge of breakdown, in spite of the rapid industrialization of the 1890s. The unsuccessful war with Japan (1904–5) was followed by "Bloody Sunday". On 9th January 1905 a peaceful demonstration carried a petition to the tsar only to be met by bullets. News of the massacre spread like wildfire and the 1905 Revolution broke out with strikes all over Russia. To avert further disaster, Nicholas II promised basic civil rights and an elected Duma (parliament) with the right to veto legislation. However, the tsar simply dissolved the parliament whenever it displeased him. This high-handed behaviour, along with the royal family's unpopular intimate friendship with Rasputin (see p121), further damaged the Romanovs' reputation.

The outbreak of World War I brought a surge of patriotism which the tsar sought to ride. But, by late 1916, Russia had lost three and a half million men, morale at the front was low and food supplies at home scarce.

Red Army badge

WORLD OF ART MOVEMENT

Costume design by Leon Bakst, 1911

The oppressive political climate at the turn of the century did not prevent art from flourishing. A small group of St Petersburg artists, including Bakst and Benois, grew into an influential creative movement under the inspired leadership of Sergey Diaghilev. Western art was introduced in their stylish World of Art magazine, while their stage designs and costumes for the Ballets Russes (see p118) brought Russian culture to the west.

REVOLUTION AND CIVIL WAR

In February 1917 strikes broke out in the capital, now renamed Petrograd. The tsar was forced to abdicate, his family put under arrest and a Provisional Government set up. But revolutionaries returning from exile organized themselves and, in October, an armed revolution overthrew the government (see pp28–9).

TIMELINE

The Romanov family in 1913

1881 Alexander II is assassinated by the "People's Will" group. Alexander III becomes tsar.	**1902** Lenin publishes *What is to be Done?*
	1898 Social-Democratic Workers' party is founded. Russian museum opens
	1913 300th anniversary of Romanov rule

1880   **1900**

1881–2 Anti-semitic pogroms		**1903** Pro-violence Bolsheviks (under Lenin) secede from Social-Democratic Workers' party	**1905** The 1905 Revolution is followed by the inauguration of the first Duma in 1906
1887 Lenin's brother is hanged for attempt on the tsar's life	**1894** Alexander III dies, Nicholas II accedes	**1904–5** Russo-Japanese War	**1914** Outbreak of WWI; St Petersburg changes name to Petrograd

The leading Bolshevik party proved to be as careless of democracy as the tsar but, in March 1918, they kept their promise to take Russia out of the war. The army was desperately needed at home to fight the developing civil war.

The Bolsheviks (Reds) found themselves threatened by a diverse coalition of anti-revolutionary groups which came to be known as the "Whites", initially supported by foreign intervention. It was the threat of the Whites rallying opposition around the royal family that led to their execution in July 1918. But the Whites were a disparate force and, by November 1920, the last troops had abandoned the struggle, leaving a devastated Soviet Russia to face two years of appalling famine. To manage, Lenin had to revise his aggressive "War Communism" nationalization project. His slightly milder New Economic Policy allowed for private enterprise.

The imperial palaces around St Petersburg were totally destroyed by the Germans in World War II. This photo shows Pavlovsk *(see pp156–9)* in 1944

THE STALIN YEARS

In the five years after Lenin's death in 1924, Joseph Stalin used his position as General Secretary of the Communist Party to eliminate all rivals. He then established his long dictatorship.

The terror began in earnest with the collectivization of agriculture which forced the peasants to give up all livestock, machinery and land to collective farms. During this time, and in the ensuing famine of 1931–2, up to 10 million people are thought to have died.

Joseph Stalin on a propaganda poster from 1933

A first major purge of intellectuals took place in urban areas in 1928–9. Then, in December 1934, Sergey Kirov, the party leader in Leningrad, was assassinated on the secret orders of Stalin *(see p72)*. Blamed on an anti-Stalinist cell, the assasination was used as the catalyst for five years of purges throughout the country. By the time they were over, some 15 million people had been arrested, many sent to the Gulag (labour camps) and over a million executed.

Stalin's purge of the Red Army boded badly for World War II, for he had got rid of three quarters of his officers. When the Germans invaded Russia in 1941 they cut off Leningrad in less than three months, subjecting the city to a 900-day siege *(see p131)* which left more than two million people dead, half of them civilians. Leningrad came to be known as a "Hero City". The Germans were eventually defeated, but the Russian people, who lost 20 million souls to the war, were subjected to a renewed terror by Stalin, which lasted until his death in March 1953.

1917 The Russian Revolution *(see p29)*

1918 Civil War starts. Capital moves to Moscow

1924 Lenin dies; Petrograd is named Leningrad

1929 Collectivization of private land

1934 Leningrad Party Secretary Kirov is killed; Stalin's purges intensify

1939 Nazi-Soviet pact

1941 Nazis attack Russia; Siege of Leningrad starts

1947 The term "Cold War" is coined

1920

1940

1921 Lenin bans all opposition after the Kronstadt mutiny

1922 Stalin becomes General Secretary of the Party

1925 Trotsky is expelled from the Politburo

1932 Socialist Realism is the only officially approved style in art

Sergey Kirov

1942 First performance of Shostakovich's Seventh Symphony in besieged Leningrad

1944 The Siege ends

The Russian Revolution

ST PETERSBURG IS KNOWN as the cradle of the Russian
Revolution, a central event in the history of the
20th century. After the 1917 February Revolution which
led to the abdication of Tsar Nicholas II, the Provisional Government declared a political amnesty. Exiled
revolutionaries such as Lenin and Trotsky flooded
into the city. By setting up a network of Workers' and
Soldiers' Soviets, representative councils elected by the
people, they established an alternative government. In
October, when soldiers had deserted from the front in
droves, the revolutionary leaders decided on an armed
uprising which brought the Communists to power.

EXTENT OF THE CITY
■ *1917*   □ *Today*

The Ex-Tsar
*Nicholas II, seen
here clearing
snow at Tsarskoe
Selo during his
house arrest in
March 1917, was
later taken with
his family to
Yekaterinburg
where they were
murdered.*

Looting was tempting
for the mob of sailors
and soldiers, especially
in the palace's well-
stocked wine cellars.

**Soldier of the
Red Guard**

STORMING THE WINTER PALACE
Late on the evening of 25 October 1917
the battleship *Aurora (see p73)* fired some
blank shots at the Winter Palace. The Red
Guard, trained by Trotsky at the Smolnyy
Institute, stormed the palace. Their aim was
the arrest of the Provisional Government,
unsuccessfully defended by 300 Cossacks.

The Cossacks,
who defended
the palace with
some cadets
and members
of the Women's
Battalion, were
too few to offer
any serious
resistance.

Lenin, Leader of the People
*A charismatic speaker, as shown
in this painting by Victor Ivanov,
Lenin returned from exile in April
to lead the Revolution. By 1918,
his Bolshevik faction had shown
their determination to rule.*

Revolutionary Plate
*Various ceramics
with revolutionary
themes, mixed
with touches of
Russian folklore,
were produced to
celebrate every
occasion, in this
case the Third
International.*

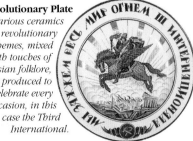

Leon Trotsky
The intellectual Trotsky played a leading military role in the Revolution. In 1927, during the power struggle after Lenin's death, he was exiled by Stalin. In 1940 he was murdered in Mexico by a Stalinist agent.

Propaganda
One hallmark of the Soviet regime was its propaganda. Artists were employed to design posters spreading its message through striking graphics. War Communism during the Civil War (1918–20) was encouraged by posters such as this one, extolling the "Workers' and Peasants' Defence".

Avant Garde Art
Even before 1917, Russia's artists had been in a state of revolution, producing the world's first truly abstract paintings. A great example of this new movement is Supremus No. 56, painted in 1916 by Kazimir Malevich.

Ministers of the Provisional Government tried to keep order but were arrested.

New Values
Traditions were radically altered by the Revolution; instead of church weddings, couples exchanged vows under the red flag. Loudly trumpeted sexual equality meant that women had to work twice as hard – at home and in the factories.

TIMELINE

1917 The February Revolution	**March** The tsar is persuaded to abdicate. Provisional Government is led by Prince Lvov	**October** Bolsheviks storm Winter Palace after signal from *Aurora* and expel Provisional Government	**March** Bolsheviks sign Brest-Litovsk peace treaty with Germany. Capital is moved to Moscow
1917		**1918**	
July Kerensky becomes Prime Minister of Provisional Government		**1918 January** Trotsky becomes Commissar of War	**July** Start of Civil War. Tsar and family are murdered in prison at Yekaterinburg
		December Lenin forms the CHEKA (secret police)	

Cruiser Aurora

The Washington Dove of Peace, a Russian caricature (1953) from the days of the Cold War

THAW AND STAGNATION

Three years after Stalin's death his successor Nikita Khrushchev denounced Stalin's crimes at the Twentieth Party Congress and the period known as "The Thaw" began. Political prisoners were released, and Solzhenitsyn's *One Day In the Life of Ivan Denisovich*, about life in the Gulag, was published.

In foreign affairs, things were not so liberal. Soviet tanks invaded Hungary in 1956 to prevent the country seceding from the Warsaw Pact and, in 1962,

Khrushchev's decision to put nuclear missiles on Cuba brought the world to the brink of nuclear war.

When Leonid Brezhnev took over in 1964, the intellectual climate froze once more and the persecution of political dissidents was stepped up. The first ten years of his regime were a time of relative plenty. But beneath the surface a vast black market and network of corruption was growing. The party apparatchiks, who benefited most from the corruption, had no interest in rocking the boat. When Brezhnev died in 1982, the politburo was determined to prevent the accession of a younger generation. He was followed by 68-year-old Yuriy Andropov and, when he died, 72-year-old Chernenko.

GLASNOST AND PERESTROIKA

When 53-year-old Mikhail Gorbachev announced his policies of *glasnost* (openness) and *perestroika* (restructuring), when he took over in 1985, he had no idea what would follow. By the end of 1991 the Soviet Union and its empire were no more.

For the first time since 1917 the elections to the Congress of People's Deputies in 1989 contained

Mikhail Gorbachev and George Bush

an element of genuine choice, with rebels such as Boris Yeltsin and human rights campaigner Andrey Sakharov winning seats. In 1991, local elections brought nationalist candidates to power in the

---

FIRST IN SPACE

It was under Krushchev that the Soviet Union achieved her greatest coup against the West, launching the first Sputnik into space in 1957. That same year the dog Laika was the first living creature in space, aboard Sputnik II. She never came down again, but four years later Yuriy Gagarin made spectacular history as the first man in space, returning to a hero's welcome. The Soviets lost the race to put a man on the moon, but their space programme worked as powerful propaganda, backing up the claims of politicians that Russia would soon catch up with and overtake the prosperity of the West.

Spuknik II and the space dog Laika, 1957

Demonstrations on Palace Square during the 1991 coup

republics, and democrats in the major Russian local councils. Russia and the Baltic Republics seceded from the Soviet Union, while the people of Leningrad, always in the vanguard of progressive movement and now led by the reformist lecturer in law, Anatoly Sobchak, voted to restore the city's original name, St Petersburg.

The new Russian State Emblem

With his great victory in the election for President of the Russian Republic, Yeltsin was able to deal the death blow to the Soviet Union. It came after the military coup against Gorbachev in August 1991, when Yeltsin's stand against tanks in Moscow made him a hero. In St Petersburg no tanks were on the street, but nonetheless Sobchak rallied supporters of democracy. By the end of the year, the Soviet Union no longer existed.

St Petersburg Today

The economic reforms which Russia has undergone since 1991 have widened the gap between rich and poor and, while some revel in the new opportunities for work and travel, others cry out for a return to Communism and the albeit limited social protection it offered.

The social problems are still being resolved, and were not helped by a financial crisis in August 1998. Major companies have, however, continued to invest, and by early 1999 relative stability had been achieved. The elections of December 1999 dramatically reduced the power of the Communists, bringing in young liberal reformers and confirming optimism about Russia's future. Meanwhile, the religious revival continues, and churches of all denominations have been restored to their original purpose, having been used as warehouses in the Soviet era.

In March 2000, Vladimir Putin was elected President of the Russian Republic. Putin is a graduate of the St Petersburg State University and was Vice-Governor of the city.

A church wedding, popular again since religion has gained new importance among the young

St Petersburg at a Glance

A CITY BUILT ON WATER, St Petersburg offers beautiful scenery and a wide range of sights. The Peter and Paul Fortress *(see pp66–7)*, the city's first building, contrasts with Baroque monasteries and Neo-Classical palaces. The city's short but stormy history is reflected in many of its museums, which display everything from Catherine the Great's fine art collection in the Hermitage to memorabilia of the Revolution in the Kshesinskaya Mansion *(see p72)*.

To help you make the most of your stay, the following 12 pages are a time-saving guide to the best museums and palaces and the most interesting of the many bridges and waterways. The cultural figures that made St Petersburg a city of importance are also featured. Below is a selection of sights that should not be missed by any visitor.

St Petersburg's Top Ten Attractions

Russian Museum
See pp104–7

Mariinskiy Theatre
See p119

Nevskiy Prospekt
See pp46–9

Stieglitz Museum
See p127

The Hermitage
See pp84–93

Church on Spilled Blood
See p100

Cathedral of Our Lady of Kazan
See p111

St Isaac's Cathedral
See pp80–81

SS Peter and Paul Cathedral
See p68

Alexander Nevsky Monastery
See pp130–31

◁ The Neo-Classical Kazan Cathedral with its impressive semi-circle of granite columns

St Petersburg's Best: Bridges and Waterways

Lᴵᴷᴱ ɪᴛs ᴡᴀᴛᴇʀʙᴏᴜɴᴅ sɪsᴛᴇʀs, Amsterdam and Venice, St Petersburg is built around a network of canals and rivers which are still the life-blood of the city. They contribute to its unique atmosphere by creating eerie mists which rise from the ice-laden waters in winter and, in summer, a glittering mirror of façades during the glowing sunsets and bright White Nights.

Bridges, necessary for communication between the islands, were also an excellent means to adorn the city with decorative sculptures, elaborate lampposts and wrought-iron work.

A walk or a boat trip *(see p134–5 and 218–19)* is the best way to enjoy them.

Winter Canal
Laid out in 1718–20, this narrow canal is crossed by three bridges and Yuriy Velten's Hermitage Theatre foyer (1783–7).

Lieutenant Shmidt Bridge
Rebuilt in 1936–8, this bridge still retains its original cast-iron seahorse railings, designed by Bryullov.

Lion Bridge
One of the earliest of its kind, this pedestrian suspension bridge dates from 1825–6. Its cables are anchored inside four cast-iron lions, by sculptor Pavel Sokolov.

Egyptian Bridge
This bridge spanning the Fontanka was decorated in the Egyptian style fashionable at the time of its construction, in 1826.

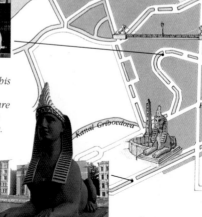

Malaya Neva

Vasilevskiy Island

Bolshaya Neva

Palace Embankment

Moyka

Sennaya Ploshchad

Kanal Griboedova

Fontanka

| 0 metres | 500 |
| 0 yards | 500 |

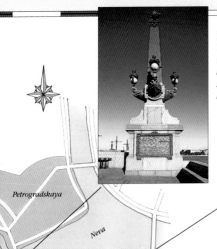

Trinity Bridge

The ten-arched Trinity Bridge (1897–1903) is famous for its Style-Moderne lampposts and railing decorations, the work of the skilful French engineers Vincent Chabrol and René Patouillard.

Swan Canal

This tree-lined canal (1711–19) leading out to the Neva is named after the swans which were once drawn to its peaceful waters.

Petrogradskaya

Neva

Bridge Passage

Cleverly designed to span the confluence of the Moyka and the Griboedov, the Theatre and Small Stable bridges were constructed by Traitteur and Adam in 1829–31.

Gostinyy Dvor

Anichkov Bridge

This three-span bridge, carrying Nevskiy prospekt across the Fontanka, was built in 1839–41. At each corner are Pyotr Klodt's impressive sculptures of men taming wild horses.

Lomonosov Bridge

The distinctive domed granite towers, built in 1785–7, originally contained the bridge's opening mechanism. The bridge was rebuilt in 1912, but the towers were kept.

Bank Bridge

Dating from the same time as the Lion Bridge, and designed by the same team, this bridge is adorned by four magnificent cast-iron griffons. Its name derives from the nearby former Assignment Bank.

Exploring St Petersburg's Bridges and Waterways

A BOAT TRIP on St Petersburg's canals and waterways is one of the highlights of any visit to the city. From the Anichkov Bridge the river boats *(see p217–8)* loop along the Neva, Fontanka and Moyka rivers, taking in many impressive bridges and landmarks. Alternatively, you can choose your own route to explore the city's rich architectural heritage by taking a water taxi *(see p219)*. A pleasant wander along the embankments of the Griboedov Canal leads past imposing 19th-century apartment houses and fancifully decorated bridges. In the winter months, one can walk on the frozen Neva.

The ice-laden Neva river in front of the Peter and Paul Fortress

THE NEVA AND ITS BRANCHES

G REATEST OF St Petersburg's numerous waterways, the Neva flows from Lake Ladoga in the east through the city to the Gulf of Finland, a distance of only 74 km (46 miles) in total. Vasilevskiy Island, one of more than 100 islands in the Neva Delta, divides the river into two separate branches, Bolshaya (Great) Neva and Malaya (Small) Neva.

Icebound for at least four months of the year, the Neva usually shows the first signs of cracking in March. The official Opening of Navigation is announced by the port authority in mid-April. Until the Revolution the event was marked with great ceremony. The Commander of the Peter and Paul Fortress *(see pp66–7)*, at the head of a naval flotilla, would scoop some icy water into a silver goblet which he presented to the tsar in the Winter Palace *(see pp92–3)*.

RIVERS AND CANALS

I NSPIRED BY AMSTERDAM, Peter the Great kept the many streams of the delta as canals, which also helped to drain the swampy ground. As the city grew new ones were dug to improve the canal network.

The **Moyka** originally flowed from a swamp near the Field of Mars *(see p94)*. In the 19th century the aristocracy lined its quays with impressive Neo-Classical mansions which are still their main attraction. Canal boats and barges ply the 7-km (4-mile) long **Fontanka**, widest and busiest of the waterways, which was once the border of the city. These two rivers are linked by the **Kryukov Canal**, dug in the 18th century.

The **Griboedov Canal**, first known as the Catherine Canal in honour of Catherine the Great, was designed to move cargo from Sennaya Ploshchad. Today the atmosphere here is more tranquil. The stretch of water running south from the Lion Bridge is particularly picturesque. The narrowest

waterway is the **Winter Canal**, just to the east of the Winter Palace. Nearby is the delightful **Swan Canal** which runs along the Summer Garden *(p95)*.

Steady industrial growth in the 19th century prompted the construction of a new canal, the **Obvodnyy**, in 1834, to take the increasing number of heavy cargo barges and supply water to the city outskirts.

NEVA BRIDGES

T HE MOST CENTRAL of the Neva bridges is the **Palace Bridge** (Dvortsovyy most). The present structure, built early in the 20th century, replaced a seasonal pontoon bridge which linked the mainland to Vasilevskiy Island.

View of the Moyka and its south bank with a water taxi in foreground

Peter the Great Bridge, crossing the Neva near Smolnyy Institute

The other bridge to this island, **Lieutenant Shmidt Bridge** (Most Leytenanta Shmidta, *see p63),* is named after a naval officer who led a rebellion of sailors of the Black Sea Fleet in 1905. The **Trinity Bridge** (Troitskiy most, *see p73)* was built in 1897–1903, in time for the city's bicentenary, by the French Batignolles company. At 582 m (1,910 ft), the Trinity Bridge was the Neva's longest, until the construction of the **Alexander Nevsky Bridge** (Most Aleksandra Nevskovo) in the 1960s, which is some 900 m (2,950 ft). Between these two is the **Liteynyy Bridge** (Liteynyy most) built in 1874–9. In 1917, the city authorities tried to prevent rebel workers crossing the Neva from the Vyborg Side by raising the central bridge span. The tactic failed since the re-volutionaries decided to cross on foot over the frozen ice.

Near the Smolnyy Institute is the **Peter the Great Bridge** (Most Petra Velikovo), also known by its Soviet name Bolsheokhtinskiy most. It has a central drawbridge and distinctive steel twin arches, erected in 1909–11.

From April to November all Neva bridges are raised at night to allow ships to pass to and from the Volga *(see p201).*

DECORATIVE BRIDGES

IN THE BEGINNING, wooden bridges spanned the canals and rivers of St Petersburg. They were usually known by their colour – red, blue, green, and so on. The **Red Bridge** (Krasnyy most) which carries Gorokhovaya ulitsa over the Moyka, has pre-served its original name. Built in 1808–14, this iron bridge is decorated with picturesque lamps on four granite obelisks. Lamps are also a feature of the **Lantern Bridge** (Fonarnyy most) which crosses the Moyka river near to the Yusupov Palace *(see p120).* Here the gilded lampposts are shaped to look like treble clefs. **Singer's Bridge** (Pevcheskiy most) at the other end of the Moyka takes its name from the choir of the nearby Glinka Capella. Its engineer, Yegor Adam, also designed the lace-like patterning of the railings.

At the junction where the Griboedov meets the Moyka is an interesting ensemble, formed by the wide **Theatre Bridge** (Teatralnyy most) and

Lamppost, St Panteleymon's Bridge

Small Stable Bridge (Malo-Konyushennyy most). The latter is cunningly designed to look like two bridges.

Among the more attractive bridges is Georg von Traitteur's pedestrian **Bank Bridge** (Bankovskiy most), crossing the Griboedov. Its cables are held up by two pairs of gold-winged griffons. The **Lion Bridge** (Lvinyy most), also by Traitteur, uses a similar device; in this case the suspension cables emerge from the open jaws of four proud lions.

St Panteleymon's Bridge (Panteleymonovskiy most, *see p99)* spans the Fontanka near the Summer Gardens. It was Russia's first chain bridge (1823–4). The Empire-style decoration has survived and includes gilded fasces and double-headed eagles perched on laurel wreaths. Next to the Nevskiy prospekt, the **Anichkov Bridge** (Anich-kovskiy most) is famous for its four vibrant bronze sculptures of wild horses and their powerful tamers, all of them in different poses. Further down the Fontanka, framed by a handsome Neo-Classical square by Carlo Rossi, is the **Lomonosov Bridge** (Most Lomonosova) with its unusual stone turrets.

The **Egyptian Bridge** (Egipetskiy most) spans the Fontanka close to the Kryukov Canal. It is ornamented with bronze sphinxes and bridgeheads resembling the entrance to an Egyptian temple. Originally constructed in 1826, the bridge collapsed under the weight of a passing cavalry squadron but was rebuilt in 1955.

A CITY UNDER WATER

Peter the Great should have known it was a bad idea to found a city here. The first flood, just three months after he started the fortress in 1703, swept away his building mater-ials. The water rises dangerously high on average once a year, but four floods, in 1777, 1824, 1924 and 1955, wrought massive damage. In 1824 the whole city went under water and 462 buildings were totally destroyed. This inspired Pushkin's poem *The Bronze Horseman (see p78).* Markers showing record waterheights can be found by the Winter Canal and the Peter and Paul Fortress. In 1989 construction of a dam was begun to prevent future destruction.

A 19th-century illustration of one of the many floods in St Petersburg

St Petersburg's Best: Palaces and Museums

S T PETERSBURG BOASTS more than 90 museums, many of them housed in palaces or other buildings of historical importance. Some are well known throughout the world, such as the Hermitage which began as Catherine the Great's private collection of European art. Others, including the Russian Museum and the Summer Palace, highlight local art, history and culture. Some of the most evocative museums are those commemorating the lives and work of famous artists, writers and musicians. This selection represents the most interesting in each category.

Petrogradskaya

The Hermitage
Incorporating the breathtaking state rooms of the Winter Palace, the world-famous Hermitage holds nearly three million exhibits which range from Fine Arts to archaeological finds.

Malaya Neva

Vasilevskiy Island

Bolshaya Neva

Menshikov Palace
This grandiose Baroque palace on Vasilevskiy Island is testimony to the power of Peter the Great's friend and advisor, Prince Menshikov.

Palace Embankment

Sennaya Ploshchad

IMPERIAL COUNTRY PALACES

To escape the pressures of the capital, successive Russian rulers built sumptuous retreats in the rural hinterland of St Petersburg. These offer a fascinating insight into the lifestyle of the Romanov dynasty.

Tsarskoe Selo's Catherine Palace was built by Rastrelli in a flamboyant Baroque style.

Peterhof's palace and pavilions are enhanced by the splendid cascades and fountains adorning the attractive grounds.

```
0 km      15

0 miles      15
```

Pavlovsk's Great Palace is set in an extensive naturalistic landscaped park, embellished with ponds, pavilions and monuments.

Kshesinskaya Mansion
Built for a prima ballerina of the Mariinskiy Theatre, this attractive Style-Moderne mansion now houses the Museum of Russian Political History containing souvenirs from the Revolution.

Neva

Summer Palace
Interiors and furniture, such as Peter the Great's original four-poster bed, give an idea of the tsar's relatively modest lifestyle.

Stieglitz Museum
A rich collection of applied art is displayed in Messmacher's magnificent building which was inspired by palaces of the Italian Renaissance.

Gostinyy Dvor

Russian Museum
Carlo Rossi's Mikhaylovskiy Palace is the splendid setting for an outstanding collection of Russian art, ranging from medieval icons to contemporary paintings and sculptures. This semi-abstract work Blue Crest *by Vasily Kandinsky dates from 1917.*

Pushkin House-Museum
Period furnishings and personal belongings such as this inkstand recreate the atmosphere of Alexander Pushkin's last home.

| 0 metres | 500 |
| 0 yards | 500 |

Exploring St Petersburg's Palaces and Museums

THE CITY'S PALACES range from imperial excess to the tasteful homes of the nobility, while art museums cover the fine and applied arts and folk crafts. The history of St Petersburg, from its foundation as Peter the Great's "window on the West" to its role as the "cradle of the Revolution", is covered by a variety of museums while its culture is documented in the apartments of writers, composers and artists. More specialist interests, from railway engines and military paraphernalia to insects and whales, also find reflection in the wealth of museums.

Bedroom in the Chinese Palace (1760s), Oranienbaum

Peter the Great's Summer Palace overlooking the Fontanka

PALACES

THE FABULOUS WEALTH of imperial St Petersburg is reflected in the magnificence of its palaces. No trip to the city is complete without a visit to at least one of the specta-cular out-of-town imperial summer residences, **Peterhof** *(see pp146–9)*, **Pavlovsk** *(see pp156–9)* or the Catherine Palace *(see pp150–151)* at **Tsarskoe Selo**. These palaces, built and added to in the last 200 years of Romanov rule, illustrate the extravagance of the imperial court and the wealth of the empire's natural resources. An abundance of gold, lapis lazuli, malachite, marble and other precious minerals decorates many of the rich palace interiors. The palace parks and grounds are landscaped and filled with follies and monuments.

At the centre of the city, the **Winter Palace** *(see pp92–3)* is home to the Hermitage art museum and epitomizes the opulence of the court. Peter the Great's more intimate

Summer Palace is nearby *(see p95)* and makes a pleasing contrast. Peter's friend and counsellor, Prince Alexander Menshikov, also built two sumptuous residences, the **Menshikov Palace** *(see p62)* on Vasilevskiy Island, and his summer country palace at **Oranienbaum** *(see p144).*

Overlooking the Moyka river is the **Yusupov Palace** *(see p120)* which is famed as the murder scene of Rasputin, the extraordinary peasant who exerted his malign influence over the Russian court.

For those in search of a tranquil setting, a pleasant day can be spent exploring the **Yelagin Palace** *(see p126)* and the island of the same name.

ART MUSEUMS

ONE OF THE WORLD'S greatest collections of Western art is housed in the **Hermitage** *(see pp84–93)* which owns an astounding 2.8 million pieces of art. With collections rang-ing from Egyptian mummies to Scythian gold, Greek vases, Colombian emeralds and a vast and dazzling array of Old Master, Impressionist and Post-Impressionist paintings, it is essential to be selective.

The **Russian Museum** *(see pp104–107)* is a showcase for Russian art, including the 20th-century avant-garde and the folk crafts which influenced it. Exhibitions from its holdings are also in the **Mikhaylovskiy Castle** *(see p101)*, **Marble Palace** *(see p94)* and **Stroganov Palace** *(see p112).*

The **Academy of Arts** *(see p63)* exhibits work by past students as well as models of the city's notable buildings.

There are fascinating displays of applied arts from around the world in the **Stieglitz Museum** *(see p127)* which includes cera-mics, wood carving, ironwork and embroidery. Its interiors and the glass-roofed exhibition hall are equally impressive.

***The Cyclist* (1913) by Natalya Goncharova, Russian Museum**

HISTORY MUSEUMS

ST PETERSBURG'S dramatic 300-year history is proudly recorded in a number of the city's museums. The **Cabin of Peter the Great** *(see p73)* was the earliest building to be constructed in the city and it offers an intriguing insight into the surprisingly humble lifestyle of this tsar.

A group of historic sights lies within the Peter and Paul Fortress. The **Cathedral of SS Peter and Paul** *(see p68)* houses the tombs of all but two of Russia's tsars since Peter the Great. The preserved cells of the grim **Trubetskoy Bastion** *(see p69)* act as a reminder of the hundreds of political prisoners to be confined within the fortress walls. In the **Commandant's House** *(see p69)*, the courthouse where prisoners were once interrogated, an exhibition looks at medieval settlements in the area, while the **Engineer's House** *(see p68)* focuses on daily life in St Petersburg before the Revolution.

A wealth of revolutionary memorabilia, including Stalin era posters and a huge propaganda stained-glass panel, can be found in the **Museum of Russian Political History**. The museum is located within the Kshesinskaya Mansion *(see p72)* which, in 1917, housed the Bolshevik headquarters. The **Cruiser Aurora** *(see p73)* also played a part in the Revolution, having fired a warning shot before the storming of the Winter Palace in October 1917.

For an impression of the prestigious pre-revolutionary school where poet Alexander Pushkin was a student, some of the class rooms of the **Lycée** at Tsarskoe Selo *(see p153)* have been restored to their 19th-century appearance.

On the southern outskirts of the city, in Victory Square *(see p131)*, the **Monument to the Heroic Defenders of Leningrad** poignantly evokes the Siege of Leningrad (1941–4) and acts as an important reminder of the great hardships endured by St Petersburgers during World War II.

Office of Leningrad party secretary Sergey Kirov, Kirov Museum

SPECIAL INTEREST MUSEUMS

REMNANTS of Peter the Great's legendary "cabinet of curiosities" can be found in the city's oldest museum, the **Kunstkammer** *(see p60)*. Housed under the same roof is a **Museum of Anthropology and Ethnography**, displaying a large collection of artifacts from all over the world. For natural history, the **Zoological Museum** *(see p60)* encompasses most known life forms, including a unique collection of molluscs and blue corals.

The **Naval Museum** *(see p60)* fascinates all ages with its model ships, small boats, figureheads and flags, while the **Artillery Museum** *(see p70)* covers military hardware, from pikes to ballistic missiles. Train enthusiasts will find plenty to enjoy in the **Railway Museum** *(see p123)*, including an 1835 engine built for the Tsarskoe Selo railway.

The **Museum of Musical Life** in the Sheremetev Palace *(see p129)* displays period

18th-century violin and score in Museum of Musical Life, Sheremetev Palace

instruments and explains the role of the Sheremetev family as leading music patrons in 19th-century St Petersburg. A stunning array of beautiful stage costumes are on display alongside photos, set designs and other theatrical ephemera in the **Theatre Museum** which is situated on Ostrovskiy Square *(see p110)*.

HOUSE-MUSEUMS

A HANDFUL of evocative museums commemorates some of the city's most famous residents. Two lovingly preserved museums, the **Pushkin House-Museum** *(see p113)* and the **Dostoevsky House-Museum** *(see p130)*, recapture something of the life and character of their former residents.

The **Anna Akhmatova Museum** in the former service quarters of the Sheremetev Palace *(see p129)* traces the dramatic life of the poetess who lived here for many years.

For an insight into the life of a powerful Communist official of the 1930s, visit the **Kirov Museum** *(see p72)*. The museum is devoted to the popular leader whose assassination on Stalin's orders initiated the Great Terror *(see p27)*.

Outside the city in **Repino** *(see p144)*, the house of the painter Ilya Repin is set in beautiful woodland on the Gulf of Finland.

Celebrated St Petersburgers

As the residence of the Russian imperial family and court from the early 18th century, St Petersburg was the focus of patronage and an almost boundless source of wealth. It was the perfect seed bed for creativity and the flowering of ideas. Institutions such as the Academy of Arts, the University, the Kunstkammer and the Imperial School of Ballet trained generations of cultural figures and scientists to the highest standards. So successful were they that, by the dawn of the 20th century, St Petersburg had become one of the most important cultural centres in Europe.

Grigoriy Kozintsev
Director Kozintsev confirmed his reputation in the West with his interpretation of Shakespeare's Hamlet *(1964), made at Lenfilm (see p70).*

Nikolai Gogol
A merciless satirist of St Petersburg society, Gogol lived on Malaya Morskaya ulitsa (see p82) for three years.

Malaya Neva

Vasilevskiy Island

Bolshaya Neva

Ilya Repin
This outstanding realist painter is seen here teaching life drawing at the Academy of Arts (see p63) where he was a professor.

Sennaya Ploshchad

Petrogradskaya

Pyotr Tchaikovsky
Tchaikovsky graduated from the Conservatory (see p120) in 1865 and went on to compose his world-famous operas and ballets.

Anna Pavlova
A prima ballerina at the Mariinskiy Theatre (see p119), Pavlova took Paris by storm in 1909 when she toured in Les Sylphides with the Ballets Russes.

Alexander Pushkin
The great poet, who sketched this self-portrait on a manuscript, died in the flat which is now a house-museum (see p113).

Sergey Diaghilev
Driving force behind the Ballets Russes, Diaghilev also produced the influential World of Art *magazine in his flat on 45 Liteynyy prospekt. He is shown here with Jean Cocteau (left).*

Neva

Palace Embankment

Anna Akhmatova
The poetess' most famous poem, Requiem, *is a powerful and moving indictment of the Stalinist regime. Akhmatova, seen here in a portrait by Nathan Altman, lived in the service quarters of the Sheremetev Palace (see p129).*

Gostinyy Dvor

Dmitriy Shostakovich
Shostakovich's Seventh Symphony *was broadcast live on the radio from the Great Hall of the Philharmonia (see p98) in August 1942, while the city was under siege. Many testified to its role in boosting the morale of the besieged citizens.*

Fyodor Dostoevsky
The novelist Dostoevsky lived for many years among the slums of Sennaya Ploshchad (see p122) which provided the setting for his greatest work, Crime and Punishment.

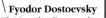

0 metres	500
0 yards	500

Remarkable St Petersburgers

THE STREETS of St Petersburg are redolent with literary and artistic associations. Fascinating art collections, house-museums, theatres and concert halls evoke the memory of famous St Petersburgers. The world of the 18th-century genius Lomonosov and 19th-century writers Pushkin and Dostoevsky can be imagined. So too, can the spirit of Russian ballet when dancers such as Anna Pavlova and Vaslaw Nijinsky thrilled the Mariinskiy audiences. During these early years of the 20th century, writers, musicians, dancers and painters flocked to St Petersburg, bringing with them a wealth of creativity.

Symbolist "Silver Age" poet, Andrei Bely (1880–1934)

WRITERS

CONSIDERED THE FATHER of modern Russian literature, **Alexander Pushkin** (1799–1837) was simultaneously intoxicated by St Petersburg's beauty and sensitive to the underlying climate of political suspicion and intolerance which constrained writers in the wake of the Decembrist rebellion of 1825 *(see p23)*. **Nikolai Gogol** (1809–52) responded to these constraints by satirising the status quo. In *The Nose*, he targeted the city's bureaucrats with their inflated sense of self worth and mind-numbing conformity.

Another aspect of the city altogether is revealed by **Fyodor Dostoevsky** (1821–81). His novel *Crime and Punishment*, one of more than 30 works set in the city, takes place against a backdrop of squalor in the notorious slums of Sennaya Ploshchad *(see p122)*. The story of the murder of an old moneylender was based on a real crime and the novel's publication in 1866 was blamed for a series of subsequent copy-cat killings.

Poetry, which flourished in the "Golden Age" of Pushkin, only regained its ascendancy over the novel in the "Silver Age" during the first decade of the 20th century. Some of the most exciting poets of the period, including **Aleksandr Blok** (1880–1921), **Andrei Bely** (1880–1934) and **Anna Akhmatova** (1889–1966), gathered at The Tower, a flat overlooking the Tauride Gardens *(see p128)*. Bely later wrote *Petersburg*, one of the earliest stream-of-consciousness novels. Akhmatova is honoured by a museum in the Sheremetev Palace *(see p129)* while one of her protégés, **Joseph Brodsky** (1940–96) went on to receive the Nobel Prize for literature in 1987. Brodsky became the bête-noire of the Leningrad literary establishment in the 1960s. The refusal of the authorities to publish his poetry, which they condemned as decadent, finally forced him to emigrate in 1972.

MUSICIANS

THE FIRST important composer to emerge from the nationalist movement was **Mikhail Glinka** (1804–57), the earliest composer of Russian opera. In 1862, the Conservatory *(see p120)* was founded by **Anton Rubinstein** (1829–94) and this became the focus of musical life in St Petersburg. **Nikolai Rimsky-Korsakov** (1844–1908) taught here for 37 years and together with composers such as **Modest Mussorgsky** (1839–81), and **Aleksandr Borodin** (1834–87), he formed "the mighty handful". They were a largely self-taught group aiming to develop a musical language based on Russian folk music and Slav traditions. Many of them wrote operas premiered at the Mariinskiy *(see p119)*.

One of the musical geniuses of the 20th century was **Igor Stravinsky** (1882–1971). He spent much time abroad but, as works like *The Rite of Spring* testify, his cultural roots were firmly in his homeland.

The city's most important concert venue is the Great Hall of the Philharmonia *(see p194)* where **Pyotr Tchaikovsky**'s (1840–93) *Sixth Symphony* was premiered in 1893 and **Dmitriy Shostakovich**'s (1906–75) *Seventh Symphony*, his most famous work, was performed in 1942.

Portrait of composer Mikhail Glinka painted by Ilya Repin in 1887

The Circus (1919) by avant-garde artist Marc Chagall

ARTISTS

FROM THE 18th century, the Academy of Arts *(see p63)* was the centre of artistic life in St Petersburg. **Dmitriy Levitskiy** (1735–1822), **Orest Kiprenskiy** (1782–1836), **Silvestr Shchedrin** (1791–1830), and Russia's first internationally recognised artist, **Karl Bryullov** (1799–1852), were all trained here.

In 1863, a group of students rebelled against the Academy and went on to establish the Wanderers movement *(see p106)*. To some extent the Academy and the Wanderers became reconciled when the most versatile of these artists, **Ilya Repin** (1844–1930), was appointed professor of painting at the Academy in 1893.

Five years later **Sergey Diaghilev** (1872–1929) and painter **Alexandre Benois** (1870–1960) launched the *World of Art* magazine *(see p107)*, proclaiming "Art for art's sake". Another collaborator, **Leon Bakst** (1866–1924), designed the most famous of the Ballets Russes costumes. Bakst also taught **Marc Chagall** (1889–1985) who later settled in France and had a profound impact on art in the West as well as in Russia. Other members of the Russian avant-garde include **Kazimir Malevich** (1878–1935) and **Pavel Filonov** (1883–1941).

Works by all of these artists can be seen at the Russian Museum *(see pp104–107)*.

DANCERS AND CHOREOGRAPHERS

THE SKILLS of Russian dancers are legendary and the performances of the Mariinskiy (Kirov) Ballet Company continue to enthral audiences all over the world. Since 1836 the dancers have been trained at the former Imperial Ballet School *(see p110)*. In 1869–1903 the outstanding choreographer at the Mariinskiy was **Marius Petipa**. He inspired a generation of dancers including **Matilda Kshesinskaya** *(see p72)*, **Vaslaw Nijinsky** (1890–1950) and the legendary **Anna Pavlova** (1885–1931).

Petipa's successor, **Michel Fokine** (1880–1942), is famous as the principal choreographer of the Ballets Russes *(see p119)*. The Mariinskiy tradition was revived after the Revolution by another graduate of the Ballet School, **Agrippina Vaganova** (1879–1951). Her groundwork paved the way for the modern generation of dancers including **Rudolf Nureyev** (1938–93) and more recently, **Galina Mezentseva** and **Emil Faskhoutdinov**.

FILM DIRECTORS

THE LENFILM STUDIOS *(see p70)* were founded in 1918 on the site where the first Russian cine film had been shown in 1896. In its heyday Lenfilm produced 15 movies a year. Its two most remarkable

Poster for *The Youth of Maxim* (1935) directed by Kozintsev

directors, **Grigoriy Kozintsev** (1905–73) and **Leonid Trauberg** (1902–90), first joined forces in 1922 and began making short experimental films. The pair then went on to direct *The New Babylon* (1929), remarkable for its montage and lighting effects, and *The Maxim Trilogy* (1935–39). Kozintsev's versions of *Hamlet* (1964) and *King Lear* (1970), with music composed by Shostakovich for both films, mark the height of his success in the West.

SCIENTISTS

The great polymath Mikhail Lomonosov

THE FOUNDATIONS of modern Russian science were laid in the 18th century by **Mikhail Lomonosov** (1711–65) *(see p61)* who worked for over 20 years in the Kunstkammer *(see p60)*. His treatise, *Elementa Chymiae Mathematica*, published in 1741, anticipates Dalton's theory of the atomic structure of matter.

In 1869, **Dmitriy Mendeleev** (1834–1907), a professor of chemistry, compiled the Periodic Table of Elements.

Many people believe that the world's first radio signal was sent by **Aleksandr Popov** (1859–1906) from the laboratories of St Petersburg University on 24 March 1896.

In 1904, the world-famous physiologist **Ivan Pavlov** (1849–1936) won the Nobel Prize for medicine for his theory of conditioned reflexes which he demonstrated by experimenting on dogs and their hearing responses.

Nevskiy Prospekt

From the Admiralty to the Griboedov Canal

A PLEASANT STROLL ALONG this first stretch of St Petersburg's main artery reveals a wealth of attractive buildings. A profusion of architectural styles ranges from the Baroque Stroganov Palace to the magnificent Neo-Classical Cathedral of Our Lady of Kazan and the striking Style-Moderne House of Books. The stately avenue was once known as the "Street of Tolerance", referring to the clutch of churches of different denominations which were established here in the late 18th and early 19th centuries. *(See also p108.)*

Literary Café
Once called the Wolf and Beranger, this café was known for its fashionable clientele. Pushkin left from here for his fatal duel in 1837 (see p83).

Admiralty
(p78)

Palace Square *(p83)* **and the Hermitage** *(pp84–93)*

ADMIRALTEYSKIY PROSPEKT

NEVSKIY PROSPEKT

The 1760s' apartment blocks at Nos. 8 and 10 are an example of early St Petersburg Neo-Classicism.

BOLSHAYA MORSKAYA ULITSA

MALAYA MORSKAYA ULITSA

BOLSHAYA MORSKAYA ULITSA

POLIT

The Admiralty Garden was laid out in 1872–4. Near the fountain are busts of composer Mikhail Glinka, writer Nikolai Gogol and poet Mikhail Lermontov.

St Isaac's Cathedral *(pp80–81)* **and Astoria Hotel** *(p79)*

Aeroflot Building
Marian Peretyatkovich's severe granite building (1912) is uncharacteristic of the city's architecture. The upper storeys were inspired by the Palazzo Medici in Florence, the arcades by the Doge's Palace, Venice.

0 metres   100

0 yards   100

ГРАЖДАНЕ!
ПРИ АРТОБСТРЕЛЕ
ЭТА СТОРОНА УЛИЦЫ
НАИБОЛЕЕ ОПАСНА

Sign at School No. 210
This school carries a sign, dating from the Siege, warning "Citizens! This side of the street is more dangerous during artillery bombardment".

Barrikada Cinema
Now a cinema, this handsome building was erected in 1768–71, for the city's police chief Nikolai Chicherin.

STAR SIGHT

★ **Cathedral of Our Lady of Kazan**

LOCATOR MAP

Dutch Church Building
The Dutch church was housed behind the central Neo-Classical portico of Paul Jacot's seemingly secular building (1831–7). The elongated wings are still occupied by offices, flats and shops.

Stroganov Palace
The façade of this splendid Baroque palace, one of the oldest buildings on the street (1753), is embellished with sculptural ornaments and the Stroganov coat of arms (see p112).

The Fashion House
Marian Lyalevich designed this building for Mertens Furriers in 1911–12. The impact of the Neo-Classical arches is heightened by the beautiful plate glass.

NAB REKI MOYKI

BOLSHAYA KONYUSHENNAYA UL

MALAYA KONYUSHENNAYA ULITSA

N E V S K I Y   P R O S P E K T

KAZANSKAYA ULITSA

KAZANSKIY MOST

KANAL GRIBOEDOVA

The House of Books
(Dom Knigi) was built for the Singer Sewing Machine Company in 1902–4 by Pavel Syuzor. The building, now a bookshop, is distinguished by a glass globe on a conical tower.

➤ **Continued (pp48–9)**

The Lutheran Church
(1833) was an important centre for the evangelical community. Converted into a swimming pool during the Soviet era, it is once again open as a church *(see p112).*

The Griboedov Canal,
originally known as the Catherine Canal, was renamed in 1923 after the 19th-century Russian playwright Aleksandr Griboedov.

★ **Cathedral of Our Lady of Kazan**
Ninety-six Corinthian columns, arranged in four rows, form an arc facing Nevskiy prospekt. Andrey Voronikhin's design was inspired by Bernini's colonnade for St Peter's in Rome (see p111).

Nevskiy Prospekt

From the Griboedov Canal to the Fontanka

Nevskiy prospekt has been the main focus for St Petersburg's shopping and entertainment since the mid-18th century. As the prospekt continues towards the handsome Anichkov Bridge on the Fontanka river, there are growing numbers of cafés, bars and restaurants as well as three historic shopping arcades, the Silver Rows, Gostinyy Dvor and Passazh. Bustling with life, this stretch of the avenue also has many sights of historic and architectural interest, including the Anichkov Palace.

Passazh Arcade
This popular shopping mall is covered by a glass canopy stretching 180 m (590 ft). The arcade opened in 1848 and was reconstructed in 1900.

Church on Spilled Blood (p100)

The Small Hall of the Philharmonia was the city's main concert hall in the early 19th century.

The Church of Saint Catherine (1762–82), by Vallin de la Mothe, is a mixture of Baroque and Neo-Classical styles. It is the oldest Roman Catholic church in Russia.

Grand Hotel Europe (p101)

Russian Museum (pp104–107)

The Armenian Church (1771–80) is a fine example of Yuriy Velten's decorative Neo-Classical style (see p108).

Gostinyy Dvor

KANAL GRIBOEDOVA

MIKHAYLOVSKAYA ULITSA

N E V S K I Y   P R O S P E K T

Nevskiy Prospekt M

Gostinyy Dvor M

DUMSKAYA ULITSA

SADOVAYA ULITSA

PLOSHC

Silver Rows Arcade (1784–7)

The Duma Tower was built in 1804 as a watchtower for fires. The Duma building was the centre of local government from 1786–1918.

The Russian National Library houses over 33 million items, including the earliest surviving handwritten Russian book (1057).

Portik Rusca
Now standing alone, the six-columned portico by Luigi Rusca was originally the entrance to a long arcade of shops. The portico was dismantled during the construction of the metro and rebuilt in 1972.

| 0 metres | 100 |
| 0 yards | 100 |

★ *Gostinyy Dvor*
This striking arcade has been St Petersburg's main bazaar since the mid-18th century (see p108). It houses more than 300 outlets which sell everything from clothes and cosmetics to souvenirs and chocolates.

★ Yeliseev's
Famous for its beautiful Style-Moderne decor, this building houses Yeliseev's delicatessen on the ground floor (see p109).

see p109

LOCATOR MAP

STAR SIGHTS

* **★ Yeliseev's**

* **★ Gostinyy Dvor**

Beloselskiy-Belozerskiy Palace
Now a cultural centre and Waxworks Museum, this sumptuous palace was designed in Neo-Baroque style by Andrey Stakenschneider in 1847–8. The faded red façade is decorated with Corinthian pilasters and atlantes upholding balconies.

Quarenghi's Stalls were built in 1803–6 as trading rows. They were then handed over to the imperial chancellor and became known as the Cabinet.

Number 66 was occupied by the music publishers Bessel and Co in the 19th century. Tchaikovsky was one of many composers who frequented their offices.

The Central District Tax Office has a Neo-Classical appearance, but was not built until the 1940s.

NEVSKIY PROSPEKT

OSTROVSKOVO

FONTANKA

ANICHKOV MOST

FONTANKA

Aleksandrinskiy Theatre

A statue of Catherine the Great stands in Ostrovskiy Square *(see p110).*

Moskovskiy railway station

The Anichkov Palace was first built as a present from Tsarina Elizabeth to her lover, Aleksey Razumovskiy. It later became the winter residence of the heir to the throne *(see p109).*

Anichkov Bridge
Four dynamic bronze statues of rearing horses and their tamers adorn this well-known landmark. They were designed in the 1840s by Pyotr Klodt (see p35).

ST PETERSBURG THROUGH THE YEAR

WHATEVER THE weather, Russians are always ready to celebrate and consequently take their public holidays very seriously. Flowers have great symbolic significance, from mimosa for International Women's Day, to lilac to mark the beginning of summer. Every official holiday, as well as some local festivals such as City Day, are celebrated both in the centre of town and in the many

Lilac, a symbol of summer

different districts, with regattas, balloon rides and fireworks at night, when the torches on the Rostral Columns *(see p60)* are lit. Classical music is the central theme of a large number of festivals each year, attracting talented performers from all over the world. But even without an official holiday, Russian people love to get out and about, whether to ski or ice-skate in the winter months or gather mushrooms in late summer and autumn.

SPRING

SPRING HAS SET IN for good when the first sunbathers gather on the beaches outside the Peter and Paul Fortress *(see pp66–7)* and when, in early April after the waterways have thawed, the city's bridges open to allow ships through.

To warm themselves up after the months of cold, locals celebrate "maslennitsa", the making of pancakes (*blini*) prior to Lent. They then gather bunches of willow as a symbol of the approaching Palm Sunday. On the eve of Lent, "Forgiveness Sunday", it is common practice to ask forgiveness of those you might have offended during the year.

Once the snows have gone, the first trips to the *dacha*, or country house, are made to put the gardens in order.

Early sunbathers on the banks of the Peter and Paul Fortress

MARCH

International Women's Day (*Mezhdunarodnyy zhenskiy den*), 8 Mar. Men rush around the city buying flowers for their womenfolk. It is a

Candles lighting up Russian Orthodox church during Easter service

tradition to say *s prazdnikom* (congratulations on the holiday) to everyone. There are even special performances and concerts and, however sexist it may seem to non-Russians, it is a very popular day.
From the Avant Garde to the Present (*Ot avangarda do nashih dney*), mid-Mar. A celebration of 20th-century art and music in a city-wide festival.
Virtuosi 2000, late Mar/early Apr. Aspiring young musicians from all over the world come together to perform and compete on St Petersburg's stages.
Easter Sunday (*Paskha*). The dates on which Lent and Easter fall change every year. On Easter Sunday, St Petersburg churches are filled with worshippers, the evocative sound of ethereal music and chanting and the smell of incense. Russians traditionally greet each other with *Khristos voskres* (Christ is risen), to which the reply is *Voistine voskres* (He is truly risen).

APRIL

Musical Spring in St Petersburg (*Muzikalnaya Vesna v Sankt-Peterburge*), mid-Apr. As warm clothing and heavy boots are laid aside after the cold winter months, the public flock to concert halls throughout the city.
Cosmonauts' Day (*Den Kosmonavtiki*), 12 Apr. Space exploration was one of the glories of the Soviet Union and this occasion is celebrated with fireworks at 10pm.

MAY

Labour Day (International Workers' Solidarity Day, *Den Solidarnosti Trudyashchihsya*), 1 May. Public holiday.
Peterhof Fountains (*Fontany v Petergofe*), first weekend in May. Bands and orchestras accompany the switching on of the famous fountains at Peterhof *(see p149)*. **Victory Day** (*Den Pobedy*), 9 May. After a sombre ceremony at Piskarevskoe Cemetery *(see p126)*, smartly-dressed veterans fill Nevskiy prospekt *(see pp46–9)* and Palace Square *(see p83)* in commemoration of the Nazi surrender in 1945.
City Day (*Den goroda*), last week of May. A great variety of events, mainly taking place around the Peter and Paul Fortress *(see pp66–7)*, mark the founding of the city on 27 May 1703.

Proud war veteran on Victory Day

AVERAGE DAILY HOURS OF SUNSHINE

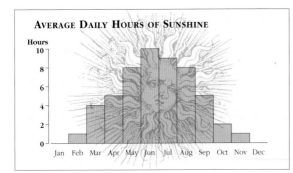

Hours: 10, 8, 6, 4, 2, 0

Jan Feb Mar Apr May Jun Jul Aug Sep Oct Nov Dec

Sunshine Hours
St Petersburg's climate can vary dramatically from hot, sunny days and occasional heavy downpours during the summer months, to winters with sub-zero temperatures and snow. From mid-June to mid-July, it never gets dark. During the winter months the days are extremely short, but there can be days of bright sunshine.

SUMMER

A LILAC IN FLOWER is the real symbol that warm weather has set in and there is an air of excitement once the Field of Mars (see p94) comes into bloom. Throughout the warm months, the city is deserted at weekends when people go off to their *dacha*, usually situated around the pine forests in the area northwest of the city.

St Petersburg's main festive season is during the acclaimed White Nights in June, when the sun hardly sets and it never quite gets dark. Concerts, ballets and other performances take place all over the city, which fills with thousands of visitors (see p193). The most favoured place to be at night-time is on the embankments of the Neva, which are crowded with revellers watching the bridges being raised at 2am.

JUNE

International Protection of Children Day (*Den Zatschity detey*), 1 Jun.

Performances and events for children are held throughout the city.

Independence Day (*Den nezavisimosti*), 12 Jun. The day Russia became "independent" of the Soviet Union is marked with fireworks at 10pm.

Trinity Sunday (*Troytsa*), 50 days after Easter. Believers and atheists alike go to tidy the graves of their loved ones and raise a glass of vodka for their souls.

The White Nights Swing, Jazz Festival, mid-June. A large jam session supported by local and visiting musicians for anyone with an interest in jazz.

Stars of the White Nights, Classical Music Festival (*Zvezdy Belykh nochey*), late Jun. This is the original White Nights festival, with first-class opera, classical music and ballet concerts performed at all major venues.

White Nights, Rock Music Festival (*Belye nochi*), late Jun. Numerous outdoor rock concerts are held at the Peter and Paul Fortress (see pp66–7).

Festival of Festivals (*Festival-festivaley*), last week

Russian battleships moored on the Neva, Navy Day

in Jun. This is an international non-competitive film festival showing the best international films released over the past year. The festival attracts film stars from all over the world.

Tsarskoe Selo Carnival (*Tsarskoselskiy karnaval*), last weekend in June. Funny costumes, music and mayhem fill the centre of Tsarskoe Selo (see pp150–53).

JULY

Sporting Competitions St Petersburg has become an increasingly popular sporting venue in recent years, offering everything from tennis to yachting.

Navy Day (*Den Voenno-morskovo Flota*), first Sun after 22 July. The Neva resembles a shipyard, with submarines and torpedo boats adorned with flags and bunting.

AUGUST

With schools on holiday and temperatures at their highest, most families escape to their *dacha* in the pine forests around the city.

Bridge opening in front of the Peter and Paul Fortress on a White Night

AVERAGE MONTHLY RAIN AND SNOWFALL

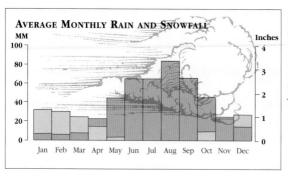

Jan Feb Mar Apr May Jun Jul Aug Sep Oct Nov Dec

Rain and Snowfall Chart

St Petersburg summers are humid and wet, but the downpours are a welcome relief from the summer heat. In winter frequent snowfalls build up to create metre-high drifts, usually not thawing until late March.

☐ Rainfall (from axis)

☐ Snowfall (from axis)

AUTUMN

CITY LIFE begins to gain pace as people return from their *dacha* and families begin to prepare for the start of school.

In September, when theatres re-open after the summer break, the city's cultural life resumes. The Mariinskiy (Kirov) returns from touring, and new plays and operas are premiered. October marks the start of the festival season, with guest musicians and theatre groups from all over the world taking part.

The crisp autumn weather is ideal for gathering mushrooms.

Chanterelle mushrooms

Popular hunting spots can be found to the northwest of the city around Zelenogorsk and Repino *(see p144)*. Enthusiastic mushroom-gatherers rise early to hunt for chanterelles, oyster mushrooms, *podberyozoviki* (brown mushrooms) and *podosinoviki* (orange-cap bolens). The locals are skilled in identifying edible mushrooms while amateur pickers should be aware of the dangers of poisonous ones. An activity with fewer potential side-effects might be a trip on the hydrofoil to Peterhof *(see pp146–9)* to see the magnificent fountains before they are switched off for the winter.

Children dressed up for Teachers' Day, the first day of school

SEPTEMBER

Knowledge Day
(Den znaniy), 1 Sep. The city is full of children heading for their first day back at school, laden with flowers.

OCTOBER

Theatre Festival of the Baltic Countries *(Teatralnyy festival Baltiyskikh stran)*, Oct. Actors, clowns and pantomime artists gather from the Baltic countries to perform in theatres and on the streets with two weeks of mayhem.

NOVEMBER

Day of Reconciliation, 7 Nov. A reminder that the Russian Federation is a multi-national country with various religions and political parties.
Sound Ways, Modern Music Festival *(Zvukovyye puti)*, mid-Nov. A chance to catch up with some of the most avant-garde trends in jazz and contemporary classical music from Russia and the rest of Europe. Musicians invited from abroad abound, and many of Russia's most renowned performers refuse international engagements in order to take part in this exciting home-grown festival.

Autumn colours in the park at Tsarskoe Selo

AVERAGE MONTHLY TEMPERATURE

Temperature Chart
St Petersburg's climate is maritime and milder than might be expected. Summers are warm and often punctuated with hot days as early as May, though during the winter months temperatures often fall below freezing. St Petersburg's average minimum and maximum temperatures throughout the year are shown in this chart.

WINTER

As the ice thickens on the waters and the snow deepens, people head for the outdoors once more. Children's sledges are not expensive to buy, and all other equipment can be hired. Cross-country skiing needs no lessons to make it fun. Tsarskoe Selo *(see pp150–53)* and Pavlovsk *(see pp156–9)* parks both provide ski and sledge hire at the ski bases *(lyzhnaya baza)*. Skates can be hired for use in the rink at Moskovskiy Park Pobedy, by Park Pobedy metro station in the southern suburbs, and also at the Central Park of Culture and Rest (Krestovskiy Ostrov metro station).

The truly hardened members of the local "walruses" swimming club break the ice by the Peter and Paul Fortress *(see pp66–7)* every day to take an early morning dip.

In the midst of winter activities come New Year and Christmas. New Year is the big holiday, while Christmas itself is celebrated according to the Orthodox calendar, on 7 January. Many people also still

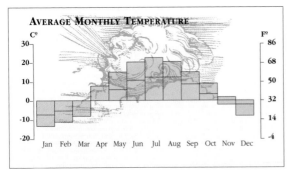

Sledging on the frozen Neva outside the Hermitage *(see pp84–93)*

Drilling a hole through the ice for winter-time fishing

celebrate Old New Year, which falls on 14 January. A seasonal delight is the Christmas ballet, *The Nutcracker*, at the Mariinskiy Theatre *(see p119)*.

DECEMBER

Constitution Day *(Den konstitutsii)*, 12 Dec. When Yeltsin's new constitution replaced the Brezhnev version, a new constitution day replaced the old one. Fireworks are set off all over town at 10pm.
Musical Encounters in the Northern Palmyra *(Muzykalnyye vstrechi v Severnoy Palmire)*, Dec–Jan. This classical music festival is the last one of the year and is made even more magical by the outside backdrop of snowy streets and frozen waterways.
New Year's Eve *(Novyy god)*, 31 Dec. Still the biggest holiday of the year, New Year's Eve is best celebrated with the local "champagne", Shampanskoye *(see p179)*. This is considered to be a family celebration, with people dressed as Grandfather Frost (the Russian equivalent of Santa Claus) and the Snow Maiden, the traditional bearers of gifts.

JANUARY

Russian Orthodox Christmas *(Rozhdestvo)*, 7 Jan. Christmas is celebrated in a quieter fashion than Easter, with a traditional visit to an evening service on Christmas Eve (6th), when the church bells ring out all over the city.

FEBRUARY

Defenders of the Motherland Day *(Den zashchitnikov rodiny)*, 23 Feb. The male equivalent of Women's Day. Men are congratulated and given flowers and presents.

PUBLIC HOLIDAYS

New Year's Day (1 Jan)
Russian Orthodox Christmas (7 Jan)
International Women's Day (8 Mar)
Easter Sunday (Mar/Apr)
Labour Day (1 May)
Victory Day (9 May)
Independence Day (12 Jun)
Day of Reconciliation (7 Nov)
Constitution Day (12 Dec)

St Petersburg Area by Area

VASILEVSKIY ISLAND

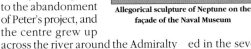

IT WAS PETER THE GREAT'S intention that Vasilevskiy Island *(Vasilevskiy ostrov),* the largest island in the Neva delta, was to be the administrative heart of his new capital. However, lack of access (the first permanent bridge was not built until 1850) and the hazards of floods and stormy crossings led to the abandonment of Peter's project, and the centre grew up

Allegorical sculpture of Neptune on the façade of the Naval Museum

across the river around the Admiralty *(see p78)* instead. The island's original street plan, based on canals that were never dug *(see p20),* survives in the numbered streets known as lines

(linii), which run from north to south. The focal point of the island is at the east end with the fine ensemble of public buildings around the spit or Strelka. The rest of the island developed with the spread of industrialization in the 19th century and it became a middle-class haven. There was also a thriving German community here which is reflected in the several Lutheran churches. Today much of the island has a sedate air, with broad tree-lined avenues, a clutch of museums and some attractive 19th-century architecture.

SIGHTS AT A GLANCE

Museums
Kunstkammer ❹
Menshikov Palace ❻
Naval Museum ❷
Zoological Museum ❸

Historic Buildings and Monuments
Academy of Arts ❾
Rostral Columns ❶
Twelve Colleges ❺

Churches
St Andrew's Cathedral ❽

Streets and Bridges
Bolshoy Prospekt ❼
Lieutenant Shmidt Bridge ❿

KEY

▨	Street-by-Street map See p58–9
Ⓜ	Metro
▥	Tram stop

0 metres 400
0 yards 400

◁ **One of the two imposing 14th-century BC sphinxes situated in front of the Academy of Arts**

Street-by-Street: the Strelka

T HE EASTERN END of Vasilevskiy Island is known as the Strelka, or "spit". Once St Petersburg's main centre of commerce, it has become an area of learning. The Academy of Sciences and St Petersburg University are situated here, as are various museums, institutes and libraries, housed in the former warehouses and customs buildings. The nautical theme is preserved in the Naval Museum and the two Rostral Columns. In front of these lighthouses is a lawn, a popular spot for newly married couples to have their picture taken. From here there are views across the Neva towards the Peter and Paul Fortress *(see pp66–7)* and the Hermitage *(see pp84–93)*.

The Naval Museum and Rostral Columns from across the Neva

The Lomonosov Monument honours Mikhail Lomonosov (1711–65), who taught at the Academy of Sciences.

Twelve Colleges
Originally erected to house the 12 ministries of Peter the Great's government, they now form the main building of St Petersburg University ❺

The Academy of Sciences was founded in 1724. The present building was constructed by Giacomo Quarenghi in 1783–5.

★ Kunstkammer
The Kunstkammer houses Peter the Great's collection of biological curiosities. Its tower, crowned by a sundial, is a St Petersburg landmark ❹

Zoological Museum
With over 1.5 million specimens the museum is one of the finest of its kind in the world. The exhibits include a set of stuffed animals that belonged to Peter the Great and a world-famous collection of mammoths ❸

MENDELEEVSKAYA LINIYA

BIRZHEVOY PROEZD

UNIVERSITETSKAYA NABEREZHNAYA

DVORTSOVYY MOST

Palace Embankment

STAR SIGHTS

★ **Naval Museum**

★ **Kunstkammer**

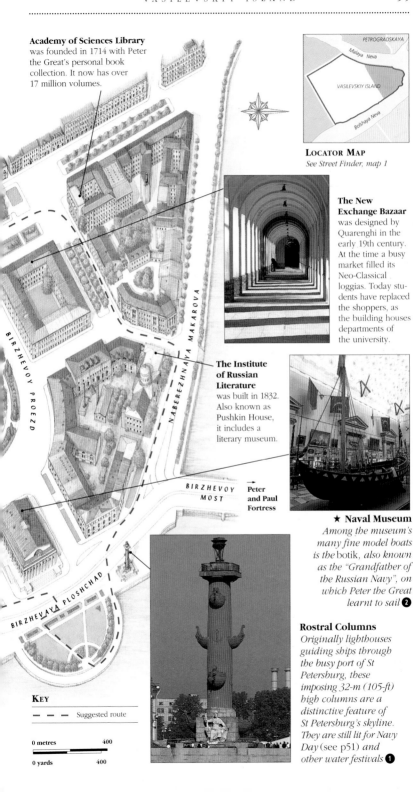

Academy of Sciences Library was founded in 1714 with Peter the Great's personal book collection. It now has over 17 million volumes.

LOCATOR MAP
See Street Finder, map 1

The New Exchange Bazaar was designed by Quarenghi in the early 19th century. At the time a busy market filled its Neo-Classical loggias. Today students have replaced the shoppers, as the building houses departments of the university.

The Institute of Russian Literature was built in 1832. Also known as Pushkin House, it includes a literary museum.

BIRZHEVOY PROEZD

NABEREZHNAYA MAKAROVA

BIRZHEVOY MOST

Peter and Paul Fortress

BIRZHEVAYA PLOSHCHAD

★ **Naval Museum**
Among the museum's many fine model boats is the botik, *also known as the "Grandfather of the Russian Navy", on which Peter the Great learnt to sail* ❷

Rostral Columns
Originally lighthouses guiding ships through the busy port of St Petersburg, these imposing 32-m (105-ft) high columns are a distinctive feature of St Petersburg's skyline. They are still lit for Navy Day (see p51) and other water festivals ❶

KEY

– – – Suggested route

0 metres 400

0 yards 400

Rostral Columns ❶

Ростральные колонны

Rostralnye kolonny

Birzhevaya ploshchad. **Map** 1 C5.
🚌 7, 10, 47, K-47, K-129, K-147,
K228, K-252. 🚎 1, 7, 10.

Situated on the Strelka before the Naval Museum, the impressive twin russet-coloured Rostral Columns were designed as lighthouses by Thomas de Thomon in 1810. During the 19th century the oil lamps were replaced by gas torches which are still lit on ceremonial occasions such as Navy Day *(see p51)*. Following a Roman custom, the columns are decorated with protruding ships' prows in celebration of naval victories. The monumental figures around the base represent four of Russia's great rivers, the Neva, Volga, Dnieper and Volkhov.

Rostral Column on the Strelka

Naval Museum ❷

Центральный
Военно-Морской музей

Tsentralnyy Voenno-Morskoy muzey

Birzhevaya ploshchad 4. **Map** 1 C5.
📞 328 2502. 🚌 7, 10, 47, K-47, K-128, K-129, K-147. 🚎 1, 7, 10. ⏰
11am–6pm Wed–Sun.
📷 ⬜ 🚻 ♿ English.
🌐 www.museum.navy.ru

The former Stock Exchange *(birzha)* was built in 1805–10 as the focal point of the Strelka. The building was designed by the Swiss architect Thomas de Thomon and was modelled on one of the famous Greek temples at Paestum in Italy. Above the columned east façade is an allegorical sculpture featuring the sea-god Neptune in a chariot drawn by sea horses; a reminder that maritime commerce was traditionally the lifeblood of this sea-oriented city.

The exchange became redundant after the Revolution and in 1940 it was turned into a museum. Beneath the magnificent coffered ceiling of the spacious trading hall is an exhibition on the history of the Russian and Soviet navy from its origins under Peter the Great to the present day. Pride of place belongs to the *botik*, the small masted wooden vessel on which Peter learned to sail. There is plenty of interest besides, from model ships and carved prow figureheads to uniforms, flags and guided missile submarines. There is also a superb diorama of the storming of the Winter Palace *(see pp28–9)* on the second-floor landing.

The photographic displays around the hall concentrate on the revolutionary period. These were redesigned only in 1995 to present a more balanced view of events, such as the involvement of Western powers in World War II.

Neo-Classical façade of the Naval Museum, overlooking the Strelka

Zoological Museum ❸

Зоологический музей

Zoologicheskiy muzey

Universitetskaya naberezhnaya 1/3.
Map 1 C5. 📞 328 0112. 🚌 7, 10, 47, K-47, K-128, K-129, K-147. 🚎 1, 7, 10. ⏰ 11am–6pm Sat–Thu.
📷 (free Thu). ⬜ 🚻 ♿ English.

Housed in a former customs warehouse designed by Giovanni Lucchini in 1826, this museum has one of the world's largest natural history collections containing more than 1.5 million specimens. Some of the stuffed animals belonged to Peter the Great's *Kunstkammer* collection, including the horse he rode at the Battle of Poltava *(see p18)*.

Dioramas atmospherically recreate natural habitats for giant crabs, weasels, polar bears and blue whales. The museum is renowned for its collection of mammoths. The most prized carcass was exhumed from the frozen wastes of Siberia in 1902 and is almost 44,000 years old.

Weasel in the Zoological Museum

Kunstkammer ❹

Кунсткамера

Kunstkamera

Universitetskaya naberezhnaya 3.
Map 1 C5. 📞 328 1412. 🚌 7, 10, 47, K-47, K-128, K-129, K-147. 🚎 1, 7, 10. ⏰ 11am–6pm Tue–Sun. 📷
♿ English.

The delicate, sea green lantern tower of the Baroque Kunstkammer ("art chamber") is visible across this part of Vasilevskiy Island. The building, by Georg Mattarnoviy, was constructed in 1718–34 to exhibit Peter the Great's infamous *Kunstkammer* collection. While touring Holland in 1697 Peter attended the lectures of Frederik Ruysch (1638–1731),

The restrained Baroque façade of the Kunstkammer (1718–34), St Petersburg's first museum

the most celebrated anatomist of his day. He was so impressed with Ruysch's collection of rarities that on a return visit in 1717, he purchased the entire collection of over 2,000 anatomical preparations. He transported it to St Petersburg and exhibited it to a wide-eyed public, who were enticed by free glasses of vodka. At the time, Peter's collection also included bizarre, live exhibits of deformed or unusual people, including an hermaphrodite. This, Russia's first museum, also included a library, an anatomical theatre and an observatory.

Today the Kuntskammer houses the Museum of Anthropology and Ethnography, with the remnants of Peter's bizarre collection on display in the central rotunda. Included are the heart and skeleton of Peter's personal servant, "Bourgeois", a giant at 2.27 m (7.5 ft), and a cabinet of teeth extracted by the tsar who was an enthusiastic amateur dentist. Most gruesome of all is the collection of pickled oddities which include Siamese twins and a two-headed sheep.

The halls surrounding the *Kuntskammer* collection contain exhibitions on the peoples of the world. Unfairly neglected by most foreign visitors, these marvellously old-fashioned displays present a vast and informative range of artifacts, from an Inuit kayak to Javanese shadow puppets.

Twelve Colleges ❺

Двенадцать коллегий

Dvenadtsat kollegiy

Universitetskaya naberezhnaya 7.
Map 1 C5. ▦ 7, 47, K-47, K-128, K-129, K-147. ▦ 1, 10. ⬤ to public.

THIS DISTINGUISHED Baroque building of red-and-white stuccoed brick is almost 400 m (1,300 ft) in length. It was intended for Peter the Great's newly-streamlined administration of 12 colleges or ministries. The single, uninterrupted façade was designed to symbolize the government's unity of purpose, while the curious alignment, at right angles to the embankment, is explained by Peter's unrealized plan for a large

Mikhail Lomonosov (1711–65)

A section of the west façade of Trezzini's Twelve Colleges

square with an unbroken view across the Strelka. Another popular theory is that Prince Menshikov changed the plan in Peter's absence so that the building would not encroach on his grounds. Domenico Trezzini won the competition for the design in 1723, but subsequent bureaucratic wrangling delayed its completion for 20 years. The building's function gradually changed and in 1819 part of it was acquired by St Petersburg University. A string of revolutionaries, including Lenin in 1891, were educated here. Among the famous Russian lecturers to teach here were the chemist Dmitriy Mendeleev (1834–1907) *(see p45)* and the physiologist Ivan Pavlov (1849–1936) *(see p45)*.

Overlooking the Neva, outside the Twelve Colleges, is an engaging bronze statue of the great 18th-century polymath Mikhail Lomonosov (unveiled in 1986). The son of a fisherman, Lomonosov was the first Russian-born member of the nearby Academy of Sciences. A "universal genius", he wrote poetry, systematized Russian grammar and was a pioneer in mathematics and the physical sciences. Thanks to his scientific discoveries, the art of porcelain, glass and mosaic production began in Russia.

The southern façade of Prince Menshikov's 18th-century palace

Menshikov Palace ⑥
Меншиковский дворец
Menshikovskiy dvorets

Universitetskaya naberezhnaya 15. **Map** 5 B1. 🇨 323 1112. 🚎 7, 47, K-47, K-128, K-129, K-147. 🚋 1, 10. 🚌 1, 11. ⭕ 10:30am–4:30pm Tue–Sun. 📷 📹 compulsory (English, French, German available).

The ochre-painted Baroque Menshikov Palace, with its beautifully carved pilasters, was one of the earliest stone buildings in St Petersburg. Designed by Giovanni Fontana and Gottfried Schädel for the infamous Prince Menshikov, the palace was completed in 1720. The palace estate originally extended as far as the Malaya Neva river to the north.

Prince Menshikov entertained here on a lavish scale, often on behalf of Peter the Great, who adopted the palace as a pied-à-terre. Guests would cross the Neva by boat and arrive to the grand welcome of a liveried orchestra.

The palace is now a branch of the Hermitage *(see pp84–93)* with exhibitions on early 18th-century Russian culture, revealing the extent to which Peter the Great's court was influenced by Western tastes.

The conducted tour begins on the ground floor; besides the kitchen there are displays of Peter's cabinet-making tools, period costumes, sturdy oak chests and ships' compasses. Adorning the beautiful vaulted hallway are marble statues imported from Italy which include a Roman Apollo dating to the 2nd century AD.

Upstairs, the secretary's rooms are decorated with 17th-century Dutch engravings of Leyden, Utrecht and Kraków. A series of breathtaking rooms are lined with hand-painted blue and white 18th-century Dutch tiles. Tiles were not only fashionable, but also a very practical means of deterring flies and dust.

In the tiled bedroom of Varvara (Menshikov's sister-in-law and confidante) is a German-made four-poster bed, with a Turkish coverlet woven from cotton, silk and silver thread. Hanging behind it is an exquisite 17th-century Flemish tapestry.

Menshikov and Peter often received guests in the aptly named Walnut Study which has Persian walnut panelling and commanding views of the Neva. Paintings hang from coloured ribbons, as was the fashion, including a late 17th-century portrait of Peter the Great by the Dutch painter Jan Weenix. The mirrors were a novelty at that time and such displays of vanity were anathema to the Orthodox Church.

The Great Hall, decorated in gold and stucco, is where balls and banquets were held. On one famous occasion, it was the setting for a "dwarfs' wedding" which Menshikov arranged for the amusement of his royal master.

The fine, Style-Moderne *apteka*, just off Bolshoy prospekt

Bolshoy Prospekt ⑦
Большой проспект
Bolshoy prospekt

Map 1 A5. Ⓜ *Vasileostrovskaya*. 🚎 7, 128, 151, 152, K-47, K-124, K-128, K-129. 🚋 10.

This imposing avenue was opened early in the 18th century to connect Menshikov's estate to the Gulf of Finland.

The mix of architectural styles ranges from the elegant Neo-Classicism of St Catherine's Lutheran Church (1768–71) at No. 1 to the simple Troyekurov House (No. 13, 6-ya liniya) in 17th-century Petrine Baroque.

Other buildings of note include the arcaded St Andrew's food market (1789–90) and two Style-Moderne edifices. One of these is the former pharmacy or *apteka* (1907–10) around the corner on 7-ya liniya, and the other is Adolph Gaveman's Lutheran orphanage at No. 55 (1908).

PRINCE MENSHIKOV

A leading advisor, comrade-in-arms and friend of Peter the Great, Aleksandr Menshikov (1673–1729) rose from humble origins to his position as the first governor of St Petersburg. After Peter's death in 1725, Menshikov engineered the ascension of Catherine I (Peter's wife, and Menshikov's former mistress) to the throne, thus maintaining his power until her demise. His notorious extravagance and venality eventually caught up with him. Accused of treason, he died in exile in 1729.

The Academy of Arts (1764–88) on the Neva embankment, an example of early Russian Neo-Classicism

St Andrew's Cathedral ❽

Андреевский собор
Andreevskiy sobor

6-ya liniya 11. **Map** 5 B1. 323 3418. 7, 128, K129. 10.

FIRST BUILT on the initiative of Peter the Great's second wife, Catherine I *(see p21)*, who donated 3,000 roubles towards its construction, the original wooden church on this site was destroyed by fire.

The present Baroque church with its distinctive steeple-like bell tower was constructed by Aleksandr Vist in 1764–80. The most stunning feature of the interior is the elaborately carved 18th-century iconostasis which incorporates icons from the original church.

The treasure of St Andrew's Cathedral, its beautiful Baroque iconostasis

Situated next door is Giuseppe Trezzini's small Church of the Three Saints (1740–60) which is dedicated to SS Basil the Great, John Chrysostom and Gregory of Nazianzus.

Academy of Arts ❾

Академия Художеств
Akademiya Khudozhestv

Universitetskaya naberezhnaya 17.
Map 5 B1. 323 3578. 7, 47, K129. 10. 1, 11.
11am–6pm Wed–Sun.

FOUNDED in 1757 to train home-grown artists in the preferred Western styles and techniques of art, the Academy spawned a galaxy of talent, including the great painter Ilya Repin *(see p42)* and architects Andrey Zakharov (1761–1811) and Andrey Voronikhin (1759–1814).

The innate conservatism of the Academy tended to discourage innovation and experiment and in 1863 a band of 14 students walked out of their graduation exams in protest. They went on to found a realist art movement and became known as the Wanderers or *peredvizhniki (see pp106–7)*.

The imposing Academy, built between 1764–88 by Aleksandr Kokorinov and Vallin de la Mothe, is an example of the transition from Baroque to Neo-Classicism. Still

an art school, it exhibits the work of students past and present, including canvases, plaster casts of famous sculptures, architectural drawings and models of many of the city's notable buildings, such as the magnificent Smolnyy Convent *(see p128)*.

The splendid Neo-Classical halls and galleries, though faded, retain something of their original grandeur. Of note are the Conference Hall on the first floor, with its ceiling painting by Vasiliy Shebuev, and the adjoining Raphael and Titian galleries, adorned with copies of Vatican frescoes.

Flanking the river stairs outside the Academy are two sphinxes from the 14th century BC. Discovered among the ruins of Thebes in ancient Egypt, they were installed here in 1832. The faces are thought to bear a likeness of the pharaoh Amenhotep III.

Lieutenant Shmidt Bridge ❿

Мост Лейтенанта Шмидта
Most Leytenanta Shmidta

Map 5 B2. K-62, K-124, K-144, K-154, K-186, K-222, K-350. 1, 11.

ORIGINALLY KNOWN as the Nicholas Bridge, this was the first permanent crossing of the Neva when it opened in 1850. The reconstruction of the bridge which was carried out in 1936–8 incorporated Aleksandr Bryullov's original railings, fancifully decorated with sea horses and tridents.

The bridge commemorates Lieutenant Pyotr Shmidt, a sailor on the cruiser *Ochakov*, who led an uprising of the Black Sea fleet in 1905.

PETROGRADSKAYA

THE CITY was founded on the northern banks of the Neva river in 1703, at the height of the Great Northern War *(see p18)*. Building began with the construction of a wooden fortress and Petrogradskaya, or the Petrograd Side, soon became a marshy suburb of wooden cabins occupied by craftsmen working on Peter the Great's new city.

Nearby, the area around Trinity Square was originally a small merchants' quarter centred around a now demolished church and St Petersburg's first stock exchange.

Detail on bridge to Peter and Paul Fortress

Petrogradskaya was sparsely populated until the late 1890s when the construction of the Trinity Bridge made the area accessible from the city centre. The bridge caused a housing boom at the height of a fashion for Style-Moderne architecture which is still in evidence today. The population quadrupled and the area became very popular with artists and professionals.

The highlight of the area, which is still largely residential, is the Peter and Paul Fortress with its cathedral, museums and grim history.

SIGHTS AT A GLANCE

Museums
Artillery Museum **7**
Cabin of Peter the Great **13**
Commandant's House **4**
Cruiser Aurora **12**
Engineer's House **2**
Kirov Museum **10**
Kshesinskaya Mansion **11**
Trubetskoy Bastion **6**

Gates
Neva Gate **5**
St Peter's Gate **1**

Cathedrals
Cathedral of SS Peter and Paul **3**

Streets, Squares and Parks
Aleksandrovskiy Park **8**
Kamennoostrovskiy Prospekt **9**
Trinity Square **14**

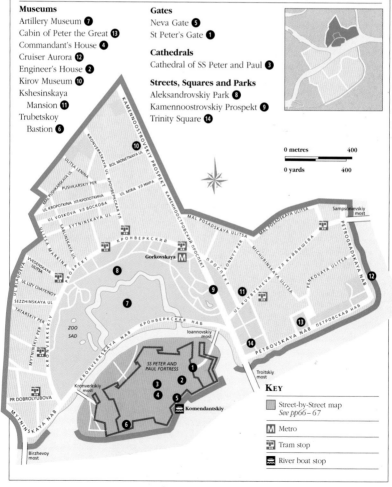

```
0 metres        400
0 yards         400
```

KEY

	Street-by-Street map See pp66–67
M	Metro
	Tram stop
	River boat stop

◁ **The Baroque Cathedral of SS Peter and Paul in the Peter and Paul Fortress**

Street-by-Street: Peter and Paul Fortress

THE FOUNDING OF the Peter and Paul Fortress on 27 May 1703, on the orders of Peter the Great, is considered to mark the founding of the city. It was first built in wood and was later replaced, section by section, in stone by Domenico Trezzini. Its history is a gruesome one, since hundreds of forced labourers died while building the fortress and its bastions were later used to guard and torture many political prisoners, including Peter's own son Alexis.

The cells where prisoners were once kept are open to the public, alongside a couple of museums and the magnificent cathedral which houses the tombs of the Romanovs.

The Archives of the War Ministry occupy the site of the "Secret House", a prison for political criminals in the 18th and 19th centuries.

Artillery Museum (see p70)

Kronverkskiy most

Zotov Bastion

Trubetskoy Bastion
From 1872–1921 the dark, damp, solitary-confinement cells in the bastion served as a grim prison for enemies of the state. Today, the bastion is open to visitors **6**

The Mint, founded in 1724, still produces ceremonial coins, medals and badges.

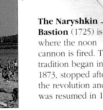

The beach is popular in summer and in winter, when members of the "walruses" swimming club break the ice for an invigorating dip.

The Naryshkin Bastion (1725) is where the noon cannon is fired. The tradition began in 1873, stopped after the revolution and was resumed in 1957.

Commandant's House
For 150 years this attractive Baroque house was the scene of interrogations and trials of political prisoners. It now houses a museum of local history **4**

Neva Gate
This riverside entrance, also known as "Death Gateway", leads to the Commandant's pier from which prisoners embarked on their journey to execution or exile. The Neva river's flood levels (see p37) are recorded under the arch **10**

★ **SS Peter and Paul Cathedral**
Marbled columns, glittering chandeliers and painted decor combine with Ivan Zarudnyy's carved and gilded iconostasis to create a magnificent setting for the tombs of the Romanov monarchs ❸

The Boat House is now a souvenir shop.

Golovkin Bastion

The Grand Ducal burial vault is the last resting place of several Grand Dukes shot by the Bolsheviks in 1919 and of Grand Duke Vladimir who died in exile in 1992.

LOCATOR MAP
See Street Finder, map 2

St Peter's Gate
The entrance to the fortress, by Domenico Trezzini, completed in 1718, features the Romanov double eagle with an emblem of St George and the dragon ❶

STAR SIGHT

★ **SS Peter and Paul Cathedral**

0 metres	100
0 yards	100

Ticket office

Ivan Gate, in the outer wall, was constructed from 1731–40.

Ioannovskiy most

Kamennoostrovskiy prospekt, Gorkovskaya Metro and Trinity Bridge

This statue of Peter the Great is by Mikhail Chemiakin (1991).

Peter I Bastion

KEY

– – – Suggested route

Engineer's House
This building, dating from 1748–9, houses temporary exhibitions of artifacts used in everyday life in St Petersburg before the revolution ❷

St Peter's Gate ❶

Петровские ворота
Petrovskie vorota

Petropavlovskaya krepost.
Map 2 E3. **M** *Gorkovskaya.*

THE MAIN ENTRANCE to the
Peter and Paul Fortress is
through two contrasting arches.
The plain Neo-Renaissance
Ivan Gate (1730s) leads to the
more imposing St Peter's Gate
(1717–18), an ornate Baroque
structure with scrolled wings
and a rounded-gable pediment.
Domenico Trezzini redesigned
the Peter Gate, retaining Karl
Osner's expressively carved
bas-relief which allegorizes
Peter the Great's victory over
Charles XII of Sweden *(see
p18)*. It depicts St Peter
casting down the winged
sorcerer Simon Magus who
attempts to soar above him.

Peter Gate, entrance to fortress

Engineer's House ❷

Инженерный дом
Inzhenernyy dom

Petropavlovskaya krepost. **Map** 2 D3.
C *232 9454.* **M** *Gorkovskaya.*
O *11am–6pm Thu–Mon; 11am–
4pm Tue.* 🎟 ✅ *English.*

THE ENGINEER'S HOUSE, built
in 1748–9, has a changing
exhibition which gives a
fascinating glimpse of daily
life in St Petersburg before
the Revolution. Architectural
backdrops and historical paintings give way to an engaging
miscellany of artifacts, ranging
from old shop fronts to model
boats, duelling pistols, court
costumes and ball masks.
 In 1915 there were more
than 100 outlets selling musical instruments in the city

**An accordion and organ surrounded by Style-
Moderne furniture, Engineer's House**

and the museum displays
an excellent collection which
includes phonographs, gramo-
phones, symphoniums and
piano accordions of the period.
 A section on vintage tech-
nology features Singer sewing
machines, typewriters, Bakelite
telephones and box cameras.

Cathedral of SS Peter and Paul ❸

Петропавловский собор
Petropavlovskiy sobor

Petropavlovskaya krepost. **Map** 2 D4.
C *232 9454.* **M** *Gorkovskaya.*
O *11am–6pm Thu–Mon; 11am–
4pm Tue.* 🎟 ✅ *English.*

DOMENICO TREZZINI designed
this magnificent church
within the fortress in 1712.
Employed by Peter the Great,
who wished to turn his back
on traditional Russian church
architecture, Trezzini produced
a Baroque master-
piece of singular
elegance. The bell
tower was com-
pleted first to test
the foundations and
this served as an
excellent viewpoint
from which Peter
could oversee the
construction work
of his new city. The
cathedral was com-
pleted in 1733, but
was badly damaged
by fire in 1756 when
the soaring 122-m
(400-ft) spire was struck by
lightning. The gilded needle
spire, crowned by a weather-
vane angel, remained the
tallest structure in St Petersburg until the building of the
TV transmitter in the 1960s.
 The interior, with its glittering chandeliers, pink and
green Corinthian columns and
overarching vaults, is also a
far cry from the traditional
Russian Orthodox church.
Even the iconostasis, culminating in a triumphal arch, is a
Baroque flight of fancy. This
masterpiece of gilded wood-
carving was designed by Ivan
Zarudnyy and executed in the
1720s by Moscow craftsmen.
 After Peter's death in 1725,
the cathedral became the last
resting place of the tsars. The
sarcophagi are all of a uniform
white Carrara marble, except
the tombs of Alexander II and
his wife Maria Alexandrovna,
which are carved from Altai

Cathedral of SS Peter and Paul, with Dvortsovyy most in foreground

jasper and Ural rhodonite. Peter the Great's tomb lies to the right of the iconostasis.

The only tsars who are not buried here are Peter II, Ivan VI and, until recently, Nicholas II. In 1998 a controversial decision was taken to rebury the remains of the last Romanov tsar, his wife and children, and the servants that died together with them, in a chapel by the entrance to the cathedral.

The Grand Ducal Mausoleum, where relatives of the tsars are buried, was added to the northeast of the cathedral at the end of the 19th century.

Commandant's House ❹
Комендантский дом
Komendantskiy dom

Petropavlovskaya krepost. **Map** 2 D4.
📞 232 9454. Ⓜ *Gorkovskaya.*
🕐 11am–6pm Thu–Mon; 11am–4pm Tue. 📷 ✔ English.

DATING FROM the 1740s, the plain brick, two-storey Commandant's House served both as the residence of the fortress commander and as a courthouse. Over the years, political prisoners, including the Decembrist rebels *(see p23)*, were brought here for interrogation and sentencing.

The house is now a museum, with a ground-floor exhibition on medieval settlements in the St Petersburg region, and temporary exhibitions upstairs.

Neva Gate ❺
Невские ворота
Nevskie vorota

Petropavlovskaya krepost. **Map** 2 E4.
Ⓜ *Gorkovskaya.*

THIS AUSTERE river entrance to the fortress was once known as the "Death Gate". Prisoners to be transported to the even more notorious Schlüsselburg Fortress (to the east of St Petersburg) for capital punishment, or to a "living death" in penal servitude, were led down the granite steps and taken away by boat. The appropriately dour, grey gateway dates from

Neva Gate leading from the river into the Peter and Paul Fortress

1784–7 and is unornamented apart from an anchor in the pediment. In the archway, brass plaques mark record flood levels. The catastrophic inundation of November 1824 is the one commemorated in Pushkin's poem, *The Bronze Horseman (see p78).*

Trubetskoy Bastion ❻
Трубецкой бастион
Trubetskoy bastion

Petropavlovskaya krepost. **Map** 2 D4.
📞 232 9454. Ⓜ *Gorkovskaya.*
🕐 11am–6pm Thu–Mon; 11am–4pm Tue. 📷 ✔ English.

PETER THE GREAT'S SON, the Tsarevich Alexis, was the first political prisoner to be detained in the grim fortress prison. Unjustly accused of treason in 1718 by his overbearing father, Alexis escaped abroad only to be lured back to Russia with the promise of

a pardon. Instead, he was tortured and beaten to death, almost certainly with Peter's consent and participation.

For the next 100 years prisoners were incarcerated in the much feared Secret House, since demolished. In 1872 a new prison block opened in the Trubetskoy Bastion which has existed as a museum since 1924. On the ground floor there is a small exhibition of period photographs, prison uniforms and a model of the guardroom. Upstairs are 69 isolation cells, restored to their original appearance, while downstairs there are two unheated, unlit punishment cells where the recalcitrant were locked up for 48 hours at a time. Once every two weeks, all detainees were taken to the Bath House in the exercise yard for de-lousing. Here prisoners were also put in irons before being carted off to penal servitude in Siberia.

POLITICAL PRISONERS

The fortress' sinister role as a prison for political activists continued until after the Revolution. Generations of rebels and anarchists were interrogated and imprisoned here, including Leon Trotsky in the wake of the 1905 Revolution. Other prominent detainees were the leading Decembrists in 1825 *(see p23)*, Dostoevsky in 1849 *(see p123)* and, in 1874–6, the anarchist Prince Pyotr Kropotkin. In 1917 it was the turn first of the tsar's ministers, then of members of the Provisional Government. Then, in the Civil War *(see p27)*, the Bolsheviks held hostage four Romanov Grand Dukes who were subsequently executed in 1919.

Leon Trotsky (1879–1940) in the Trubetskoy Bastion

Rocket launcher in the courtyard of the Artillery Museum

Artillery Museum **❼**

Музей Артиллерии

Muzey Artillerii

Kronverk. **Map** 2 D3. [📞] 232 0296.
[Ⓜ] *Gorkovskaya.* [🕐] 11am–5pm
Wed–Sun. [♿]

THIS VAST, horseshoe-shaped building in red brick stands on the site of the Kronverk, the outer fortifications of the Peter and Paul Fortress *(see pp66–67)*. Designed by Pyotr Tamanskiy and constructed in 1849–60, the building was originally used as the arsenal.

The museum boasts more than 600 pieces of artillery and military vehicles, including tanks. There are uniforms, regimental flags, muskets and small arms dating back to medieval times, as well as several rooms devoted to World War II. A star exhibit is the armoured car in which Lenin rode in triumph from Finland Station *(see p126)* to Kshesinskaya Mansion *(see p72)* on 3 April 1917.

Aleksandrovskiy Park **❽**

Александровский парк

Aleksandrovskiy park

Kronverkskiy prospekt. **Map** 2 D3.
[Ⓜ] *Gorkovskaya.* [♿]

THE PARK'S UNIQUE character as a centre of popular culture and entertainment was established in the year 1900 with the inauguration of the Nicholas II People's House. This was where pantomime artists, wild animal trainers, magicians and circus acts

entertained the crowds, while the more serious-minded were drawn to the lecture halls, reading galleries and tea rooms. The *pièce de résistance* was the magnificent domed Opera House (1911), where the legendary bass singer, Fyodor Chaliapin, sometimes gave performances.

Today the Opera House offers less highbrow entertainment, as its change of name to Music Hall suggests. The adjoining buildings, erected in the late 1930s, include the innovatory Baltic House Theatre and the Planetarium.

The park still draws crowds on summer weekends and public holidays, although some of the attractions, especially the zoo, are now rather tawdry.

Kamennoostrovskiy Prospekt **❾**

Каменноостровский проспект

Kamennoostrovskiy prospekt

Map 2 D2. [Ⓜ] *Gorkovskaya or Petrogradskaya.* [🚌] 46, K-63, K-76, K-223.

DEVELOPED DURING the construction boom of the late 1890s, this eye-catching avenue is noted for its Style-Moderne architecture. The first house, at No. 1–3 (1899–1904) was designed by Fyodor Lidval. The multi-textured façade, windows of contrasting shapes and sizes, ornate iron balconies and fanciful carvings are the most typical features of this Russian version of Art Nouveau. The neighbouring

**Griffon, No. 1–3
Kamennoostrovskiy**

house (No. 5) was once occupied by Count Sergey Witte, a leading industrialist who negotiated the peace treaty with Japan in 1905 *(see p26)*.

Situated just off the start of the avenue is the city's only mosque (1910–14). Designed by Russian architects, its minarets, majolica tiling and the rough granite surfaces of the walls are fully in keeping with the surrounding Style-Moderne architecture. The mosque was, in fact, modelled on the Mausoleum of Tamerlane in Samarkand and involved Central Asian craftsmen.

At No. 10 is the tall portico of the Leningrad Film Studios (Lenfilm). It was on this site, in May 1896, that the Lumière brothers showed the first moving picture in Russia. Since its founding in 1918, some of the most innovative Soviet film directors such as Leonid Trauberg and Grigoriy Kozintsev *(see p45)* have worked there.

At the intersection with ulitsa Mira, each house has individually designed turrets, spires, reliefs and iron balconies, forming a handsome Style-Moderne ensemble. Other buildings of interest include No. 24 (1896–1912), with its red brick majolica and terracotta façade; No. 26–28 where Sergey Kirov lived *(see p72)*; and on the corner of Bolshoy prospekt, the "Turreted House" with its Neo-Gothic portal.

**Turreted House (1913–15),
Kamennoostrovskiy prospekt**

Style Moderne in St Petersburg

Kshesinskaya
Mansion railing detail

IN VOGUE throughout Europe from the 1890s to the 1900s, Art Nouveau marked a break with imitation of the past. The movement, known as Style Moderne in Russia, began in the decorative arts and was then reflected in architecture, where it led to an abundance of ornamental elements. Inspired by new industrial techniques, artists and architects made lavish use of natural stone and brick, wrought iron, stucco, coloured glass and ceramic tiles.

Dominated by sinuous and undulating lines, with a predominance of floral and vegetal elements, even traditional forms such as doors and windows are broken up, distorted or given unexpected curves. In fin-de-siècle St Petersburg, the Style Moderne flourished as the city underwent a building boom, particularly on Petrogradskaya. The city became a showcase for the talents of leading architects such as Fyodor Lidval and Aleksandr von Gogen.

Kshesinskaya Mansion *reveals von Gogen's relatively severe version of Style Moderne. Asymmetrical in composition, it is enlivened with wrought iron and glazed tiles* (see p72).

Yeliseev's *is evidence of the skill of Gavriil Baranovskiy, who made excellent use of industrial techniques in the creation of large window spaces. The rich exterior detailing is matched by elegant shop-fittings and chandeliers inside* (see p109).

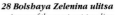

28 Bolshaya Zelenina ulitsa *is one of the most outstanding examples of the use of stylized animal and fish motifs and a variety of surface decoration techniques. Fyodor von Postel's 1904–5 apartment block is reminiscent of the work of his contemporary, the Catalan architect Gaudí.*

1–3 Kamennoostrovskiy pr *is the work of St Petersburg's master of Style Moderne, Fyodor Lidval. Delicate details such as floral and animal reliefs stand out against a background of discreetly elongated proportions and unusual window shapes.*

House of Books *(1910–14) reveals Pavel Syuzor's use of an unusually eclectic mix of architectural styles. Ornate Style-Moderne wrought-iron balconies and decorative wooden window frames combine with elements of Renaissance and Baroque revivals.*

PALACE EMBANKMENT

IN TERMS OF SHEER SCALE and grandeur, St Petersburg's magnificent south waterfront has few equals. Its formidable granite quays, stretching over 2 km (1 mile) from the Senate building in the west to Peter the Great's Summer Palace in the east, and the surrounding area of stately aristocratic palaces and ornamental canal bridges are justly famous worldwide.

Every aspect of the city's history is juxtaposed in this rich area. Falconet's statue of Peter the Great, the Bronze Horseman, is an eloquent testimony to imperial ambition while the square in which it stands is named

Alexander Column, Palace Square

in honour of the Decembrist rebels who rose up against the tsarist regime in 1825. In Palace Square, Rastrelli's Winter Palace (part of the Hermitage) evokes the opulence of Imperial Russia while the Eternal Flame, flickering in the Field of Mars, is a more sombre reminder of revolutionary sacrifice.

Dominating St Petersburg's skyline are the magnificent dome of St Isaac's Cathedral and the gilded spire of the Admiralty. Some of the best views can be appreciated by making a boat trip along the waterways (see pp218–19), or by strolling through the Summer Gardens.

SIGHTS AT A GLANCE

Palaces and Gardens
Marble Palace ⑭
Summer Garden ⑯
Summer Palace ⑰

Museums
The Hermitage pp84–93 ⑫

Historical Buildings and Monuments
The Admiralty ❶
The Bronze Horseman ❸
Horseguards' Manège ❹
House of Fabergé ❾

Churches
St Isaac's Cathedral pp80–81 ❺

Streets and Squares
Decembrists' Square ❷
Field of Mars ⑮
Malaya Morskaya Ulitsa ❽
Millionaires' Street ⑬
Palace Square ⑪
St Isaac's Square ❻

Hotels and Cafés
Astoria Hotel ❼
Literary Café ⑩

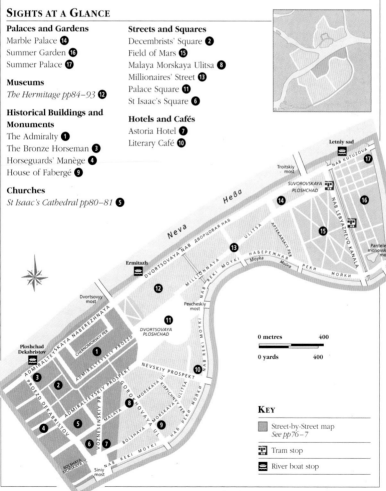

KEY

| | Street-by-Street map See pp76–7 |
| Tram stop |
| River boat stop |

◁ **The golden dome** of St Isaac's Cathedral above elegant façades along the Neva

Street-by-Street: St Isaac's Square

Detail from the frieze on the Admiralty gate tower

THE HIGHLIGHT OF St Isaac's Square is the imposing cathedral at its centre, which opened in 1858 and is the fourth church to stand on this site. The cathedral, and subsequently the square, were named after St Isaac of Dalmatia, because Peter the Great's birthday fell on this saint's day. The busy square, used as a market place in the first half of the 19th century, is now at the heart of an area teeming with buildings and statues of historical and architectural interest. Among them are the Admiralty, the Mariinskiy Palace and the Bronze Horseman.

Horseguards' Manège
Built in 1804–7 by Giacomo Quarenghi, this building housed the Life Guards' Mounted Regiment ❹

The Bronze Horseman
Etienne Falconet's magnificent statue of Peter the Great, his horse trampling the serpent of treason, captures the spirit of the city's uncompromising and wilful founder ❸

Decembrists' Square
Dominating the western side of the square are Carlo Rossi's monumental Senate and Synod buildings, linked by a triumphal arch ❷

The Glory Columns, topped by bronze angels, were erected in 1845–6.

Myatlev House

The Former German Embassy was designed by Peter Behrens in 1911–12.

★ St Isaac's Cathedral
The magnificent golden dome of the cathedral is visible all across the city. 100kg (220lb) of gold leaf were needed to cover the dome's surface ❺

ADMIRALTEYSKAYA NABEREZHNAYA

PROEZD DEKABRISTOV

UL YAKUBOVICHA

ISAAKIEVSKAYA PLOSCHAD

BOLSHAYA

MOYK

0 metres   100

0 yards   100

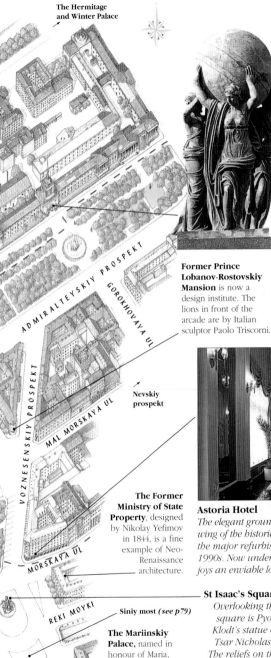

The Hermitage and Winter Palace

ADMIRALTEYSKIY PROSPEKT

GOROKHOVAYA UL

VOZNESENSKIY PROSPEKT

MAL MORSKAYA UL

Nevskiy prospekt

MORSKAYA UL

REKI MOYKI

Siniy most *(see p79)*

The Mariinskiy Palace, named in honour of Maria, daughter of Nicholas I, now houses the St Petersburg city hall.

KEY

- - - Suggested route

LOCATOR MAP
See Street Finder maps 2, 5 & 6

The Admiralty

Sculptures and reliefs, celebrating the power of Russia's navy, decorate the Admiralty's façade. The archway of the main entrance is framed by nymphs carrying globes on their shoulders ❶

Former Prince Lobanov-Rostovskiy Mansion is now a design institute. The lions in front of the arcade are by Italian sculptor Paolo Triscorni.

STAR SIGHT

★ **St Isaac's Cathedral**

The Former Ministry of State Property, designed by Nikolay Yefimov in 1844, is a fine example of Neo-Renaissance architecture.

Astoria Hotel

The elegant ground floor hallway of the Angleterre wing of the historic Astoria Hotel (see p173) reflects the major refurbishment undertaken in the early 1990s. Now under new management, the hotel enjoys an enviable location in the heart of the city ❼

St Isaac's Square

Overlooking the square is Pyotr Klodt's statue of Tsar Nicholas I. The reliefs on the pedestal depict episodes from his reign. Tellingly, two of them show the suppression of rebellions ❻

The Admiralty ❶
Адмиралтейство
Admiralteystvo

Admiralteyskaya naberezhnaya 2.
Map 5 C1. 🚌 *7, 10, K-129.* 🚎 *1, 7, 10, 17, 22.*

HAVING FOUNDED a city and built a fortress, Peter the Great's next priority was to create a Russian navy to guarantee access to the sea and dominance over Sweden.

The Admiralty began life as a fortified shipyard built on this site between 1704–11. Two years later, some 10,000 men were employed in building the first battleships of the embryonic Russian navy.

One of Russia's most inspired architects, Andrey Zakharov, began to rebuild the Admiralty in 1806. The remarkable façade is 407 m (1,335 ft) in length and is adorned with an abundance of sculptures and reliefs which document the glory of the Russian fleet. Zakharov retained some of the original features, including the central gate tower and spire which he recast in Neo-Classical style with columned porticos and pavilions. The heightened spire was gilded and topped with a model frigate. This has become a symbol of the city, just like the trumpet-blowing pair of angels on the portals of the façade overlooking the Neva.

In the 1840s, shipbuilding was moved downstream and the Admiralty was handed over to the Russian navy. It has been occupied by the Naval Engineering School since 1925.

Tower and spire of the Admiralty (1806–23)

Decembrists' Square ❷
Площадь Декабристов
Ploshchad Dekabristov

Map 5 C1. 🚌 *3, 10, 22, 27.* 🚎 *5, 22.*

THE NAME of this square alludes to the momentous event which took place here on 14 December 1825 *(see p23)*. During the inauguration of Nicholas I, Guards officers intent on imposing a constitutional monarchy attempted to stage a coup d'état in the square. After a confused standoff which lasted several hours, the rebel forces were routed with grapeshot by the new tsar and loyalist troops. Five of the ringleaders were later executed and 121 others exiled to Siberia, thus effectively ending Russia's first revolution.

The imposing Neo-Classical buildings that command the western side of Decembrists' Square were intended to harmonize with the Admiralty. Designed by Carlo Rossi between 1829–34, they were the headquarters of two important institutions which were originally created by Peter the Great: the Supreme Court, or Senate, and the Holy Synod which was responsible for the administration of the Orthodox Church. The two buildings, which now house historical archives, are linked to each other by a triumphal arch supported by Corinthian columns and decorated with a Neo-Classical frieze and a plethora of statuary.

The Bronze Horseman (1766–78)

The Bronze Horseman ❸
Медный Всадник
Mednyy Vsadnik

Ploshchad Dekabristov. **Map** 5 C1. 🚌 *3, 10, 22, 27.* 🚎 *5, 22.*

THE MAGNIFICENT equestrian statue of Peter the Great was unveiled in Decembrists' Square in 1782, as a tribute from Catherine the Great. The statue is known as the Bronze Horseman after Pushkin's famous poem. A French sculptor, Etienne Falconet, spent more than 12 years overseeing this ambitious project. The pedestal alone weighs

---

THE BRONZE HORSEMAN BY PUSHKIN

1956 stamp of Pushkin and the statue that inspired his poem

The famous statue of Peter the Great is brought to life in Alexander Pushkin's epic poem *The Bronze Horseman* (1833). In this haunting vision of the Great Flood of 1824 *(see p37)*, the hero is pursued through the mist-shrouded streets by the terrifying bronze statue. Pushkin's words evoke the domineering and implacable will for which the tsar was renowned: *"How terrible he was in the surrounding gloom! ... what strength was in him! And in that steed, what fire!"*

1,625 tonnes and was hewn from a single block of granite, which was hauled from the Gulf of Finland. It bears the simple inscription "To Peter I from Catherine II" in Latin and Russian. A serpent, symbolizing treason, is crushed beneath the horse's hooves.

Newlyweds often pose for photographs under the statue which is meant to bring luck.

Horseguards' Manège ❹
Конногвардейский манеж
Konnogvardeyskiy manezh

Isaakievskaya ploshchad 1. **Map** 5 C2. ▌ *312 2243.* ○ *11am–6pm Fri–Wed.* ▥ *3, 22, 27.* ▥ *5, 22.* ▥ ▢

T HE ENORMOUS INDOOR riding school of the Life Guards' Mounted Regiment was built by Giacomo Quarenghi in 1804–7 to resemble a Roman basilica. Two clues to the building's original function are the dynamic frieze of a horse race beneath the pediment and the statues on either side of the portico. The statues of the unclad twin sons of Zeus reining in wild horses are copies from the Quirinale Palace in Rome. The Holy Synod, scandalized by this display of nakedness so near to St Isaac's Cathedral, ordered their removal. The statues were re-erected in 1954.

Next to the manège, which is now used as an exhibition hall, are two marble pillars surmounted by bronze angels cast in Berlin, which were sent over as a gift in 1840.

St Isaac's Cathedral ❺

See pp80–81.

St Isaac's Square ❻
Исаакиевская площадь
Issakievskaya ploshchad

Map 5 C2. ▥ *3, 10, 22, 27.* ▥ *5, 22.*

D OMINATED BY Auguste de Montferrand's majestic St Isaac's Cathedral, this impressive square was created during the reign of Nicholas I,

St Isaac's Cathedral, statue of St Nicholas I and the Astoria, St Isaac's Square

although a few of its earlier buildings date from the 18th century. The monument to Nicholas I at its centre was also designed by Montferrand. Erected in 1859 and sculpted by Pyotr Klodt, it depicts the tsar in the uniform of one of Russia's most prestigious regiments, the Kavalergardskiy guards. The pedestal is embellished with allegorical sculptures of his daughters and his wife who represent Faith, Wisdom, Justice and Might.

On the western side of the square at No. 9, the Myatlev House is a Neo-Classical mansion, dating from the 1760s, which belonged to one of Russia's most illustrious families. The French encyclopedist, Denis Diderot, stayed here in 1773–4 following an invitation from Catherine the Great. In the 1920s it became the premises of the State Institute of Artistic Culture where some of Russia's most influential avant-garde artists, including Kazimir Malevich and Vladimir Tatlin *(see p107),* worked.

The forbidding granite-faced building alongside is the former German embassy, designed in 1911–12 by the German architect, Peter Behrens.

Across the 100-m (330-ft) wide Siniy most (Blue Bridge), which was the site of a serf market until 1861, the Mariinskiy Palace *(see p77)* dominates the southern end of the square.

Astoria Hotel ❼
Гостиница Астория
Gostinitsa Astoriya

Bolshaya Morskaya ulitsa 39. **Map** 6 D2. ▌ *313 5757.* ▥ *3, 10, 22, 27, K-169, K-180, K-190, K-252, K-289.* ▥ *5, 22. See* Where to Stay *p180.*

N OW ONE of St Petersburg's leading hotels, the seven-storey Astoria was designed by Fyodor Lidval in the Style Moderne *(see p71)* in 1910–12.

American writer, John Reed, author of the famous eyewitness account of the Revolution *Ten Days that Shook the World,* was staying here when the Bolsheviks seized power.

In 1925, the poet Sergey Yesenin, husband of Isadora Duncan, hanged himself in the annexe, after daubing the walls of his room with a farewell verse in his blood "To die is not new – but neither is it new to be alive".

The hotel's banqueting hall was to be the venue for Hitler's prematurely planned victory celebration, so sure was he that he would conquer the city.

Restored Style-Moderne foyer in the Astoria Hotel, on the eastern edge of St Isaac's Square

St Isaac's Cathedral ⑤

Исаакиевский собор
Isaakievskiy sobor

St Isaac's, one of the world's largest cathedrals, was designed in 1818 by the then unknown architect Auguste de Montferrand. The construction of the colossal building was a major engineering feat. Thousands of wooden piles were sunk into the marshy ground to support its weight of 300,000 tonnes and 48 huge columns were hauled into place. The cathedral opened in 1858 but was designated a museum of atheism during the Soviet era. Officially still a museum today, the church is filled with hundreds of impressive 19th-century works of art.

The Dome
From the dome there are panoramic views over the city which include the Admiralty (see p78) and the Hermitage (see pp84–93). Adorning the gilded dome are angels sculpted by Josef Hermann.

The mosaic icons on the iconostasis are by Bryullov, Neff and Zhivago.

Angels with Torch
Ivan Vitali created many of the cathedral's sculptures, including the pairs of angels supporting gas torches which crown the four attic corners.

This chapel honours Alexander Nevsky who defeated the Swedes in 1240 *(see p17).*

The north pediment is ornamented with a bronze relief (1842–4) of the Resurrection designed by François Lemaire.

Exit

★ **Iconostasis**
Three rows of icons surround the royal doors through which a stained-glass window (1843) is visible. Above the doors is Pyotr Klodt's gilded sculpture, Christ in Majesty (1859).

Malachite and lapis lazuli columns frame the iconostasis. About 16,000 kg (35,280 lbs) of malachite decorate the cathedral.

St Catherine's Chapel has an exquisite white marble iconostasis, crowned by a sculpted Resurrection (1850–4) by Nikolay Pimenov.

The silver dove (1850) hanging in the cupola is a symbol of the Holy Spirit.

VISITORS' CHECKLIST

Isaakievskaya ploshchad. **Map** 5 C2. 315 9732. Nevskiy Prospekt, Sadovaya. 3, 10, 22, 27, K-169, K-180, K-190, K-252, K-289. 5, 22. 11am–7pm Thu–Tue (Oct–Apr: 11am–6pm). religious festivals.

★ Ceiling Painting
The celestial Virgin in Majesty by Karl Bryullov (see p105), dating to 1847, covers an area of 816 sq m (8,780 sq ft). It is ringed by exuberant gilded stucco mouldings and white marble.

Portraits of apostles and evangelists

Statue of St Matthew

The entrance is through the side doors on St Isaac's Square.

South Doors
Three great doors of oak and bronze (1841–6), weighing 20 tonnes, are decorated with carved reliefs by Ivan Vitali. The exteriors of the doors show scenes from the life of Christ and saints, including Alexander Nevsky (see p17).

The relief of St Isaac blessing the Emperor Theodosius and his wife Flaccilla is by Ivan Vitali. On the extreme left, Montferrand is depicted clutching a model of his cathedral.

The walls are adorned with 14 coloured marbles and 43 other types of semi-precious stones and minerals.

The vast interior covers 4,000 sq m (43,000 sq ft).

Red granite columns, each weighing 114 tonnes, were transported from Finland by specially constructed ships.

STAR SIGHTS

★ **Iconostasis**

★ **Ceiling Painting**

Malaya Morskaya ulitsa with No. 13 in the middle

Malaya Morskaya Ulitsa ❽

Малая Морская улица
Malaya Morskaya ulitsa

Map 6 D1. 🚌 *3, 10, 22, 27.*
🚎 *5, 22.*

MALAYA MORSKAYA ULITSA is
sometimes still referred
to as ulitsa Gogolya after the
great prose-writer, Nikolai
Gogol (1809–52) who lived
at No. 17 from 1833–6. It was
here that Gogol wrote *The
Diary of a Madman* and *The
Nose,* two biting satires on the
archetypal Petersburg bureau-
crat "drowned by the trivial,
meaningless labours at which
he spends his useless life".
Gogol's bitingly humorous,
fantastical and grotesque
tales reveal a nightmarish
and deeply pessimistic
view of modern urban life.
   The composer, Pyotr
Tchaikovsky *(see p42),* died
in the top floor apartment
of No. 13 shortly after the
completion of his *Pathétique*
symphony in November 1893.
Officially he was supposed to
have died of cholera, but it is
commonly believed that he

committed suicide, due to
pressure from Conservatory
colleagues wishing to avoid a
scandal after Tchaikovsky's
alleged homosexual affair.
   The house at No. 23 was
occupied by the novelist
Fyodor Dostoevsky *(see p123)*
from 1848–9. It was here that
he was arrested and charged
with political conspiracy for
his participation in the
socialist Petrashevsky circle
(see p123). Today, the street
manages to exude a 19th-
century feel despite the many
busy shops and businesses.

House of Fabergé ❾

Дом Фаберже
Dom Faberzhe

Bolshaya Morskaya ulitsa 24.
Map 6 D1. ⬤ *to public.* 🚌 *3, 22,
27.* 🚎 *5, 22.*

THE WORLD-FAMOUS Fabergé
jeweller's was established
in Bolshaya Morskaya ulitsa
in 1842 by Gustav Fabergé, of
French Huguenot origin. It was
not until the 1880s that his sons
Carl and Agathon abandoned
conventional jewellery-making
for intricate and exquisitely
crafted *objets d'art* of a highly
innovative design. Most famous of all their works are the
imaginatively designed Easter
eggs made for the tsars.
   In 1900 Carl moved the
business from No. 16–18 into
purpose-built premises at No.
24, where it remained until
the Revolution. The exterior,
designed by his relative, Karl
Schmidt, has striking triangular
roof gables and multi-textured
stonework. The original showroom, with its squat red granite
pillars, was on the ground
floor. It is still a jeweller's, but
with no connection to Fabergé.
In the workshops above, boy
apprentices were trained by
master craftsmen in the arts
of enamelling, engraving,
stone cutting and jewelling.
   In 1996, the 150th anniversary of Carl Fabergé's birth was
marked by the unveiling of a
memorial plaque at No. 24
and of a monument, designed
by the sculptor Leonid Aristov
and others, on the corner of
Zamnevskiy prospekt and
prospekt Energetikov.

FABERGÉ EGGS

**The Kelch Bon-
bonnière Egg**

In 1885 Alexander III commissioned the
Fabergé brothers to create an Easter egg for
Tsarina Maria Fyodorovna. Inside the shell
of gold and white enamel was a beautifully
sculpted golden hen. A tradition was
established and, by the Revolution, there
were 54 Fabergé Easter eggs, no two of
which were alike. The *pièce de résistance*
is the Siberian Railway Egg, commissioned
by Nicholas II in 1900. It contains a miniature replica of the royal train, complete with
ruby headlamps, rock crystal windows and
a clockwork engine. The Bonbonnière Egg
was commissioned by Kelch, a wealthy
industrialist, for his wife Varvara in 1903.

DEATH OF A POET

In November 1836 Pushkin received an anonymous letter which awarded him the title of "Grand Master of the Most Serene Order of Cuckolds". It had been sent by Georges d'Anthès, a ne'er-do-well cavalry officer who for some time had been making overtures towards Pushkin's wife, the beauty and socialite Natalya Goncharova. Pushkin challenged d'Anthès to a duel

A Naumov's painting of Pushkin, fatally wounded after his duel

and, on the afternoon of 27 January 1837, he met his opponent in snow-bound woodland to the north of the city. D'Anthès fired first and Pushkin was mortally wounded. He died two days later, aged 38. D'Anthès was later reduced to the ranks and banished from Russia.

Sign outside the Literary Café

Literary Café ⓾

Литературное кафе
Literaturnoe kafe

Nevskiy prospekt 18. **Map** 6 E1.
📞 *312 6057.* ⏰ *11am–1am.*
Ⓜ *Nevskiy Prospekt.* ♿
See Restaurants and Cafés p180.

ALSO KNOWN AS the Café Wulf et Beranger after its original owners, this café is famous for its association with Alexander Pushkin, Russia's greatest poet *(see p43)*. It was here that Pushkin met his second, Konstantin Danzas, before setting out for his ill-fated duel with Baron d'Anthès. The café was a popular haunt for St Petersburg writers from its beginning, frequented by Fyodor Dostoevsky and the poet Mikhail Lermontov (1814–41), among others.

Despite its hallowed literary importance and elegant setting, in Vasiliy Stasov's handsome building of 1815, the café itself does not merit the high prices.

Palace Square ⓫

Дворцовая площадь
Dvortsovaya ploshchad

Map 6 D1 🚌 *7, 10, K-47, K-128, K-129, K-147.* 🚎 *1, 7, 10.*

PALACE SQUARE has played a unique role in Russian history. Before the Revolution the square was the setting for colourful military parades, often led by the tsar on horseback. In January 1905, it was the scene of the massacre of "Bloody Sunday" *(see p26)* when gathered troops fired on thousands of unarmed demonstrators. Then, on 7 November 1917, Lenin's Bolshevik supporters secured the Revolution by attacking the Winter Palace *(see pp28–9)* from the square, as well as its west side. Today it is still a favourite venue for political meetings and for popular entertainment such as rock concerts *(see p51)*.

The resplendent square is the work of the inspired architect Carlo Rossi *(see p110)*. Facing the Winter Palace on its southern side is Rossi's magnificent General Staff Building (1819–29), the headquarters for the Russian army. Rossi demolished an entire row of houses to make room for it.

The two graceful, curving wings (the eastern one now a branch of the Hermitage) are connected by a double arch leading to Bolshaya Morskaya ulitsa. The arch is crowned by a sculpture of Victory in her chariot (1829), by Stepan Pimenov and Vasiliy Demut-Malinovskiy. Forming the eastern side of this striking architectural ensemble is the Guards Headquarters, designed by Aleksandr Bryullov in 1837–43. To the west lies the Admiralty *(see p78)*.

The Alexander Column in the centre of the square is dedicated to Tsar Alexander I for his role in the triumph over Napoleon *(see pp22–3)*. On the pedestal are inscribed the words "To Alexander I, from a grateful Russia". The red granite pillar is balanced by its 600-tonne weight, making it the largest free-standing monument in the world. The column was designed by Auguste de Montferrand in 1829 and it took 2,400 soldiers and workmen two years to hew and transport the granite. It was erected in 1830–34. The column is topped by a bronze angel, and together they stand 47 m (154 ft) high.

The Alexander Column and General Staff Building in Palace Square

The Hermitage ⑫

Эрмитаж
Ermitazh

ONE OF THE MOST FAMOUS museums in the world, the Hermitage has a vast collection occupying a grand ensemble of buildings. The most impressive is Rastrelli's Baroque Winter Palace *(see pp92–3)*, to which Catherine the Great soon added the more intimate Small Hermitage. In 1771–87, she erected the Large Hermitage to house her rapidly growing collection of art. The Theatre was built in 1785–7, and finally the New Hermitage in 1839–51. The New and Large Hermitages were opened by Nicholas I in 1852 as a public museum. Between 1918 and 1939, after the establishment of Soviet power, the Winter Palace was slowly incorporated into the Hermitage museum ensemble.

The New Hermitage (1839–51) was designed by Leo von Klenze to form a coherent part of the Large Hermitage. It is the only purpose-built museum within the whole complex.

Court ministries were located here until the 1880s.

Atlantes
Ten 5-m (16-ft) tall granite Atlantes hold up what was the public entrance to the Hermitage museum from 1852 until after the Revolution.

The Winter Canal *(see p36)*

A gallery spanning the canal connects the Theatre to the Large Hermitage and forms the theatre foyer.

Theatre
During Catherine's reign, there were regular performances held in Quarenghi's theatre. Today it hosts exhibitions and concerts (see p194).

The Large Hermitage was designed by Yuriy Velten to house Catherine's paintings.

★ Raphael Loggias
Catherine was so impressed by engravings of Raphael's frescoes in the Vatican that in 1787 she commissioned copies to be made on canvas. Small alterations were made, such as replacing the Pope's coat of arms with the Romanov two-headed eagle.

Hanging Gardens

This unusual raised garden is decorated with statues and fountains. During the Siege of Leningrad (see p27) Hermitage curators grew vegetables here.

The Small Hermitage (1764–75), by Vallin de la Mothe and Yuriy Velten, served as Catherine's retreat from the bustle of the court.

VISITOR'S CHECKLIST

Dvortsovaya nab 34–6. **Map** 2 D5.
110 3420. 7,10, Э47, T129. 1, 7,10. 10:30am–6pm Tue–Sat; 10.30am–5pm Sun. Last adm 1 hour before closing. in English (219 4751 to book).

Winter Palace Façade

Rastrelli embellished the palace façades with 400 columns and 16 different window designs.

STAR SIGHTS

★ **Winter Palace State Rooms**

★ **Pavilion Hall**

★ **Raphael Loggias**

Palace Square

Main entrance

River Neva

The Winter Palace (1754–62) was the official residence of the Imperial family until the Revolution.

★ **Pavilion Hall** (1850–8) *Andrey Stakenschneider's striking white marble and gold hall replaced Catherine's original interior. It houses Englishman James Cox's famous Peacock Clock (1772), which was once owned by Catherine's secret husband, Prince Grigory Potemkin.*

★ **Winter Palace State Rooms** *The tsars spared no expense in decorating rooms such as the Hall of St George. These rooms were not intended for private life, but were used for state ceremonies.*

The Hermitage Collections

CATHERINE THE GREAT purchased some of Western Europe's best collections between 1764 and 1774, acquiring over 2,500 paintings, 10,000 carved gems, 10,000 drawings and a vast amount of silver and porcelain with which to adorn her palaces. None of her successors matched the quantity of her remarkable purchases. After the Revolution, the nationalization of both royal and private property brought more paintings and works of applied art, making the Hermitage one of the world's leading museums.

The Knights' Hall (1842–51) is used for displays of armour and weapons from the former Imperial arsenal.

Stairs to ground floor

The Litta Madonna (c.1491)
One of two works by Leonardo da Vinci in the museum, this masterpiece was admired by his contemporaries and was frequently copied.

Skylight Rooms

Raphael Loggias (*see p84*)

First Floor

The Gallery of Ancient Painting (1842–51) is decorated with scenes from ancient literature. It houses a superb display of 19th-century European sculpture.

Ground Floor

European Gold Collection

STAR EXHIBITS

★ **Abraham's Sacrifice by Rembrandt**

★ **Ea Haere Ia Oe by Gauguin**

★ **La Danse by Matisse**

GALLERY GUIDE

Individual visitors enter from the Neva embankment, group tours from Palace Square. Start with the interiors of the Winter Palace state rooms on the first floor to get an overview of the museum. Select one or two topics of interest to concentrate on. 19th- and 20th-century European Art is best reached by either of the staircases on the Palace Square side of the Winter Palace.

The Hall of Twenty Columns (1842–51) is painted in Etruscan style.

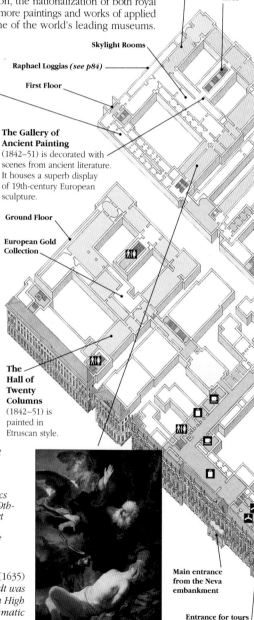

★ **Abraham's Sacrifice** (1635)
In the 1630s Rembrandt was painting religious scenes in a High Baroque style, using dramatic and striking gestures rather than detail to convey his message.

Main entrance from the Neva embankment

Entrance for tours and guided groups

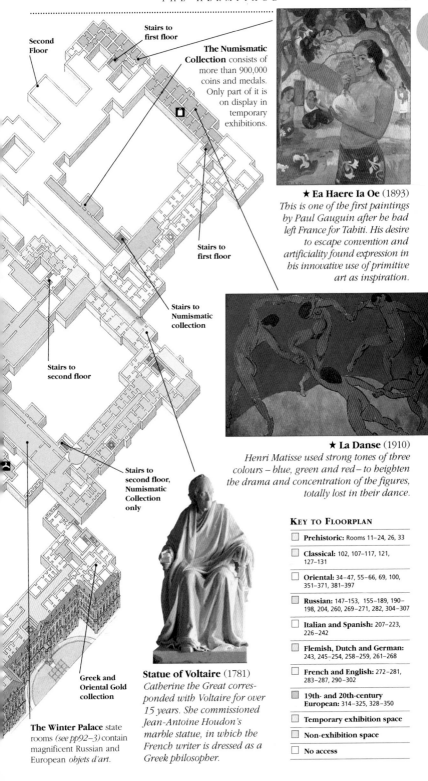

Second Floor

Stairs to first floor

The Numismatic Collection consists of more than 900,000 coins and medals. Only part of it is on display in temporary exhibitions.

★ **Ea Haere Ia Oe** (1893)
This is one of the first paintings by Paul Gauguin after he had left France for Tahiti. His desire to escape convention and artificiality found expression in his innovative use of primitive art as inspiration.

Stairs to first floor

Stairs to Numismatic collection

Stairs to second floor

★ **La Danse** (1910)
Henri Matisse used strong tones of three colours – blue, green and red – to heighten the drama and concentration of the figures, totally lost in their dance.

Stairs to second floor, Numismatic Collection only

KEY TO FLOORPLAN

- **Prehistoric:** Rooms 11–24, 26, 33
- **Classical:** 102, 107–117, 121, 127–131
- **Oriental:** 34–47, 55–66, 69, 100, 351–371, 381–397
- **Russian:** 147–153, 155–189, 190–198, 204, 260, 269–271, 282, 304–307
- **Italian and Spanish:** 207–223, 226–242
- **Flemish, Dutch and German:** 243, 245–254, 258–259, 261–268
- **French and English:** 272–281, 283–287, 290–302
- **19th- and 20th-century European:** 314–325, 328–350
- **Temporary exhibition space**
- **Non-exhibition space**
- **No access**

Greek and Oriental Gold collection

Statue of Voltaire (1781)
Catherine the Great corresponded with Voltaire for over 15 years. She commissioned Jean-Antoine Houdon's marble statue, in which the French writer is dressed as a Greek philosopher.

The Winter Palace state rooms *(see pp92–3)* contain magnificent Russian and European *objets d'art*.

Exploring the Hermitage Collections

IT IS IMPOSSIBLE to absorb the Hermitage's vast, encyclopedic collection in one or even two visits. Whether it be Scythian gold, antique vases and cameos, or Iranian silver, every room has something to capture the eye. The furniture, applied art, portraits and rich clothing of the imperial family went to make up the Russian section, which also includes the superb state rooms. The collection of European paintings was put together largely according to the personal taste of the imperial family while most of the 19th- and 20th-century European art, notably the Impressionists, Matisse and Picasso, came from private collections after the Revolution. These are now the most popular exhibits.

Scythian gold stag dating from 7th–6th century BC

PREHISTORIC ART

PREHISTORIC artifacts found all over the former Russian Empire include pots, arrow heads and sculptures from Palaeolithic sites, which date back nearly 24,000 years, and rich gold items from the time of the Scythian nomads living in the 7th–3rd centuries BC.

Peter the Great's famous Siberian collection of delicate gold work includes Scythian animal-style brooches, sword handles and buckles. Objects continued to be discovered in Siberia and in 1897 a large stylized stag, which once decorated an iron shield, was found at Kostromskaya. This and other gold pieces are held in the Gold Collection (for which a separate ticket is required). A copy is on display in the Scythian rooms.

Greek masters also worked for the Scythians, and from the Dnepr region came a late 5th-century comb decorated with amazingly naturalistic figures of Scythians fighting, as well as the late 4th-century Chertomlyk Vase with scenes depicting animal taming.

Excavations in the Altai, notably at Pazyryk in 1927–49, uncovered burials nearly 2,500 years old. Many perishable materials were preserved by the frozen land, including textiles, a burial cart and even a man's heavily tatooed skin.

Gonzaga Cameo (285–246 BC), made in Alexandria

CLASSICAL ART

THE LARGE NUMBER of Graeco-Roman marble sculptures range from the famous Tauride Venus of the 3rd century BC, acquired by Peter the Great in

1720, to Roman portrait busts. The smaller objects, however, are the real pride and joy of the Classical department.

The collection of red-figured Attic vases of the 6th–4th centuries BC is unequalled anywhere in the world. Exquisitely proportioned and with a lustrous shine, they are decorated with scenes of libation, episodes from the Trojan War, and in one case a famous image of the sighting of the first swallow (c.510 BC).

In the 4th and 3rd centuries BC, Tanagra was the centre for the production of small, elegant terracotta figurines. They were discovered in the 19th century and became so popular that fakes were produced on a grand scale. The Russian ambassador in Athens, Pyotr Saburov, put his collection together in the 1880s before the copies appeared, making it unusually valuable.

Catherine the Great's true passion was for carved gems, which she bought en masse. In just ten years, she purchased some 10,000 pieces. The largest and most stunning gem in the Classical collection, however, is the Gonzaga Cameo, which was presented by Napoleon's ex-wife Josephine Beauharnais to Tsar Alexander I in 1814.

The Gold Collection contains some items of 5th-century gold jewellery made by Athenian craftsmen. They used a filigree technique for working gold so finely that the detail can only be seen properly through a magnifying glass.

ORIENTAL ART

THIS SELECTION of artifacts covers a wide range of cultures; from ancient Egypt and Assyria, through Byzantium, India, Iran, China, Japan and the marvels of Uzbekistan and Tajikistan. The most complete sections are those where excavations were conducted by the Hermitage, mainly in China and Mongolia before the Revolution, and in Central Asia during the Soviet period.

Dating back to the 19th century BC, at the time of the Middle Kingdom, is a seated porphyry portrait of Pharaoh

8th-century fresco of a wounded warrior from Tajikistan

Excavations and expeditions to Central Asia have produced carpets, bronzes and wonderful glazed tiles. Uzbekistan and Tajikistan revealed marvellous complexes of 8th-century buildings at Varaksha, Adjina-Tepe and Pendzhikent, which have been a source of beautiful frescoes, such as the one depicting the wounded warrior.

RUSSIAN ART

Aᴌᴛʜᴏᴜɢʜ ᴍᴀᴊᴏʀ Russian works of art were transferred from the Winter Palace to the Russian Museum (see pp104–107) in 1898, everything else that belonged to the imperial family was nationalized after the Revolution. This included anything from official portraits and thrones to looking glasses and petticoats. Over 300 items of apparel belonging to Peter the Great alone survive. Later, the department also began acquiring medieval Russian art, including icons and church utensils.

The tsars from Peter the Great onwards invited foreign craftsmen and artists to train

Universal sundial (1714–19) from Peter the Great's collection

locals. Peter studied with them and his fascination for practical things is reflected in his large collection of sundials, instruments and wood-turning lathes which includes the universal sundial by Master John Rowley. A bust by Bartolomeo Carlo Rastrelli (1723–30), however, portrays Peter as the mighty and cruel emperor, rather than the rough workman.

Russian artists were soon combining traditional art forms with European skills to create such intricate marvels as the openwork walrus ivory vase by Nikolay Vereshchagin (1798), and the large silver sarcophagus and memorial to Alexander Nevsky, truly Russian in scale (1747–52).

The gunsmiths of Tula (south of Moscow) perfected their technique to such an extent that they began producing unique furniture in steel inlaid with gilded bronze, such as the decorative, Empire-style dressing table set (1801).

The state interiors (see pp92–3) are the pride of the Russian department, revealing the work of Russian and foreign craftsmen from the mid-18th to the early 20th century. The discovery of large deposits of coloured stones in the Urals inspired Russian artists to decorate whole rooms with malachite and to fill every corner of the Winter Palace with marble vases. It was through these rooms that the imperial family paraded on state occasions, greeting courtiers and ambassadors en route in the Field Marshals' Hall.

Amenemhet III. The star of the Egyptian collection is an extremely rare, small, wooden statue of a standing man from the 15th century BC.

From the Far East – Japan, India, Indonesia, China and Mongolia – comes an array of objects ranging from Buddhist sculptures and fabrics to a display of tiny netsukes (ivory toggles). Excavations at the cave temple of the Thousand Buddhas near Dun Huan in western China revealed 6th–10th-century icons, wall paintings and plaster sculptures, including the lions that once guarded the cave. During the 13th-century Mongol invasion, the town of Khara-Khoto was destroyed and taken over by the surrounding desert. The sand preserved many usually perishable objects, from 12th-century silks to woodcuts.

From Byzantium come early secular items, such as icons, religious utensils and a 5th-century ivory diptych with scenes from a Roman circus.

Iran produced a large number of silver and bronze vessels, many of which were taken by medieval traders to Siberia and the Urals where they were rediscovered by specialists in the 19th century. There is also a large collection of traditional Persian miniatures and a rich display of 19th-century Persian court portraits, which combine traditional elements with western oil painting, as in the *Portrait of Fatkh-Ali Shah* (1813–14).

Steel dressing table set from Tula dating from 1801

ITALIAN AND SPANISH ART

THE DISPLAY of Italian art contains some fine pieces. A few early works reveal the rise of the Renaissance in the 14th and 15th centuries and the styles then in vogue. Simone Martini's stiff *Madonna* (1340–44) contrasts with Fra Angelico's more humane fresco of the Virgin and Child (1424–30).

In the late 15th and early 16th century, artists disputed the merits of line, as practised by the Florentine school, and the merits of colour, virtue of the Venetians. The former can be seen in the *Litta Madonna* (c.1491) and the *Madonna Benois* (1478) by Leonardo da Vinci, a marble *Crouching Boy* by Michelangelo (c.1530) and two early portraits of the Virgin by Raphael (1502 and 1506). Venice is represented by *Judith* by Giorgione (1478–1510) and an array of works by Titian (c.1490–1576). The Skylight Rooms are packed with vast Baroque canvases, including works by Luca Giordano (1634–1704) and Guido Reni (1575–1642), and even larger 18th-century masterpieces by Tiepolo. The works of the Italian sculptor Antonio Canova (1757–1822) (*Cupid and Psyche, The Three Graces*) stand in the Gallery of Ancient Painting.

The Spanish collection is more modest, but Spain's Golden-Age heroes can all be seen, from El Greco with *The Apostles Peter and Paul* (1587–92), through to Ribera, Murillo, and Zurbarán with *St Lawrence* (1636). The portrait of a courtier, *Count Olivares*, painted c.1640 by Velázquez, contrasts with a much earlier genre scene of a peasant's breakfast (1617–18).

Venus and Cupid (1509) by Lucas Cranach the Elder

FLEMISH, DUTCH AND GERMAN ART

THE SMALL COLLECTION of early paintings from the Netherlands includes a marvellous, jewel-like *Madonna and Child* (1430s) by the Master of Flemalle. He is thought to have been the teacher of Rogier van der Weyden, who is represented by *St Luke Painting the Madonna* (c.1435).

Over 40 works by Rubens include religious subjects (*The Descent from the Cross*, 1617–18) and scenes from Classical mythology (*Perseus and Andromeda*, 1620–21), as well as landscapes and an immensely obese *Bacchus* (1636–40). His portraits, such as the *Infanta's Maid* (1625), reveal his common Flemish heritage with Van Dyck, whose paintings include a series of formal, full-length portraits and a dashing and romantic self-portrait from the late 1620s.

The Dutch section is rich in Rembrandts. Within a short period of time he produced the dramatic *Abraham's Sacrifice* (1636), the gentle *Flora* (1634) and the brilliant effects of *The Descent from the Cross* (1634). One of his last works was the *Return of the Prodigal Son* (1668–9), with an emotional depth unseen before.

Among the many small-genre paintings is Gerard Terborch's *Glass of Lemonade* from the mid-17th century. All the usual elements of a genre scene are imbued with psychological tension and heavy symbolism.

In the German collection, it is the works of Lucas Cranach the Elder which captivate the viewer. His *Venus and Cupid* (1509), the stylish *Portrait of a Woman in a Hat* (1526) and the tender *Virgin and Child Beneath an Apple Tree* reveal the varied aspects of his talent.

FRENCH AND ENGLISH ART

FRENCH ART was *de rigueur* for collectors in the 18th century. Major artists of the 17th century, including Louis Le Nain and the two brilliant and contrasting painters Claude Lorrain and Nicolas Poussin, are well represented. Antoine Watteau's elegant *Embarrassing Proposal* (c.1716), *Stolen Kiss* (1780s) by Jean Honoré Fragonard and François Boucher's fleshy and certainly far-from-virtuous

A Young Man Playing a Lute, by Michelangelo Caravaggio (1573–1610)

Still Life with the Attributes of the Arts (1766), by Jean-Baptiste Chardin

heroines represent the more wicked side of 18th-century taste, but Catherine the Great preferred didactic or instructional works. She bought *Still Life with Attributes of the Arts* (1766) by Chardin and, on the advice of Denis Diderot, Jean-Baptiste Greuze's moralizing *The Fruits of a Good Education* (1763). She also patronized sculptors, purchasing works by Etienne-Maurice Falconet (*Winter*, carved 1771) and Jean-Antoine Houdon (*Voltaire*, 1781).

Catherine also acquired English works, including a portrait of the philosopher John Locke (1697) by Sir Godfrey Kneller, who was also author of a portrait of Pyotr Potemkin (1682) in Russian 17th-century court dress. From Sir Joshua Reynolds Catherine commissioned *The Infant Hercules Strangling the Serpents* (1788). Her most daring purchase was of works by the still largely unknown Joseph Wright of Derby. *The Iron Forge* (1773) is a masterpiece of artificial lighting, but *Firework Display at the Castel Sant'Angelo* (1774–5) is a truly romantic fiery spectacle. She provided much work for English cabinet-makers and carvers of cameos. She became one of Josiah Wedgwood's most prestigious clients, ordering the famous Green Frog Service for her Chesma Palace *(see p130)*.

The Green Frog Service, Wedgwood (1773–4)

19TH- & 20TH-CENTURY EUROPEAN ART

ALTHOUGH THE royal family did not patronize the new movements in art in the 19th century, there were far-sighted private individuals whose collections were nationalized and entered the Hermitage after the 1917 Revolution. Thanks to them, the Barbizon school is represented by works such as Camille Corot's charming silvery *Landscape with a Lake*, French Romanticism by two richly-coloured Moroccan scenes of the 1850s by Delacroix, and German Romanticism by Caspar David Friedrich's *On the Prow of the Ship* (1818–20).

Two collectors, Ivan Morozov and Sergey Shchukin, brought the Hermitage its superb array of Impressionist and Post-Impressionist paintings. Monet's art can be admired both in his early *Woman in a Garden* (1860s) and in the later, more exploratory *Waterloo Bridge, Effect of Mist* (1903). Renoir and Degas perpetually returned to women as subjects, as in Renoir's charming *Portrait of the Actress Jeanne Samary* (1878) and Degas' pastels of women washing (1880s–90s). Pissarro's *Boulevard Montmartre in Paris* (1897) is typical of his urban scenes, while Alfred Sisley painted weather effects and light in the French countryside.

A change in colour and technique appeared as artists investigated new possibilities. Van Gogh used deeper tones in his *Women of Arles* (1888) and stronger brushstrokes in *Cottages* (1890). Gauguin turned to a different culture for inspiration, and his Tahitian period is represented by enigmatic works, such as *Ea Haere Ia Oe* (1893). In *The Smoker* (c.1890–2) and *Mont Ste-Victoire* (1896–8), Cézanne introduced experiments with plane and surface which were to have a strong influence on the next generation.

Matisse played both with colour and surface, in the carpet-like effect of *The Red Room* (1908–9) and the flatness of the panels *La Musique* and *La Danse* (1909–10). His visit to Morocco introduced new light effects, as in *Arab Coffeehouse* (1913), but it was Picasso who took Cézanne's experiments one stage further. In early works such as *Visit* (1902) from his Blue Period, Picasso concentrates on mood, but the surface destruction of the Cubist period of 1907–12, including *L'Homme aux Bras Croisés*, fills a whole room.

L'Homme aux Bras Croisés, painted by Pablo Picasso in 1909

The Winter Palace

PRECEDED BY three earlier versions on this site, the existing Winter Palace (1754–62) is a superb example of Russian Baroque. Built for Tsarina Elizabeth, this opulent winter residence was the finest achievement of Bartolomeo Rastrelli. Though the exterior has changed little, the interiors were altered by a number of architects and then largely restored after a fire gutted the palace in 1837. After the assassination of Alexander II in 1881, the imperial family rarely lived here. During World War I a field hospital was set up in the Nicholas Hall and other state rooms. Then, in July 1917, the Provisional Government took the palace as its headquarters, which led to its storming by the Bolsheviks *(see pp28–9)*.

The 1812 Gallery (1826) has portraits of Russian military heroes of the Napoleonic War, most by English artist George Dawe.

The Armorial Hall (1839), with its vast gilded columns, covers over 800 sq m (8,600 sq ft). It now houses the European silver collection and a restored imperial carriage.

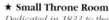

★ **Small Throne Room**
Dedicated in 1833 to the memory of Peter the Great, this room houses a silver-gilt English throne, made in 1731.

The Field Marshals' Hall (1833) was the reception room where the devastating fire of 1837 broke out.

The Hall of St George (1795) has monolithic columns and wall facings of Italian Carrara marble.

The Nicholas Hall, the largest room in the palace, was always used for the first ball of the season.

North façade overlooking the Neva

★ **Main Staircase**
This vast, sweeping staircase (1762) was Rastrelli's master-piece. It was from here that the imperial family watched the Epiphany ceremony of baptism in the Neva, which celebrated Christ's baptism in the Jordan.

★ **Malachite Room**
Over two tonnes of ornamental stone were used in this sumptuous room (1839) which is deco-rated with malachite columns and vases, gilded doors and ceiling, and rich parquet flooring.

Alexander Hall
Architect Aleksandr Bryullov employed a mixture of Gothic vaulting and Neo-Classical stucco bas-reliefs of military themes in this reception room of 1837.

BARTOLOMEO RASTRELLI

The Italian architect Rastrelli (1700–71) came to Russia with his father in 1716 to work for Peter the Great. His rich Baroque style became highly fashionable and he was appointed Chief Court Architect in 1738. During Elizabeth's reign, Rastrelli designed several buildings, including the grandiose Winter Palace and impressive Smolnyy Convent *(see p128)*. Unlike Elizabeth, Catherine the Great preferred Classical sim- plicity and Rastrelli retired in 1763, after she came to power.

The French Rooms, designed by Bryullov in 1839, house a collection of 18th-century French art.

The White Hall was decorated for the wedding of the future Alexander II in 1841.

South façade on Palace Square

Dark Corridor
The French and Flemish tapestries here include The Marriage of Emperor Constantine, *made in Paris in the 17th century to designs by Rubens.*

The Rotunda
(1830) connected the private apartments in the west with the state apartments on the palace's north side.

West wing

The Gothic Library and other rooms in the northwest part of the palace were adapted to suit Nicholas II's bourgeois lifestyle. This wood-panelled library was created by Meltzer in 1894.

STAR FEATURES

★ **Small Throne Room**

★ **Malachite Room**

★ **Main Staircase**

The Gold Drawing Room
Created in the 1850s, this room was extravagantly decorated in the 1870s with all-over gilding of walls and ceiling. It houses a display of Western European carved gems.

Millionaires' Street ⑬

Миллионная улица

Millionnaya ulitsa

Map 2 E5.

Millionaires' street takes its name from the aristocrats and members of the imperial family who once inhabited its opulent residences. Since the main façades and entrances overlook the river, some house numbers correspond to the embankment side.

On the eve of the Revolution, No. 26 (on the embankment) was the home of Grand Duke Vladimir Aleksandrovich who was responsible for firing on peaceful demonstrators on Bloody Sunday *(see p26)*. His consort, Maria Pavlovna, was one of Russia's leading society hostesses who gave soirées and balls that eclipsed even those of the imperial court. The building (1867–72), which was designed by Aleksandr Rezanov in the style of the Florentine Renaissance, is now the House of Scholars.

Putyatin's house, at No. 12 Millionaires' Street, witnessed the end of the Romanov dynasty. It was here that Grand Duke Mikhail Aleksandrovich, Nicholas II's brother, signed the decree of abdication in March 1917. Next door, No. 10, was where French novelist Honoré de Balzac stayed in 1843, while courting his future wife, Countess Eveline Hanska. The mid-19th-century house was designed by Andrey Stakenschneider for his own use.

The delicately sculpted façade of No. 10 Millionaires' Street

Gala staircase of the Marble Palace

Marble Palace ⑭

Мраморный дворец

Mramornyy dvorets

Millionnaya ulitsa 5 (entrance from the Field of Mars). **Map** 2 E4. 📞 *312 9196.* 🚌 *46.* 🚊 *2.* ⏱ *10am–5pm Wed–Sun, 10am–4pm Mon.* 🈴 🈯 *English.*

The marble palace was built as a present from Catherine the Great to her lover Grigoriy Orlov who had been instrumental in bringing her to power in 1762 *(see p22)*. An early example of Neo-Classical architecture, dating from 1768–85, the building is considered to be Antonio Rinaldi's masterpiece.

The palace takes its name from the varied marbles used in its construction. Most of the interiors were reconstructed in the 1840s by Aleksandr Bryullov, although the gala staircase and the Marble Hall are Rinaldi's originals. The latter has marbled walls of grey, green, white, yellow, pink and lapis lazuli, and a ceiling painting, the *Triumph of Venus* (1780s) by Stefano Torelli.

The palace, which housed a Lenin museum for 55 years, is now a branch of the Russian Museum *(see pp104–107)*. On display are works by foreign artists working in Russia and modern art bequeathed by the German collectors Peter and Irene Ludwig. Their collection includes a Picasso, *Large Heads* (1969), and work by post-war artists Jean-Michel Basquiat, Andy Warhol, Ilya Kabakov and Roy Lichtenstein.

In front of the palace stands a curious equestrian statue of Alexander III by Prince Pavel Trubetskoy. Unveiled on ploshchad Vosstaniya in 1911, the ridiculed statue was removed from its original site in 1937 and its vast pedestal was cut up to create statues of new heroes, such as Lenin.

Field of Mars ⑮

Марсово Поле

Marsovo Pole

Map 2 F5. 🚌 *46.* 🚊 *2.*

Once a vast marshy expanse, this area was drained during the 19th century and utilized for military manoeuvres and parades, fairs and other festivities. It was appropriately named after Mars, the Roman god of war. Between 1917 and 1923 the area, by then a sandy expanse, was nicknamed the "Petersburg Sahara". It was landscaped and transformed into a war memorial. The granite *Monument to Revolutionary Fighters* (1917–19), by Lev Rudnev, and the Eternal Flame (1957) commemorate the victims of the Revolutions of 1917 and the Civil War *(see p27)*.

Eternal Flame, Field of Mars

The west of the square is dominated by an imposing Neo-Classical building erected by Vasiliy Stasov in 1817–19. This was formerly the barracks of the Pavlovskiy Guards which were founded by Tsar Paul I in 1796. The military-obsessed tsar is said to have only recruited guardsmen with snub noses like his own. The Pavlovskiy officers were among the first to turn against the tsarist government in the 1917 Revolution *(see pp28–9)*.

Today the huge square is a popular spot for locals in the bright spring evenings, when it is alive with lilac blossom.

Summer Garden ⑯
Летний сад
Letniy sad

Letniy Sad. **Map** 2 F4. 🚌 46.
🚇 2. ⬜ 8am–8pm daily (May–Oct:
8am–10pm). ♿ ☐ 🎨 May–Oct.

I N 1704 Peter the Great commissioned these beautiful
gardens which were among
the first in the city. Designed
by a Frenchman in the style
of Versailles, the allées were
planted with imported elms
and oaks and adorned with
fountains, pavilions and some
250 Italian statues dating from
the 17th and 18th centuries.
A flood in 1777 destroyed
most of the Summer Gardens
and the English-style garden
which exists today is largely
the result of Catherine the
Great's more sober tastes. A
splendid feature is the fine
filigree iron grille (1771–84)
along the Neva embankment,
created by Yuriy Velten and
Pyotr Yegorov.

For a century the Summer
Gardens were an exclusive
preserve of the nobility. When
the gardens were opened to
"respectably dressed members
of the public" by Nicholas I,
two Neo-Classical pavilions,
the Tea House and the Coffee
House, were erected over-
looking the Fontanka. These
are now used for temporary
exhibitions of art by modern
St Petersburg artists.

Nearby, the bronze statue
of Ivan Krylov, Russia's most
famous writer of fables, is a
favourite with Russian children. It was sculpted by Pyotr
Klodt in 1854 with charming
bas-reliefs on the pedestal depicting animals from his fables.

Ivan Krylov's statue amidst autumn foliage in the Summer Gardens

Summer Palace ⑰
Летний дворец
Letniy dvorets

Naberezhnaya Kutuzova. **Map** 2 F4.
📞 314 0456. ⬜ 11am–6pm Wed–
Mon. ⬤ 11 Nov–30 Apr. 🚌 46.
🚇 2. 🎨 🎫

B UILT FOR Peter the Great,
the modest two-storey
Summer Palace is the oldest
stone building in the city. It
was designed in the Dutch
style by Domenico Trezzini
and was completed in 1714.
The celebrated Prussian sculptor Andreas Schlüter created
the delightful maritime bas-
reliefs (1713) which are an
allegorical commentary on
Russia's naval triumphs under
Peter the Great's stewardship.

Grander than his wooden
cabin (see p73), Peter's second St Petersburg residence is
still by no means comparable
to the magnificent palaces
built by his successors.

On the ground floor, the
reception room is hung with
portraits of the tsar and his
ministers and contains Peter's
oak Admiralty Chair. The
tsar's bedroom has its original four-poster bed with a
coverlet of Chinese silk, and
an 18th-century ceiling painting showing the triumph of
Morpheus, the god of sleep.
Next door is the turnery
which contains some original Russian lathes as well as
an elaborately carved wooden
meteorological instrument,
designed in Dresden in 1714.

The palace boasted the city's
first plumbing system with
water piped directly into the
kitchen. The original black
marble sink can still be seen,
along with the beautifully
tiled kitchen stove and an
array of early 18th-century
cooking utensils. The kitchen
opens onto the exquisite
dining room, imaginatively
refurbished to convey an
atmosphere of domesticity.
It was used only for small
family gatherings since major
banquets were held at the
Menshikov Palace (see p62).

An original staircase leads up
to the first floor and the
more lavish suite of Peter's second
wife, Catherine. The throne in
the aptly named Throne Room
is ornamented with Nereides
and other sea deities. The glass
cupboards in the Green Room
once displayed Peter's fascinating collection of curiosa
before it was transferred to
the Kunstkammer (see p60).

The remarkable stove in the Summer Palace's tiled kitchen

GOSTINYY DVOR

THE GREAT BAZAAR, Gostinyy Dvor, was the commercial heart of St Petersburg at the beginning of the 18th century and today it still hums with activity. A profusion of smaller retail outlets soon appeared on and around Nevskiy prospekt. Thriving communities of foreign merchants and businessmen also took up residence in the neighbourhood.

Until the mid-19th century, shops in this area catered almost exclusively for the luxury end of the market, fulfilling the limitless demand, created by the royal and aristocratic households, for gold and silverware, jewellery and haute couture. Increasing commercial and financial activity created a new middle class of business entrepreneurs. By the Revolution, banks proliferated around Nevskiy prospekt, their imposing new offices introducing diverse architectural styles to a largely Neo-Classical setting. Today the wheels of capitalism are turning again and Nevskiy prospekt still attracts a wealthy clientèle. In contrast to the bustling commercial atmosphere of much of the area is the calm oasis of Arts Square, with the Russian Museum and other institutions which act as a reminder of the city's rich cultural life.

Statues on façade of the Russian Museum

SIGHTS AT A GLANCE

Churches
Armenian Church 7
Cathedral of Our Lady of Kazan 15
Church on Spilled Blood p100 1
Lutheran Church 17

Museums
Mikhaylovskiy Castle 2
Pushkin House-Museum 19
Russian Museum pp104–107 3

Streets and Squares
Arts Square 4
Nevskiy Prospekt 6
Ostrovskiy Square 11
Ulitsa Zodchevo Rossi 12

Markets and Shops
Apraksin Market 14
Gostinyy Dvor 8
Yeliseev's 9

Palaces
Anichkov Palace 10
Stroganov Palace 16
Vorontsov Palace 13

Hotels
Grand Hotel Europe 5

Historic Buildings
Glinka Capella 18
Imperial Stables 20

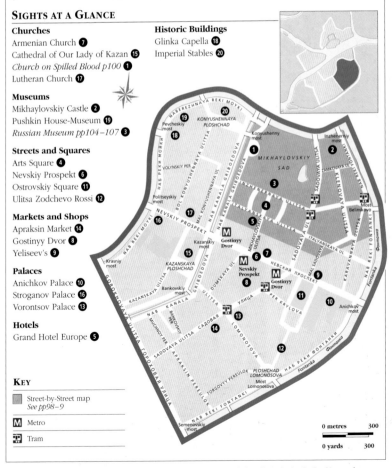

KEY

▦	Street-by-Street map *See pp98–9*
M	Metro
⬚	Tram

0 metres	300
0 yards	300

◁ **The busy Nevskiy prospekt, with the Duma tower on the left and the Admiralty in the background**

Street-by-Street: Around Arts Square

THE APTLY NAMED Arts Square, one of Carlo Rossi's finest creations, is surrounded by buildings revealing the city's impressive cultural heritage. The grand palace housing the Russian Museum is flanked by theatres and the Philharmonia concert hall. Behind it is the leafy Mikhaylovskiy Garden, a haunt of St Petersburg's intellectuals. The gardens stretch down to the beautiful Moyka river which together with two other waterways, the Griboedov and Fontanka, create a shimmering frame for this picturesque area.

Peter the Great statue

★ **Church on Spilled Blood**
Colourful mosaics and elaborate stone carving are the main features of the church's exterior, which emulates traditional 17th-century Russian style ❶

Mikhaylovskiy Garden

NABEREZHNAYA REKI MOYKI

MOYKA

★ **Russian Museum**
Located in Rossi's Mikhaylovskiy Palace, this famous gallery boasts a fabulous collection of Russian painting, sculpture and applied art. The grand staircase and White Hall are original features ❸

KANAL GRIBOEDOVA

NAB KANALA GRIBOEDOVA

INZHENERNAYA ULITSA

ITALYANSKAYA ULITSA

Statue of Pushkin (1957)

Nevskiy prospekt

The Great Hall of the Philharmonia is one of the major concert venues in St Petersburg (see p194).

Arts Square
The square's present name derives from the number of cultural institutions situated here. On the western side, the Mussorgsky Theatre of Opera and Ballet opened in 1833 ❹

Grand Hotel Europe
This famous St Petersburg hotel was constructed by Ludwig Fontana in 1873–5. Mighty atlantes adorn its eclectic façade which stretches all the way down to Nevskiy prospekt ❺

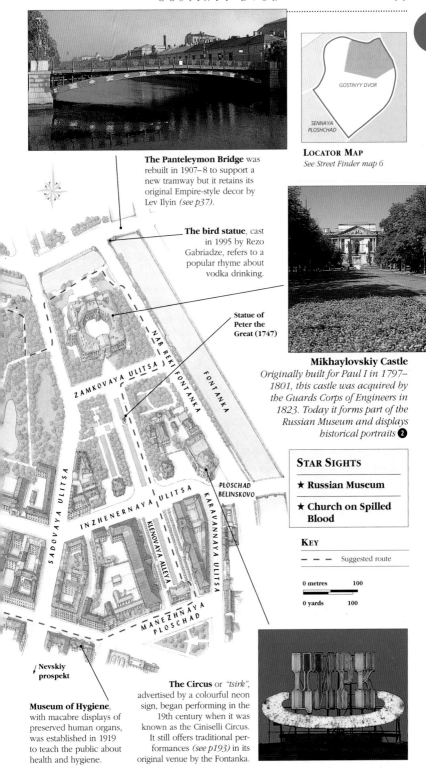

LOCATOR MAP
See Street Finder map 6

The Panteleymon Bridge was rebuilt in 1907–8 to support a new tramway but it retains its original Empire-style decor by Lev Ilyin *(see p37).*

The bird statue, cast in 1995 by Rezo Gabriadze, refers to a popular rhyme about vodka drinking.

Statue of Peter the Great (1747)

Mikhaylovskiy Castle
Originally built for Paul I in 1797–1801, this castle was acquired by the Guards Corps of Engineers in 1823. Today it forms part of the Russian Museum and displays historical portraits ❷

STAR SIGHTS

★ **Russian Museum**

★ **Church on Spilled Blood**

KEY

– – – Suggested route

0 metres 100

0 yards 100

Nevskiy prospekt

Museum of Hygiene, with macabre displays of preserved human organs, was established in 1919 to teach the public about health and hygiene.

The Circus or *"tsirk"*, advertised by a colourful neon sign, began performing in the 19th century when it was known as the Ciniselli Circus. It still offers traditional performances *(see p193)* in its original venue by the Fontanka.

Church on Spilled Blood ❶

Храм Спаса-на-Крови

Khram Spasa-na-Krovi

THE CHURCH ON SPILLED BLOOD, also known as the
Resurrection Church of Our Saviour, was built on the
spot where on 1 March 1881 Tsar Alexander II was
assassinated *(see p26)*. In 1883 his successor, Alexander
III, launched a competition for a permanent memorial.
The winning design, in the Russian Revival style
favoured by the tsar himself, was by Alfred
Parland and Ignatiy Malyshev. The foundation
stone was laid in October 1883.

A riot of colour, the overall effect of the
church is created by the imaginative juxtaposition of materials. Inside, more than 20 types of
minerals, including jasper, rhodonite, porphyry
and Italian marble are lavished on the mosaics
of the iconostasis, icon cases, canopy and
floor. The interior reopened in 1998 after
more than 20 years of restoration.

Mosaic Tympanum
*Mosaic panels showing scenes from the
New Testament adorn the exterior. They
were based on designs by artists such as
Viktor Vasnetsov and Mikhail Nesterov.*

**The tent-roofed
steeple** is 81 m
(265 ft) high.

Coat of Arms
*The 144 mosaic coats
of arms on the bell
tower represent the
regions, towns and
provinces of the
Russian empire.
They were intended
to reflect the grief
shared by all
Russians in
the wake of
Alexander's
assassination.*

Intricate Detailing
*The flamboyant
Russian Revival style
of the exterior
provides a dra-
matic contrast to
the Neo-Classical
and Baroque
architecture
which dominates
the centre of
St Petersburg.*

Jewellers' enamel was
used to cover the
1,000 sq m
(10,760 sq ft) surface
of the five domes.

Glazed ceramic
tiles enliven
the façade.

Twenty dark red
plaques of Norwegian
granite are engraved in
gilt letters with the most
outstanding events of
Alexander II's reign
(1855–81). Among the
historic events recorded
are the emancipation of
the serfs in 1861 and
the conquest of Central
Asia (1860–81).

Mosaic portraits
of the saints are
set in tiers of
kokoshniki gables.
Almost 7,000 sq m
(75,500 sq ft) of
mosaics embellish
the church's extra-
vagant exterior.

Window Frames
*The windows are
flanked by carved
columns of ornate
Estonian marble. The
casings are in the form
of double and triple
kokoshniki (tiered
decorative arches).*

South façade of Mikhaylovskiy Castle and statue of Peter the Great

Mikhaylovskiy Castle ❷

Михайловский замок

Mikhaylovskiy zamok

Sadovaya ulitsa 2. **Map** 2 F5.
313 4173. 46, 134.
2. ◯ 10am–6pm Wed–Sun, 10am–5pm Mon.

THE IMPOSING red brick castle overlooking the Moyka and Fontanka rivers is also known as the Engineers' Castle. It was erected in 1797–1801 by Vasiliy Bazhenov and Vincenzo Brenna for Tsar Paul I. The tsar's obsessive fear of being assassinated led him to surround his new residence with moats and drawbridges, and to build a secret underground passage to the barracks on the Field of Mars *(see p94)*. Unfortunately, all these precautions proved futile and, after living in his fortified castle for just 40 days, Paul fell victim to a military conspiracy which resulted in his murder *(see p22)*.

In 1823 the fortress was acquired by the Guards Corps

of Engineers and was renamed. The school's most famous graduate was the writer Fyodor Dostoevsky *(see p123)*. Today the castle serves as a branch of the nearby Russian Museum. It is used for temporary exhibitions.

The Church of the Archangel Michael is accessed via the exhibition and is a good example of Brenna's Neo-Classical style.

In front of the castle stands a bronze statue of Peter the Great on horseback, designed by Bartolomeo Carlo Rastrelli and cast in 1747.

Russian Museum ❸

See pp104–107.

Arts Square ❹

Площадь Искусств

Ploshchad Iskusstv

Map 6 F1. M *Nevskiy Prospekt, Gostinyy Dvor.*

SEVERAL OF THE CITY'S leading cultural institutions are located on this imposing Neo-Classical square, hence its name. The attractive square was designed by Carlo Rossi in the early 19th century to harmonize with the magnificent Mikhaylovskiy Palace (now the Russian Museum) which stands on its northern side.

On the opposite side of the square is the Great Hall of the St Petersburg Philharmonia, also known as the Shostakovich Hall *(see p43)*. This is where the Philharmonic Orchestra has been based since the 1920s *(see p194)*. Constructed by

Paul Jacot in 1834–9, it started as a Nobles' Club where concerts were held. Among the works premiered here were Beethoven's *Missa Solemnis* in 1824 and Tchaikovsky's *(see p42) Pathétique* in 1893.

On the square's western side is the Mussorgsky Opera and Ballet Theatre *(see p194)*, rebuilt by Albert Kavos in the mid-19th century. In the centre of the square is a sculpture of one of Russia's greatest literary figures, Alexander Pushkin *(see p43)*. The statue was executed by leading post-war sculptor, Mikhail Anikushin.

Grand Hotel Europe's elegant Style-Moderne restaurant *(see p181)*

Grand Hotel Europe ❺

Гранд Отель Европа

Grand Otel Evropa

Mikhaylovskaya ulitsa 1/7. **Map** 6 F1.
329 6000. M *Nevskiy Prospekt, Gostinyy Dvor.* See Where to Stay p173.

ONE OF RUSSIA'S most famous hotels, the ornate Grand Hotel Europe (1873–5) was designed by Ludwig Fontana. The building owes much of its character to alterations made in the 1910s by Style-Moderne architect Fyodor Lidval.

Before the Revolution, the hotel's magnificent restaurant was a favourite rendezvous for members of the diplomatic corps and secret police. In the 1970s, the hotel café became a popular meeting place for young intellectuals and artists.

Pushkin's statue in front of the Russian Museum, Arts Square

The Church on Spilled Blood, a magical reminder of old Russia ▷

Russian Museum ❸

Русский Музей

Russkiy Muzey

THE MUSEUM is housed in the Mikhaylovskiy Palace, one of Carlo Rossi's finest Neo-Classical creations which was built in 1819–25 for Grand Duke Mikhail Pavlovich. Alexander III's plans to create a public museum were realized by his son, Nicholas II, when the Russian Museum opened here in 1898. Today, the museum holds one of the world's greatest collections of Russian art.

The Benois Wing, named after its main architect Leonty Benois, was added in 1913–19.

Stairs to ground floor

A Meal in the Monastery (1865–76)
Vasiliy Perov's politically motivated canvas exposes the hypocrisy of the Orthodox clergy, with the juxtaposition of good and evil, rich and poor, false piety and true faith.

★ **Princess Olga Konstantinovna Orlova** (1911)
Although he painted various genres, by the turn of the 20th century Valentin Serov was the most successful portrait painter in Russia.

Stairs to first floor of Benois Wing

GALLERY GUIDE

The main entrance on Arts Square leads to the ticket office in the basement. The exhibition starts on the first floor. It is arranged chronologically, starting with icons in Room 1. It continues on the ground floor of the main building and Rossi Wing, then the first floor of the Benois Wing. Exhibitions are changed regularly.

STAR EXHIBITS

★ **Princess Olga Konstantinovna Orlova by Serov**

★ **The Last Day of Pompeii by Bryullov**

★ **Barge-Haulers on the Volga by Repin**

Folk Art Toy (1930s)
This clay toy from Dykomovo is part of the colourful selection of folk art which also includes lacquer boxes, painted ceramics and textiles.

★ The Last Day of Pompeii (1833)
*Karl Bryullov's Classical subject em-
bodies the aesthetic principles of the
Academy of Arts. This vivid depiction
of the eruption of Vesuvius won him
the Grand Prix at the Paris Salon.*

**★ Barge-Haulers on
the Volga** (1870–73)
*Ilya Repin was the most famous member
of the Wanderers, a group of artists
dedicated to social realism and Russian
themes. His powerful indictment of
forced labour imbues the oppressed
victims with sullen dignity.*

14

15

12

**Stairs to
ground floor**

16   13

17

11

10

9   8

**The White
Hall** contains
original Empire-
style furniture
by Carlo Rossi.

1   7

2   3   6

4   5

Rossi Wing

**Start of
exhibition**

45 44 43 42 41 40 39

49

52 53 54

33

34

32

**Entrance points
from basement
ticket office**

**Phryne at the Festival of Poseidon
in Eleusin** (1889)
*Henryk Siemiradzki's paintings are fine
examples of late European Neoclassicism.
He is renowned for his academic scenes
of life in ancient Greece and Rome.*

55

57

58

59

31   30

29   28   27

38

37   26

25   24

18   19

20

23

22   21

KEY

☐	Old Russian art
☐	18th-century art
☐	Early 19th-century art
☐	Late 19th-century art
☐	Late 19th–early 20th-century art
☐	20th-century art
☐	18th–20th-century sculpture
☐	Folk art
☐	Temporary exhibitions
☐	Non-exhibition space

The portico of
eight Corinthian
columns is the
central feature of
Rossi's façade.
Behind is a frieze
of Classical figures,
designed by Rossi
and executed by
Demut-Malinovskiy.

**Stairs to
first floor**

**The main
entrance** is
through a small door
which leads to the
basement with a ticket
office, a cloakroom,
toilets and a café.

Exploring the Russian Museum

HOUSING ONE OF THE world's greatest collections of Russian art, the museum originally comprised officially approved works from the Academy of Arts *(see p63)*. When the museum was nationalized after the Revolution, art was transferred from palaces, churches and private collections. By the 1930s, Socialist Realism had become state policy and avant-garde works were stored away, to re-emerge with the advent of *perestroika* in the 1980s.

The Angel with the Golden Hair, an icon from the early 12th century

OLD RUSSIAN ART

THE MUSEUM'S fine collection begins with icons dating from the 12th–17th centuries. Russian icons derive from the Orthodox tradition and thus, just like Byzantine icons, tend to be sombre, marked by an absence of movement and a remote, mystic characterization of the saints. A superb example is one of the earliest icons, *The Angel with the Golden Hair,* in which the large, expressive eyes and delicate modelling of the Archangel Gabriel's face convey a sense of ethereal grace.

The Novgorod School *(see p163)* encouraged a much bolder and brighter style with a greater sense of drama and movement. And yet it is the poetically expressive and technically refined work of Andrey Rublev (c.1340–c.1430) that is considered by many to mark the pinnacle of Russian icon painting.

18TH–19TH-CENTURY ART

THE FIRST secular portraits (which owed much to the static quality of the icons) appeared in the second half of the 17th century. It was, however, under Peter the Great that Russian painting fully cast off from its Byzantine moorings. Peter the Great himself was the first patron to send young artists, often serfs, to study abroad. Secular art began to gain momentum in 1757 with the establishment . of the Academy of Arts *(see p63)* which placed a heavy emphasis on Classical and mythological subjects.

European influence permeates the work of Russia's first important portrait painters, Ivan Nikitin (1688–1741) and Andrey Matveev (1701–39). The art of portraiture matured with Dmitriy Levitskiy (1735–1822), amongst whose best known works is a series of portraits of noble girls from the Smolnyy Institute.

Russian landscape painting was stimulated by the Romantic movement and in particular artists who sought inspiration abroad, including Silvestr Shchedrin (1791–1830) and

Portrait of E I Nelidova (1773), by Dmitriy Levitskiy

Fyodor Matveev (1758–1826). Ivan Aivazovskiy's (1817–1900) vast marine paintings, however, have something purely Russian in their scale and mood. Romanticism also influenced history painters such as Karl Bryullov (1799–1852), as in his depiction of *The Last Day of Pompeii.*

In 1863 a group of students, led by Ivan Kramskoy (1837–87), rebelled against the conservatism of the Academy of Arts. Seven years later they went on to set up the Association of Travelling Art Exhibitions, and came to be better known as the Wanderers *(Peredvizhniki),* or the Itinerants. They demanded that painting should be more socially relevant, and were fundamentally committed to Russian subject matter.

The most versatile of the Wanderers was Ilya Repin *(see p43)* whose bold canvas *Barge-Haulers on the Volga*

Knight at the Crossroads (1882), by Viktor Vasnetsov

The Six-Winged Seraph (1904), by Mikhail Vrubel

combines a visually powerful attack on forced labour with a romantic view of the Russian people. Meanwhile, *A Meal in the Monastery* by Vasiliy Perov (1833–82) is a satirical and equally effective attack on social injustice.

The nationalist element led history painters such as Nikolay Ge (1831–94) and Vasiliy Surikov (1848–1916) to turn to Russian history for inspiration, treating their subjects with a new psychological acuity, as in Ge's canvas of 1871–2, in which Peter the Great interrogates his sullenly resistant son.

The general Slavic revival also breathed new life into landscape painting, concentrating on the beauties of the Russian countryside. The master of the genre was Isaak Levitan (1860–1900), whose *Golden Autumn Village,* dated 1889, is almost Impressionist in style, a sign perhaps that the ascendancy of the Wanderers was coming to an end.

Viktor Vasnetsov (1848–1926) turned to Russia's heroic, and often legendary, pre-European past, in realistically painted canvases such as the *Knight at the Crossroads.* A haunting metaphor for Russia's uncertain future, the painting reveals that Vasnetsov was unable to avoid the fin-de-siècle melancholy and mysticism which was so potently expressed in the work of the next up-and-coming generation of artists, notably the Symbolists.

20TH-CENTURY ART

THE DARK, brooding canvases of Symbolist Mikhail Vrubel (1856–1910) combine Russian and religious themes with a more international outlook. Vrubel used colour and form to depict emotion and in *The Six-Winged Seraph* he employs a broken, vibrant, surface to express tension.

Another major contribution to 20th-century art was the "World of Art" movement, founded by Alexandre Benois and Sergey Diaghilev in the 1890s *(see p26).* It rejected the notion of "socially useful art" in favour of a new tenet, "art pure and unfettered", and also opened up Russian painting to Western influences. Many members of the group,

Portrait of the Director Vsevolod Meyerbold (1916), Boris Grigorev

including Benois and Leon Bakst, designed stage sets and costumes for Diaghilev's Ballets Russes *(see p119).*

The Russian avant-garde grew out of these local influences, plus the art of Cézanne, Picasso and Matisse. Mikhail Larionov (1881–1964) and Natalya Goncharova (1881–1962) both made brilliant use of Russian folk art as inspiration for primitivist works such as Goncharova's *Bleaching Canvas* (1908). They often altered their style in response to changing stimuli and later turned to Futurism's cult of the machine, as in Goncharova's *Cyclist* (1913) *(see p40).*

The link between innovation in painting and the arts in general at this time is strikingly depicted in Boris Grigorev's angular portrait of Meyerhold, himself renowned for his radical approach to theatre.

Kazimir Malevich's (1878–1935) fascination with the juxtaposition of simple geometric shapes inspired the Suprematist movement. Vasily Kandinsky (1866–1944), a leading member of Munich's Blaue Reiter group, was also a key figure in the growth of Russian abstract art.

Marc Chagall (1887–1985), El Lissitskiy (1890–1941) and Alexander Rodchenko (1891–1956) are also represented.

Due to the high demand for the loan of avant-garde works abroad, a changing selection by the major artists is on show.

FOLK ART

FOLK ART became a strong influence on the development of modern Russian art in the 1860s when the wealthy industrialist and patron Savva Mamontov established an artists' colony at Abramtsevo, near Moscow. Vasiliy Polenov (1844–1927), Ilya Repin and Viktor Vasnetsov were among the painters encouraged to work alongside, and learn from, the serf craftsmen on the estate. The museum's collection of folk art is wonderfully diverse and includes exquisitely embroidered tapestries, traditional headdresses, painted tiles, porcelain toys, and lacquered spoons and dishes.

Nevskiy Prospekt **6**
Невский проспект
Nevskiy prospekt

Map 6 D1–8 D3. **M** *Nevskiy Prospekt, Gostinyy Dvor. See also pp46–9.*

RUSSIA'S MOST famous street, Nevskiy prospekt, is also St Petersburg's main thoroughfare and artery. In the 1830s, the novelist Nikolai Gogol *(see p42)* declared with great pride: "There is nothing finer than Nevskiy Avenue ... in St Petersburg it is everything ... is there anything more gay, more brilliant, more resplendent than this beautiful street of our capital?". In this respect very little has actually changed, for Nevskiy prospekt's intrinsic "all-powerful" value still prevails today.

Laid out in the early days of the city, it was first known as the Great Perspective Road, running 4.5 km (3 miles) from the Admiralty *(see p78)* to the Alexander Nevsky Monastery *(see pp130–31)*. In spite of roaming wolves and uncontrollable flooding from the Neva *(see p37)* which made

the avenue navigable in 1721, fine mansions, such as the Stroganov Palace *(see p112)* soon started to appear. Shops and bazaars, catering for the nobility, and inns for travelling merchants followed. A magnet pulling rich and poor alike, by the mid-18th century the avenue had become the place to see and be seen, to meet for gossip, business and pleasure.

Today, the street still teems with people until late into the night throughout the year. Many of the city's sights are close to the stretch between the Admiralty and Anichkov Bridge *(see pp46–7)*. Some of the best shops *(see pp186–7)* can be found around Gostinyy dvor and Passazh arcade. Nevskiy prospekt also offers a wealth of cultural interest: the Small Philharmonia concert hall *(see p194)*, the Russian national library, Beloselskiy-Belozerskiy Palace *(see p49)* and a wide variety of museums, theatres, churches, including the Church of St Catherine *(see p48)*, shops, cinemas and eateries.

Armenian Church portico (1771–9)

Armenian Church **7**
Армянская церковь
Armyanskaya tserkov

Nevskiy prospekt 40–42. **Map** 6 F1.
C *318 4108.* **M** *Gostinyy Dvor.*
O *9am–9pm.*

YURIY VELTEN designed the beautiful blue and white Armenian Church of St Catherine, with its Neo-Classical portico and single cupola. The church, which opened in 1780, was financed by a wealthy Armenian businessman called Ioakim Lazarev, who acquired the money from the sale of a Persian diamond which Count Grigoriy Orlov purchased for Catherine the Great *(see p22)*.

Closed in 1930, the building has now been returned to the Armenian community and visitors are welcome to attend a service.

Gostinyy Dvor **8**
Гостиный двор
Gostinyy dvor

Nevskiy pr 35. **Map** 6 F2. **C** *110 5408.* **M** *Gostinyy Dvor.*
O *9am–9pm daily.*

THE TERM *gostinyy dvor* originally meant a coaching inn, but as trade developed around the inns, with travelling merchants setting up their stalls, it later came to mean "trading rows". The original wooden structure of this *gostinyy dvor* was destroyed by fire in 1736. Twenty years later, Bartolomeo Rastrelli

View along the bustle of Nevskiy prospekt, the hub of St Petersburg

designed a new building but the project proved too costly and ambitious. Building recommenced in 1761 and continued until 1785. Vallin de la Mothe created the striking sequence of columned arcades and massive porticos. The prominent yellow building forms an irregular quadrangle which is bounded on one side by Nevskiy prospekt. The combined length of its façades is nearly 1 km (3,300 ft).

In the 19th century the gallery became a fashionable promenade where more than 5,000 people were employed. Serious damage during the Siege of Leningrad (see p27) led to major reconstruction, making it more like a modern department store. Even now, with all the changes, it has retained its layout of "stalls" of individual trading units. Today it includes branches of foreign shops and a wide range of goods, making it the city's most important store (see p187).

Style-Moderne stained-glass windows in Yeliseev's food store

Columned arcades, Gostinyy dvor

Yeliseev's **9**
Елисеевский гастроном
Yeliseevskiy gastronom

Nevskiy prospekt 56. **Map** 6 F1.
📞 312 1865. **M** Gostinyy Dvor.
🕐 10am–9pm Mon–Fri, 11am–9pm Sat & Sun. ● Jan 1.

THE SUCCESSFUL Yeliseev dynasty was founded by Pyotr Yeliseev, an ambitious peasant who, in 1813, opened a wine shop on Nevskiy prospekt. By the turn of the century his grandsons owned a chocolate factory, numerous houses, inns and this famous food store. Housed in the city's most opulent Style-Moderne building, designed by Gavriil Baranovskiy in 1901–3, it is adorned with bronzes, heroic sculptures and huge windows. The equally impressive interior, with its stained-glass windows, marble counters and crystal chandeliers, steals the attention from the delicacies on sale (see p190). A plaque by the main door honours the grandsons.

Anichkov Palace **10**
Аничков дворец
Anichkov dvorets

Nevskiy prospekt 39. **Map** 7 A2.
M Gostinyy Dvor. ● to public except for special events.

IN THE EARLY days, the broad Fontanka river was lined by palaces accessible mainly by boat. One of them was the Anichkov Palace (1741–50), remodelled in Baroque style in 1754. The palace was a gift from Tsarina Elizabeth to her lover Aleksey Razumovskiy. It was named after Lieutenant Colonel Mikhail Anichkov who set up camp on this site at the time of the founding of the city. Over the years the palace was rebuilt and altered many times, according to the tastes of each successive owner. After Razumovskiy's death, Catherine the Great in turn gave the building to her lover, Prince Potemkin (see p25). In the early 19th century, Neo-Classical details were added by Carlo Rossi.

The palace then became the traditional winter residence of the heir to the throne. When Alexander III became tsar in 1881, however, he continued to live here, rather than move to the Winter Palace as was customary. After his death, his widow Maria Fyodorovna stayed on until the Revolution.

The palace originally had large gardens to the west but these were curtailed in 1816 when Ostrovskiy Square (see p110) was created and two Neo-Classical pavilions were added. The elegant colonnaded building overlooking the Fontanka to the east had been another addition to the palace, commissioned by Giacomo Quarenghi in 1803–5. It was initially built as an arcade where goods from the imperial factories were stored before being allocated to the palaces. Later it was converted into government offices and now also houses the Cultural Centre of Children's Creative Work.

Quarenghi's addition to the Anichkov Palace from Nevskiy prospekt

Porticoed façade of Aleksandrinskiy Theatre (1828–32), Ostrovskiy Square

Ostrovskiy Square ⓫

Площадь Островского
Ploshchad Ostrovskovo

Map 6 F2. Ⓜ *Gostinyy Dvor.* **Russian National Library** Ⓒ *310 7137.* ◯ *9am–9pm.* **Theatre Museum** Ⓒ *311 2195.* ◯ *11am–6pm Thu–Mon; 1–6pm Wed.* ⬤ *public hols.* 🚻 ♿

ONE OF RUSSIA'S most brilliant and prolific architects, Carlo Rossi, created this early 19th-century square which is now named in honour of the prominent dramatist Aleksandr Ostrovskiy (1823–86).

The focal point of the square is the elegant Aleksandrinskiy Theatre *(see p194)*, designed in the Neo-Classical style which Rossi favoured. The portico of six Corinthian columns is crowned by a chariot of Apollo, sculpted by Stepan Pimenov.

The building was the new home to Russia's oldest theatre company, set up in 1756. Plays premiered here included Nikolai Gogol's *The Inspector General* (1836) and Anton Chekhov's *The Seagull* (1901). In Soviet times the theatre was renamed the Pushkin Theatre.

In the garden just in front of the theatre is a monument to Catherine the Great, surprisingly the only one to be found in St Petersburg. It was designed principally by Mikhail Mikeshin and unveiled in 1873. The statue depicts Catherine surrounded by states-men and other worthies, and includes the female president (1783–96) of the Academy of Sciences, Princess Yekaterina Dashkova.

The benches behind the monument are packed during the summer months with chess players and spectators. On the west side of the square, opposite the Anichkov Palace *(see p109)* is an elegant colonnade decorated with Classical sculptures. This is the extension of the Russian Library, made by Rossi in 1828–34. Founded in 1795, the library currently holds more than 28 million items. A prized possession is the personal library of the French philosopher Voltaire, which Catherine the Great purchased to show her appreciation of her sometime mentor and correspondent.

In the southeast corner of the square, at No. 6, is the Theatre Museum which traces the evolution of the Russian stage from its origins in mid-18th-century serf and imperial theatres. Amid the eclectic array of playbills, photographs, costumes, set designs and other artifacts, there are also some set designs by one of the great innovators of modern theatre, the director Vsevolod Meyerhold (1874–1940).

Ulitsa Zodchevo Rossi ⓬

Улица Зодчего Росси
Ulitsa Zodchevo Rossi

Map 6 F2. Ⓜ *Gostinyy Dvor.*

THERE COULD BE no better memorial to Carlo Rossi than the near perfect architectural ensemble of identical arcades and colonnades forming "Architect Rossi Street". The 22-m (72-ft) high buildings stand precisely 22 m (72 ft) apart and are 220 m (720 ft) in length. Viewed from ploshchad Lomonosova, the perspective hypnotically coaxes the eye towards the Aleksandrinskiy Theatre.

At No. 2 is the home of the former Imperial School of Ballet, now named after the teacher Agrippina Vaganova (1879–1951), one of the few dancers not to emigrate after the Revolution. The school began in 1738 when Jean-Baptiste Landé began training orphans and palace servants' children to take part in court entertainment. It moved to its present quarters in 1836 and has since produced many of Russia's most celebrated dancers *(see p118)*, including Anna Pavlova and Rudolf Nureyev.

19th-century photograph of ulitsa Zodchevo Rossi (1828–34)

ARCHITECT CARLO ROSSI

Carlo Rossi (1775–1849) was one of the last great exponents of Neo-Classicism in St Petersburg. He found an ideal client in Alexander I, who shared his belief in the use of architecture to express the power of the ruling autocracy. By the time of his death, Rossi had created no fewer than 12 of St Petersburg's impressive streets and 13 of its squares, including Palace Square *(see p83)*. Rossi's status as Alexander I's favourite architect encouraged rumours that Rossi was the offspring of an affair between Tsar Paul I and Rossi's Italian ballerina mother.

Central corpus of Vorontsov Palace

Vorontsov Palace ⑬
Воронцовский дворец
Vorontsovskiy dvorets

Sadovaya ulitsa 26. **Map** 6 F2.
⬤ *to public.* Ⓜ *Gostinyy Dvor, Sennaya Ploshchad.*

THE MOST EXCLUSIVE military school in the Russian empire, the Corps des Pages, occupied the Vorontsov Palace from 1810–1918. Among those privileged enough to study here were a number of the Decembrists *(see pp22–3)* and Prince Felix Yusupov *(see p121)*. Today the palace houses the Suvorov Military Academy.

Designed by Bartolomeo Rastrelli *(see p93)*, the handsome palace, which once stood in its own extensive grounds, was built in 1749–57 for Prince Mikhail Vorontsov, one of Tsarina Elizabeth's leading ministers. Rastrelli's graceful wrought-iron railings are among the earliest examples of their kind in Russia.

Apraksin Market ⑭
Апраксин двор
Apraksin dvor

Sadovaya ulitsa. **Map** 6 E2.
Ⓜ *Gostinyy Dvor, Sennaya Ploshchad.* ⬤ *9am–5pm.*

FOUNDED in the late 18th century, the market takes its name from the Apraksin family who owned the land it was built on. When fire destroyed the original wooden stalls in 1862, the arcade was erected. By 1900 there were more than 600 outlets selling everything from food, wine and spices to furs, furniture and haberdashery. Today, street stalls extend all the way along Apraksin pereulok, and in a yard *(see p187)* behind the arcade, toys, car parts, cigarettes, watches, TV sets, alcohol and leather jackets are sold.

Cathedral of Our Lady of Kazan ⑮
Собор Казанской Богоматери
Sobor Kazanskoy Bogomateri

Kazanskaya pl 2. **Map** 6 E1. ⬤ 318 4528. Ⓜ *Nevskiy Prospekt.* ⬤ *9am–7:30pm daily.* ⬤ ⬤

ONE OF St Peterburg's most majestic churches, the Cathedral of Our Lady of Kazan was commissioned by Paul I and took over a decade to build (1801–11). The impressive design by serf architect Andrey Voronikhin was inspired by St Peter's in Rome. Its 111-m (364-ft) long, curved colonnade disguises the orientation of the building which runs parallel to Nevskiy prospekt, conforming to a religious stipulation that the main altar face east. In Voronikhin's original design he intended to duplicate the colonnade on the south side.

The cathedral is named after the miracle-working icon of Our Lady of Kazan. The icon is now kept in the cathedral.

The interior decoration is generally subdued. Its most impressive features are the great 80-m (262-ft) high dome and the massive pink Finnish granite columns with bronze capitals and bases. Occupied in the Communist era by a Museum of Atheism, the building was returned to exclusive religious use in 1999.

Completed in 1811, the cathedral is intimately linked with the wars against Napoleon *(see p22)* fought during the same period. In 1813 Field Marshal Mikhail Kutuzov (1745–1813), mastermind of a successful retreat from Moscow following the invasion of Napoleon's Grand Army in 1812, was buried here with full military honours. Kutuzov has been immortalized in Tolstoy's great novel *War and Peace* (1865–9). His statue and that of his comrade-in-arms, Mikhail Barclay de Tolly (1761–1818), both by Boris Orlovskiy, have stood in Kazanskaya ploshchad outside the cathedral since 1837.

Pink granite columns and mosaic floor in main nave, Kazan Cathedral

Stroganov Palace 16
Строгановский дворец
Stroganovskiy dvorets

Nevskiy prospekt 17. **Map** 6 E1.
Ⓜ *Nevskiy Prospekt.* 🄲 311 2360.
◔ *10am–6pm Wed–Sun
(10am–5pm Mon).*

THIS BAROQUE masterpiece
was designed in 1752–4
by Bartolomeo Rastrelli *(see
p93)*. Commissioned by the
enormously wealthy Count
Sergey Stroganov, the palace
was occupied by his descendants until the 1917 Revolution.
The vast Stroganov fortune
was amassed mainly through
the monopoly the family held
on salt, which they mined
from their territories in the
north of the Russian empire.

   The green and white palace,
which overlooks both Nevskiy
prospekt and the Moyka river,
was one of the city's most
impressive private residences.
The magnificent river façade is
decorated with Doric columns,
cornices, pediments and inven-
tive window surrounds.

   The Stroganovs were noted
collectors of everything from
Egyptian antiquities and Roman
coins to icons and Old Masters.
The palace was nationalized
after the Revolution and then
preserved for ten years as a
museum of the life of the
decadent aristocracy. When it
was closed, some of the objects

**Neo-Romanesque portal of the
Lutheran Church (1832–8)**

were auctioned in the West,
and the rest were transferred
to the Hermitage *(see pp84–
93)*. The building now belongs
to the Russian Museum *(see
pp104–107)*. It is used for
temporary exhibitions. Also on
show here is a collection of
waxworks of historical figures.

Lutheran Church 17
Лютеранская церковь
Lyuteranskaya tserkov

Nevskiy prospekt 22–24. **Map** 6 E1.
Ⓜ *Nevskiy Prospekt.*

SET BACK a little from Nevskiy
prospekt, the attractive,
twin-towered Lutheran church
is dedicated to St Peter. Built
in its present form during the

1830s, the church served
St Petersburg's ever-growing
German community *(see p57)*.
The prize-winning design by
Aleksandr Bryullov is in an un-
usual, Neo-Romanesque style.

   From 1936 the church was
used as a vegetable store until,
in the late 1950s, it was converted into a swimming pool.
The basin was carved out of
the nave floor, the gallery
lined with spectator benches
and there was a high diving
board under the apse. The
building has now been handed
back to the German-Lutheran
Church of Russia. Restoration
is under way, but the church is
open and has regular services.

Glinka Capella concert hall

Academic Capella 18
Академическая капелла
Akademicheskaya kapella

Naberezhnaya reki Moyki 20. **Map** 2
E5. 🄲 314 1058. Ⓜ *Nevskiy
Prospekt.* ◔ *for concerts only.*
🎫 See Entertainment p194.

ENCLOSED WITHIN a courtyard
off the Moyka river is this
ochre-coloured concert hall
with a façade in the French
Classical style of Louis XV.
The Academic Capella was
designed by Leontiy Benois in
1887–9 as the residence of the
Imperial Court choir. Founded
during the reign of Peter the
Great, the choir is as old as
the city itself. Its former
directors have included the
distinguished Russian composers Mikhail Glinka
(1804–57) and Nikolai
Rimsky-Korsakov (1844–1908).

   With its excellent acoustics,
the Academic Capella can
claim to be one of the best
concert halls in the world.
Outside is the aptly named
Singers' Bridge (Pevcheskiy
most), which was designed by
Yegor Adam in 1837–40.

Elaborate west façade of the Stroganov Palace overlooking the Moyka river

Personal effects in Pushkin's study, Pushkin House-Museum

Pushkin House-Museum 🄆

Музей-квартира
А. С. Пушкина
Muzey-kvartira AS Pushkina

Naberezhnaya reki Moyki 12.
Map 2 E5. 311 3531.
11am–5pm Wed–Mon.
public hols.

EVERY YEAR on the anniversary of Alexander Pushkin's death (29 January 1837), loyal devotees of Russia's greatest poet come to lay floral tributes outside his apartment. Pushkin was born in Moscow in 1799, but spent many years of his life in St Petersburg and the museum is one of several places in the city with which the poet is associated.

From the autumn of 1836 until his death, Pushkin lived in this fairly opulent apartment overlooking the Moyka, with his wife Natalya, their four children and Natalya's two sisters. It was here on the couchette in the study that he bled to death after his fateful duel with d'Anthès *(see p83)*.

Some half dozen rooms on the first floor have been refurbished in the Empire style of the period. By far the most evocative is Pushkin's study, which is arranged exactly as it was when he died. On the writing table is an ivory paper knife given to the poet by his sister, a bronze handbell and a treasured inkstand *(see p39)*. Embellished with the figure of an Ethiopian boy, the inkstand is a reminder of Pushkin's great grandfather, Abram Hannibal. Bought by the Russian ambassador in Constantinople as a slave in 1706, Hannibal served as a general under Peter the Great. He was the inspiration for the unfinished novel *The Negro of Peter the Great* on which Pushkin was working at the time of his death.

On the wall in front of his desk is a Turkish sabre presented to Pushkin in the Caucasus, where he had been exiled in 1820 for his radical views. Ironically it was there that he spent some of his happiest years. It was there too that he began his most famous work, *Eugene Onegin*, a novel in verse written in 1823–30.

The most impressive feature of the apartment is the poet's library which contains more than 4,500 volumes in a staggering 14 European and Oriental languages. Among these are works by the authors whom Pushkin most admired, including Shakespeare, Byron, Heine, Dante and Voltaire.

Imperial Stables 🄔

Конюшенное Ведомство
Konyushennoe Vedomstvo

Konyushennaya ploshchad 1.
Map 2 E5. **Church** 10am–7pm
daily.

THE LONG, salmon-coloured building running parallel to the Moyka embankment is the former Imperial stables. Originally built in the first part of the 18th century, the stables were reconstructed by Vasiliy Stasov in 1817–23.

The only part of the building open to the public lies behind the central section of the long south façade, crowned by a silver dome and cross. This is the church where Alexander Pushkin's funeral took place on 1 February 1837. Its Neo-Classical interior is in the form of a basilica and is decorated with yellow marble pillars. It is now a fully functional Orthodox church.

North façade of Imperial Stables (left) and Little Stable Bridge on the Moyka

SENNAYA PLOSHCHAD

THE WESTERN PART of St Petersburg is an area of contrasts, home to some of the city's wealthiest residences and most poverty-stricken dwellings. The palatial architecture along the English Quay is a world away from the decrepit living quarters around bustling Sennaya ploshchad, which have changed little since Dostoevsky *(see p123)* described them. In between lies the old maritime quarter, once inhabited by Peter the Great's shipwrights, many of whom were English. This area extended all the way from the New Holland warehouses to

St Nicholas' Cathedral, which stands on the site of the naval parade ground. Theatre Square has been a hub of entertainment since the mid-18th century. It is dominated by the prestigious Mariinskiy Theatre and the Rimsky-Korsakov Conservatory, where many of Russia's greatest artists began their careers. Before 1917, the streets leading off the square were home to theatre directors, actors, ballerinas, artists and musicians. Today, performing artists are once more returning to live in this shady backwater, attracted by the peace of the tree-lined canals.

Coat of arms on Yusupov Palace

SIGHTS AT A GLANCE

Cathedrals
St Nicholas' Cathedral ❷

Theatres
Mariinskiy Theatre p119 ❶

Historic Buildings and Areas
Main Post Office ❼
New Holland ❺
Rimsky-Korsakov Conservatory ❸

Palaces
Yusupov Palace ❹

Streets and Squares
Bolshaya Morskaya Ulitsa ❽
The English Quay ❻
Sennaya Ploshchad ❾

Museums
Railway Museum ❿

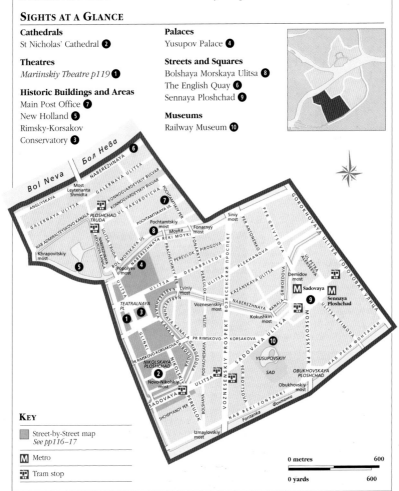

KEY

Street-by-Street map
See pp116–17

Ⓜ Metro

🚋 Tram stop

| 0 metres | 600 |
| 0 yards | 600 |

◁ **Gilded Baroque interior of the upper church of St Nicholas' Cathedral**

Street-by-Street: Theatre Square

THEATRE SQUARE WAS ONCE known as Carousel Square and was frequently used as the site for fairs and festivals. During the 19th century when St Petersburg became the cultural capital of Russia, the Mariinskiy Theatre and Rimsky-Korsakov Conservatory were established, and the neighbourhood became home to many artists. Today, the tradition of entertainment is still thriving and Theatre Square remains a focal point for theatrical and musical life *(see p194).*

Atlas on prospekt Rimskovo-Korsakova

Nearby, the tree-lined canal embankments and the gardens surrounding the beautiful St Nicholas' Cathedral are enchanting places to stroll.

NAB REKI MOYKI

ULITSA DEKABRISTOV

TEATRALNAYA PL

NAB KRYUKOVA KANALA

KRYUKO

The Monument to Rimsky-Korsakov, who taught at the Conservatory for 37 years, was designed by Veniamin Bogolyubov and Vladimir Ingal and erected in 1952.

Yusupov Palace
Historic site of the gruesome murder of Rasputin (see p121), this grand palace belonged to the wealthy Yusupov family. Its opulent interiors include this Italian marble staircase and a tiny Rococo theatre ❹

Rimsky-Korsakov Conservatory
Tchaikovsky, Prokofiev and Shostakovich (see p43) were among the talents nurtured by Russia's first conservatory, founded in 1862 by pianist and composer Anton Rubinstein ❸

Monument to Mikhail Glinka
(see p44)

★ Mariinskiy Theatre
This theatre has been home to the world-famous Mariinskiy (Kirov) Opera and Ballet Company since 1860. Hidden behind its imposing façade is the sumptuous auditorium where many of Russia's greatest dancers (see p118) have performed ❶

The Lion Bridge *(Lviny Most)* is one of a number of quaint and curious suspension bridges on the narrow, tree-lined Griboedov canal *(see p36)*. These bridges are well-known meeting places, notably for romantic trysts.

LOCATOR MAP
See Street Finder, map 5

The House of Michel Fokine at No. 109 is where the renowned ballet-master and choreographer lived before the Revolution.

The Benois House belonged to an artistic dynasty which included the co-founder of the World of Art movement, Alexandre Benois *(see p107)*.

The Belfry, an elegant four-tiered structure with a gilded spire, was built to mark the main entrance to St Nicholas' Cathedral.

St Nicholas' Cathedral
A fine example of 18th-century Russian Baroque, the lofty upper church is richly decorated with icons, gilding and this carved iconostasis. The lower church, beautifully lit with candles, is also open for worship ❷

KEY

— — — Suggested route

NABEREZHNAYA KANALA GRIBOEDOVA

PROSPEKT RIMSKOVO–KORSAKOVA

TSA GLINKI

NIKOLSKIY PEREULOK

KANAL GRIBOEDOVA

SADOVAYA ULITSA

KANAL

The former Nicholas market, characterized by its long arcade and steep roof, was constructed in 1788–9. In the 19th century it became an unofficial labour exchange as many unemployed workers gathered here.

0 metres   100

0 yards   100

Ballet in St Petersburg

ADMIRED THROUGHOUT the world, Russian ballet traces its origins back to 1738 when a French dancing master, Jean-Baptiste Landé, established a school in St Petersburg to train the children of palace employees. The Imperial Ballet School, as it soon became known, flourished under a string of distinguished foreign teachers, culminating in Marius Petipa (1818–1910). Petipa first joined the school in 1847 as a principal dancer and later choreographed over 60 ballets, inspiring such famous dancers as Matilda Kshesinskaya *(see p72).*

Matilda Kshesinskaya's ballet shoes

Following the 1905 Revolution, a reaction against Classicism led to an increasing number of defections from the Imperial theatres to the new private companies like Sergey Diaghilev's Ballets Russes. The dispersion of talent increased after the Bolsheviks seized power in 1917 and many artists went into exile abroad. Fortunately for Soviet Russia, the distinguished prima ballerina Agrippina Vaganova remained to train the next generation of dancers. St Petersburg's Russian Ballet Academy now bears her name *(see p110).*

Anna Pavlova's (1885–1931) most famous role, The Dying Swan, was created especially for her by Michel Fokine. In 1912 Pavlova left Russia to form her own touring company, spreading her enthusiasm for ballet throughout Europe.

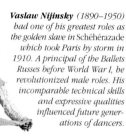

Vaslaw Nijinsky (1890–1950) had one of his greatest roles as the golden slave in Schéhérazade which took Paris by storm in 1910. A principal of the Ballets Russes before World War I, he revolutionized male roles. His incomparable technical skills and expressive qualities influenced future generations of dancers.

Rudolf Nureyev (1938–93), seen here in Sleeping Beauty at the Mariinskiy, defected to the West in 1961. As both choreographer and dancer, Nureyev continued to enthral audiences for over 30 years until his death in 1993.

The Mariinskiy Ballet, usually known abroad as the Kirov, is now reviving some of the original productions of the Ballets Russes, including their version of Giselle, previously not shown in Russia.

THE BALLETS RUSSES

The legendary touring company which revolutionized ballet between 1909 and 1929 was the brainchild of the impresario and art critic Sergey Diaghilev (*see p43*). Diaghilev found a kindred spirit in the choreographer Michel Fokine, who shared his vision of a spectacle that would fuse music, ballet and decor in a seamless artistic whole.

Diaghilev had the pick of dancers from the Mariinskiy and, in 1909, he brought his Ballets Russes to Paris. The company went from strength to strength with successful tours worldwide.

Diaghilev's new company had a remarkable impact on the contemporary art world. The ballets of Fokine, in particular, prepared audiences for greater innovation and experiment. Exciting contributions from costume and set designers Léon Bakst and Alexandre Benois, the composer Igor Stravinsky and the dancers Vaslaw Nijinsky, Anna Pavlova and Tamara Karsavina all played a part in expanding back the artistic frontiers. After Diaghilev's death in 1929, the Ballets Russes fragmented but its ethos and traditions have been preserved in many of today's leading companies.

Early 20th-century programme for the Ballets Russes

One of Russia's most important cultural institutions, the Mariinskiy Theatre

Mariinskiy Theatre ●
Мариинский театр
Mariinskiy teatr

Teatralnaya ploshchad. **Map** 5 B3.
📞 114 4344. 🚎 3, 22, 27. 🚐 5, 22. 🚊 1, 11. ◯ *for performances only (see pp194–5).* 🎭 ◻ ◻ ⊘

NAMED IN HONOUR of Tsarina Maria Alexandrovna, wife of Alexander II, this theatre is known abroad by its Soviet title, the Kirov, while at home it has reverted to its original name, the Mariinskiy Theatre. The building was erected in 1860 by the architect Albert Kavos, who designed the Bolshoy Theatre in Moscow. It stands on the site of an earlier theatre which was destroyed by fire.

In 1883–96, the Neo-Renaissance façade was remodelled by Viktor Schröter, who added most of the ornamental detail. The sumptuous pale blue and gold auditorium, where so many illustrious dancers have made their debut, creates a dazzling impression. Its architectural decoration of twisted columns, atlantes, cherubs and cameo medallions has remained unchanged since the theatre's completion, and the imperial eagles have recently been restored to the royal box. The ceiling painting of dancing

Imperial eagle on the royal box

girls and cupids by Italian artist Enrico Franchioli dates from c.1856, while the superb stage curtain was added during Russian ballet's golden age in 1914. Equally remarkable is the glittering festive foyer, decorated with fluted pilasters, bas-reliefs of Russian composers and mirrored doors.

Although the Mariinskiy is better known abroad for its ballet company, it is also one of the country's leading opera houses. Most of the great 19th-century Russian operas were premiered here, including Mussorgsky's *Boris Godunov* (1874) and Tchaikovsky's *Queen of Spades* (1890). Shostakovich's highly controversial opera *Lady Macbeth of Mtsensk* also opened here in 1934. Widely acclaimed in St Petersburg, this opera was rejected by Stalin and immediately dropped from the repertoire after the composer was denounced in a *Pravda* editorial entitled "Muddle instead of Music".

The Mariinskiy's luxuriant stage curtain, designed by Aleksandr Golovin in 1914

St Nicholas' Cathedral ②

Никольский собор

Nikolskiy sobor

Nikolskaya ploshchad. **Map** 5 C4.
[114 0862. **[=** 3, 22. **[** 1, 11.
○ 7am–noon, 4–7pm daily.

THIS STUNNING Baroque cathedral by Savva Chevakinskiy, one of Russia's great 18th-century architects, was built in 1753–62. Founded for sailors and Admiralty employees housed in the neighbourhood, and named after St Nicholas, the patron saint of sailors, the cathedral became known as the "Sailors' Church".

The beautiful exterior is decorated with white Corinthian pilasters and surmounted by five gilded cupolas. Nearby, within the cathedral's leafy grounds and overlooking the intersection of the Kryukov and Griboedov canals, is a slender four-tiered bell tower crowned by a spire.

Following the Russian tradition, there are two churches within the cathedral. The lower church, intended for daily use, is lit by icon lamps, candles and chandeliers, creating a magical effect. The icons (1755–7) are the work of the brothers Fedot and Menas Kolokolnikov. In total contrast, the upper church, used mainly on Sundays and for weddings, has a brighter, airy feel and a typically Baroque exuberance, with gilt and stucco ornamentation and Italianate paintings.

The pale blue and white Baroque façade of St Nicholas' Cathedral

Islamic arches and coffered ceiling in the Moorish Room, Yusupov Palace

The most impressive feature is the magnificent gilded iconostasis dating from 1755–60.

Rimsky-Korsakov Conservatory ③

Консерватория имени Римского-Корсакова

Konservatoriya imeni Rimskovo-Korsakova

Teatralnaya ploshchad 3. **Map** 5 B3.
[312 2519. **[=** 3, 22, 27. **[** 5, 22. **[** 1, 11. **○** for performances only. **[**📷**] [✓]** by appt.

RUSSIA'S OLDEST music school, the conservatory was founded in 1862 by the piano virtuoso Anton Rubinstein (1829–94). The present building was designed in 1896 by Vladimir Nicolas.

Among those to graduate from the school before the Revolution were Tchaikovsky *(see p42)* and Sergey Prokofiev. In the Soviet years, the school continued to flourish, and the greatest musical figure to emerge from this era was composer Dmitriy Shostakovich (1906–75) *(see p43)*.

In the forecourt outside the school are two statues. On the left, a 1952 memorial honours the school's influential teacher, Nikolai Rimsky-Korsakov, after whom the conservatory is now named. On the right, the statue of Mikhail Glinka (1906) by Robert Bach is a reminder that the conservatory stands on the original site where Russia's first opera, Glinka's *A Life for the Tsar*, was premiered in 1836 in the old Kamennyy (Stone) Theatre.

Yusupov Palace ④

Юсуповский дворец

Yusupovskiy dvorets

Naberezhnaya reki Moyki 94. **Map** 5 B3. **[** 314 8893. **[=** 3, 22, 27. **[** 1, 11. **○** noon–3pm daily. **[**📷**]**

OVERLOOKING the Moyka, this yellow, colonnaded building (1760s) was designed by Vallin de la Mothe. The palace was acquired in 1830 by the aristocratic Yusupov family to house their superb collection of paintings. Major work was then carried out on the interior by Andrey Mikhaylov and Ippolito Monighetti.

The interiors, notable among them the exotic Moorish Room, with its fountain, colourful mosaics and horseshoe arches, can be viewed by guided tour only. Separate tickets are needed for the tour of the cellars, which house an exhibition on Grigoriy Rasputin, the infamous "holy man" who was murdered here by Prince Felix Yusupov.

The elegant, Rococo-style family theatre seats just 180, and attending a concert *(see p194)* is an experience in itself.

THE GRIM DEATH OF RASPUTIN

The Russian peasant and mystic Grigoriy Rasputin (1869–1916) exercised an extraordinarily powerful influence over the court and government of Russia *(see p26)*. The mysterious circumstances of his dramatic death on 17 December 1916 are legendary. Lured to Yusupov's palace on the pretext of a party, Rasputin was poisoned, then shot by Prince Felix Yusupov and left for dead. Returning to the scene the prince found Rasputin still alive and a struggle ensued before Rasputin disappeared into the courtyard. Pursued by the conspirators he was shot another three times and brutally battered before being dumped in the river. When his corpse was found three days later, clinging to the supports of a bridge, water in his lungs indicated death by drowning.

New Holland ❺

Новая Голландия

Novaya Gollandiya

Naberezhnaya reki Moyki 103. **Map** 5 B3. 3, 22. 🚇 1, 11, 31, 42.

CREATED when the Kryukov canal was constructed between the Moyka and Neva rivers in 1719, this triangular island was originally used for storing ship timber. The name is in honour of the Dutch shipbuilders who inspired Peter the Great's naval ambitions.

In 1765, the original wooden warehouses were rebuilt in red brick by Savva Chevakinskiy. At the same time Vallin de la Mothe designed the austere but romantic arch facing onto the Moyka which creates an atmospheric entrance to the timber yard. Barges would pass through the arch and into a turning basin beyond, then return loaded with timber

Vallin de la Mothe's impressive arch on the Moyka, leading into New Holland

along the canals towards the Admiralty shipyards. Today the overgrown and inaccessible island holds a certain charm in its isolation.

The English Quay ❻

Английская набережная

Angliyskaya naberezhnaya

Map 5 A2. 🚇 1, 11, K-154, K-124, K-186.

THE FIRST English merchants settled here in the 1730s, followed by a huge influx of craftsmen, architects, artists, innkeepers and factory owners. In the 1760s the first English church opened and the embankment came to be known in the 19th century as the English Quay. By the end of the century the area boasted a string of riverside mansions and was one of the city's most fashionable addresses. It has some fine views of the river and several impressive buildings. On naval holidays, ships richly decorated with flags line the shore.

The Neo-Classical mansion (1770s) at No. 10 was the fic-

tional setting for the debutante ball of Natasha Rostova, heroine of Tolstoy's epic novel *War and Peace*. It contrasts sharply with the rusticated façade of No. 28, built in Florentine Renaissance style for the banking family of the barons von Derviz in the 1890s. No. 28 was later occupied by Grand Duke Andrey Vladimirovich, lover of ballet dancer Matilda Kshesinskaya *(see p72)*, and in 1917 it served as headquarters for the Socialist-Revolutionary Party. Its history took a final peculiar turn when it became a Palace of Weddings, or registry office. A little further along, at No. 32, is an elegant edifice built by Quarenghi in 1782–3.

Set back on ploshchad Truda is the palace of Grand Duke Nikolai Nikolaevich (son of Nicholas I), built in 1853–61 by Andrei Stakenschneider. In 1894 it became a school for young ladies of the nobility, but in 1917 the Bolshevik government gave it to the trade unions. Galas, seminars and other events are held here.

Back on the embankment, No. 44 is the Rumyantsev Palace, built in 1826–7. It is now part of the State Museum of the History of St Petersburg. There is a permanent exhibition, "Leningrad During the Second World War", as well as other exhibition spaces and halls. No. 56 is the former English church, an imposing Neo-Classical building by Quarenghi, dating from 1814.

Quarenghi's grand porticoed façade, at No. 32 on the English Quay

Main Post Office ❼
Главпочтамт
Glavpochtamt

Pochtamtskaya ulitsa 9. **Map** 5 C2.
📞 *312 8302.* 🚌 *3, 22.* 🚎 *5, 22.*
🕐 *9am–8pm Mon–Sat, 10am–6pm
Sun.* ⚫ *public hols.*

T HE MOST REMARKABLE feature
of the Main Post Office is
the arched gallery spanning
Pochtamtskaya ulitsa. Built as
an extension to Nikolay Lvov's
main building, the gallery
was added by Albert Kavos
in 1859. Under the *Pochtamt*
(Post Office) sign on the arch
is a clock showing the time in
major cities around the world.

Inside the post office, behind
Lvov's porticoed Neo-Classical
façade of 1782–9, is a splendid
Style-Moderne hall characterized by decorative ironwork
and a glass ceiling over the
vast, tiled floor space. The
hall was created in the early
20th century when a roof was
constructed over what was
originally the courtyard stables.

Porticoed façade, Main Post Office

Bolshaya Morskaya Ulitsa ❽
Большая Морская улица
Bolshaya Morskaya ulitsa

Map 5 C2. 🚌 *3, 22, 27.*

A LWAYS ONE of St Petersburg's
most fashionable streets,
shady Bolshaya Morskaya ulitsa
is the choice of the artistic
elite to this day. It has some
exceedingly handsome 19th-
century mansions hidden away
between St Isaac's Square *(see
p79)* and Pochtamtskiy most.

**Stone atlas at No. 43 Bolshaya
Morskaya ulitsa (1840)**

The mansion at No. 61 was
built by Albert Kavos in the
1840s for the St Petersburg
Stage Coach Company. No. 52,
nearby, was acquired by the
Russian Union of Architects in
1932. Built by Aleksandr Pel
in 1835–6, it was formerly the
residence of the celebrated
patron of the arts Aleksandr
Polovtsov, who built up the
impressive collection of the
Stieglitz Museum *(see p127).*
The striking late 19th-century
interiors with mahogany panelling, tapestries and carved
ceilings were designed by
Maximilian Mesmacher and
Nikolay Brullo and can be
admired from the Nikolay
restaurant within *(see p180).*

Just across the street, No. 47
is a particularly fine example
of Style-Moderne architecture
with sculpted stone rosettes,
delicate iron tracery and a
beautiful mosaic frieze of
pink flowers. This is the work
of Mikhail Geisler and Boris
Guslistiy, dating from 1901–2.
It was in this mansion that the
celebrated émigré novelist
Vladimir Nabokov (1899–1977)
grew up, and there are plans
to open a museum to him.
Admired for his linguisitic in-
genuity in both English and
Russian, Nabokov hit the head-
lines across the world with
the publication of *Lolita*, his
succès de scandale of 1959.

Next door at No. 45 is the
Union of Composers, the former home of socialite Princess
Gagarina who lived here in
the 1870s. The mansion was
reconstructed in the 1840s by
Auguste-Ricard de Montferrand,
and it retains elements of the
original 18th-century building.

Montferrand also built the
former residence of millionaire
industrialist Pyotr Demidov at
No. 43. A mass of Renaissance
and Baroque elements, with
atlantes, vases, winged glories
and rustication, the façade also
has Demidov's coat of arms.

Sennaya Ploshchad ❾
Сенная площадь
Sennaya ploshchad

Map 6 D3. Ⓜ *Sennaya Ploshchad,
Sadovaya.*

T HIS IS ONE of the oldest
squares in St Petersburg.
The square's name, meaning
Haymarket, derives from the
original market where livestock, fodder and firewood
were sold which opened in
the 1730s. Although fairly close
to the city centre, the area
around the square was inhabited by the poor and the
market was the cheapest and
liveliest in the city (the so-called
"belly of St Petersburg"). The

Style-Moderne mosaic frieze at No. 47 Bolshaya Morskaya ulitsa (1901–2)

Guardhouse and 1950s apartment blocks on bustling Sennaya ploshchad

FYODOR DOSTOEVSKY

One of Russia's greatest writers, Fyodor Dostoevsky *(see pp43–4)* was born in 1821 in Moscow but spent most of his adult life in St Petersburg, where many of his novels and short stories are set. A defining moment in his life occurred in 1849 when he was arrested and charged with revolutionary conspiracy. After eight months of solitary confinement in the Peter and Paul Fortress *(see pp66–7)*, Dostoevsky and 21 other "conspirators" from the socialist Petrashevsky Circle were subjected to a macabre mock execution before being exiled to hard labour in Siberia until 1859. The sinister experience is recalled in his novel *The Idiot* (1868). He died in 1881.

oldest building, at the centre of the square, is the former guardhouse, a single-storey Neo-Classical building with a columned portico, which dates to 1818–20. The guardsmen's duties ranged from supervising the traders to flogging serfs, mostly for minor misdemeanours. By that time the neighbourhood had become synonymous with dirt, squalor, crime and vice. At No. 3 is the site of "Vyazemskiy's Monastery", the nickname for a notorious tenement overrun with pubs, gambling dens and brothels in the 1850s and '60s.

This was the squalid world so vividly evoked in Fyodor Dostoevsky's masterpiece *Crime and Punishment.* As the

contemptuous hero of the novel, Raskolnikov, wanders around the market, he absorbs the "heat in the street.... the airlessness, the bustle and the plaster, scaffolding, bricks and dust.... that special St Petersburg stench.... and the numerous drunken men" which "completed the revolting misery of the picture". The novel was finished in 1866 while Dostoevsky was living at Alonkin's House, (No. 7 Przhevalskovo ulitsa), to the west of the square.

During the Soviet era the square was given a new image, stallholders were banished, trees were planted and it was optimistically renamed Peace Square (ploshchad Mira). The five-storey, yellow and white apartment blocks that surround the square today were also built then, in Stalin's version of Neo-Classicism. Sadly, in 1961, the square's most attractive monument, the Baroque Church of the Assumption, built in 1765, was pulled down to make way for one of the city's earliest metro stations.

Railway Museum ⑩
Музей железнодорожного транспорта
Muzey zheleznodorozhnovo transporta

Sadovaya ulitsa 50. **Map** 6 D4.
☎ 315 1476. Ⓜ *Sennaya Ploshchad, Sadovaya.* ◯ *11am–5pm Sun–Thu.*
✔ *English.*

MORE THAN 6,000 fascinating exhibits illustrate the history of the Russian railway system since 1813. The most interesting sections of the museum deal with the earliest railways, including Russia's first from Tsarskoe Selo to St Petersburg which began running in 1837, and the 650-km (404-mile) line from Moscow to St Petersburg (1851).

Exhibits include models of the first Russian steam engine, built by the Cherepanovs in 1834, and of an armoured train used by Trotsky in the defence of the city during the Civil War *(see p27).* An insight into luxury travel in the late tsarist period can be gained from the walk-through section of a first-class sleeping compartment with velvet upholstery and Style-Moderne decoration.

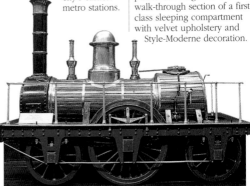

Model of 1830s engine for the Tsarskoe Selo railway, Railway Museum

FURTHER AFIELD

WHILE THE majority of St Petersburg's sights are centrally located, the outlying areas of the city have a number of places of architectural, cultural and historical importance.

To the east is the Smolnyy district, taking its name from the tar yard which supplied the city's embryonic shipbuilding industry in the 18th century. The highlight of this area is Rastrelli's dazzling Baroque Smolnyy Convent. Nearby, the Smolnyy Institute is famed for its historic role as the Bolshevik headquarters during the October Revolution (*see pp28–9*).

Ceramic tile from 1770s stove, Stieglitz Museum

Southeast of the centre lies the Alexander Nevsky Monastery where many of Russia's celebrated artists, architects and composers are buried.

The southern suburbs offer a strikingly different perspective of the city, with rows of pompous 1930s–50s houses, a reminder that Stalin sought to destroy the city's historical heart by relocating the centre from the old imperial district to the area around Moskovskaya ploshchad. The south also has the Chesma Church and the 1970s Victory Monument, a memorial to the suffering of St Petersburgers during the Siege of Leningrad.

SIGHTS AT A GLANCE

Palaces
Sheremetev Palace **9**
Tauride Palace **6**
Yelagin Palace **1**

Museums
Dostoevsky House-Museum **10**
Stieglitz Museum **4**

Churches
Alexander Nevsky Monastery **11**
Cathedral of the
   Transfiguration **5**
Chesma Church **12**
Smolnyy Convent **7**

Historic Buildings and Monuments
Finland Station **3**
Piskarevskoe Memorial
   Cemetery **2**
Smolnyy Institute **8**
Victory Monument **13**

KEY

	Central St Petersburg
	Greater St Petersburg
✈	Airport
🚉	Railway station
⛴	Ferry port
▬	Major road
═	Minor road

0 kilometres   3

0 miles   3

◁ **The Baroque Sheremetev Palace on the east bank of the Fontanka river**

East façade of Yelagin Palace with Srednaya Nevka river in foreground

Yelagin Palace ❶

Елагин дворец
Yelagin dvorets

Yelagin ostrov 1. 🅚 430 1131.
Ⓜ *Krestovskiy ostrov.*
⭕ *10am–5pm Wed–Sun.* 📷
♿ *to ground floor.* ⬛

ONE OF THE northernmost islands of St Petersburg, Yelagin Island is named after a court official who built a palace here at the end of the 18th century. Alexander I then bought the island in 1817 for his mother, Maria Fyodorovna, and commissioned Carlo Rossi to rebuild the palace. The magnificent Neo-Classical palace (1818–22), enlivened on the east façade by a half rotunda flanked by Corinthian porticoes, is part of an ensemble which includes an orangery, a horseshoe-shaped stable block and porticoed kitchens.

The palace interior was destroyed by fire during World War II but is now undergoing restoration. The Oval Hall is resplendent with statuary and trompe l'oeils while the rooms leading from it are exquisitely decorated with stucco, *faux marbre* and painted friezes, executed by a collective of gifted artists and craftsmen.

Statue of Mother Russia (1956–60), Piskarevskoe Memorial Cemetery

In the Soviet period, the whole of the wooded island became the Central Park of Culture and Rest *(see pp136–7)*. Festivals and public entertainments are held here, and there is an exhibition of decorative art in the palace's former stables.

Piskarevskoe Memorial Cemetery ❷

Пискаревское мемориальное кладбище
Piskarevskoe memorialnoe kladbishche

Prospekt Nepokorennykh 74.
🅚 247 5716. Ⓜ *Akademicheskaya.*
🚌 123, 178. ⭕ *24 hours daily.*
Memorial halls 10am–6pm daily. ⬛

THIS VAST, BLEAK cemetery is a memorial to the two million people who died during the Siege of Leningrad, 1941–4 *(see p27)*. With little food and no electricity, water or heating, the citizens of Leningrad perished in vast numbers from starvation, cold and disease. Thousands of corpses were dragged on sledges to collection points from where they were taken for burial to mass cemeteries on the outskirts of town. Piskarevskoe was the largest, with 490,000 burials.

Today the cemetery is a place of pilgrimage for those who lost relatives and friends during those desperate times. The memorial complex, designed by Yevgeniy Levinson and Aleksandr Vasiliev, opened in 1960, on the 15th anniversary of the end of the war. Two memorial halls, one of which contains an exhibition on the Siege, flank the stairs down to a 300-m (984-ft) long avenue, which culminates in a towering, heroic bronze statue of Mother Russia by Vera

Isayeva and Robert Taurit. On the wall behind are verses composed by Olga Bergholts, herself a survivor of the Siege. The funereal music broadcast over the whole cemetery adds to the sombre atmosphere.

On either side of the avenue are 186 grassy mounds, each with a granite slab marking the year and indicating, with a red star or hammer and sickle, whether those interred were soldiers or civilians.

Locomotive 293, Finland Station

Finland Station ❸

Финляндский вокзал
Finlyandskiy vokzal

Ploshchad Lenina 6. **Map** 3 B3.
Ⓜ *Ploshchad Lenina.*
See also p221.

ON THE NIGHT of 3 April 1917, the exiled Vladimir Lenin and his Bolshevik companions arrived at Finland Station after travelling from Switzerland on a sealed train. A triumphant reception awaited their return to Russia and, on leaving the station, Lenin spoke to cheering crowds of soldiers, sailors and workers. A statue erected outside the station in 1926 depicts Lenin delivering his speech.

The modern terminal was opened in the 1960s. On platform 5 there is a huge glass case containing Locomotive 293 which Lenin rode when fleeing the capital for a second time in July 1917. After spending the summer as a fugitive in Russian Finland, Lenin returned on the same train and spurred on the October Revolution *(see pp28–9)*.

Stieglitz Museum ❹

Музей Штиглица

Muzey Shtiglitsa

Solyanoy pereulok 13. **Map** 3 A5.
📞 273 3258. 🚌 46. 🚎 90.
🕐 Sep–Jul: 11am–4pm Tue–Sat.
📷 ☑ English, German.

THE MILLIONAIRE industrialist Baron Aleksandr Stieglitz founded the Central School of Industrial Design in 1876. His aim was to provide a top quality collection of original works for the use of Russian students of applied arts and design.

19th-century crystal vase, Stieglitz Museum

With a large budget and the good taste of Stieglitz's son-in-law, Aleksandr Polovtsov (*see p122*), the collection, unusual in covering both Western European and Oriental art, soon outgrew the school and in 1896 a Museum of Applied Arts opened next door. This magnificent building, designed by Maximilian Messmacher, was inspired by Italian Renaissance palaces. Inside, the halls and galleries were decorated in an impressive variety of national and period styles, echoing French and German Baroque and, above all, Italian Renaissance monuments, such as St Mark's Library in Venice, the Raphael Loggias of the Vatican and the Villa Madama, also in Rome.

After the Revolution the school was closed and the museum became a branch of the Hermitage (*see pp84–93*). Serious damage to the building was inflicted during the Siege of Leningrad (*see p27*) and restoration continues. At the end of the war the school was revived to train gilders and carvers for the huge restoration programme needed to repair the damaged city.

Situated on the ground floor, the exhibition features opulent displays of glassware, ceramics and majolica, as well as porcelain from all the great European manufacturers. One room, decorated in the style of the medieval Terem Palace in the Kremlin, provides a superb backdrop for a collection of colourfully embroidered dresses and headgear made by Russian peasant women.

Some pieces of decorative metalwork including locks, keys and craft tools date back to the Middle Ages. The workmanship seen on the wooden furniture is breathtaking. The Neo-Gothic cabinet is a beautiful example. Its finely inlaid doors, depicting church naves in skilful perspective, open to reveal sculpted biblical scenes.

One way to end your visit is with a look at the stunning Grand Exhibition Hall with its curving staircase of Italian marble and magnificent glass roof.

Cathedral of the Transfiguration ❺

Спасо-Преображенский собор

Spaso-Preobrazhenskiy sobor

Preobrazhenskaya ploshchad 1. **Map** 3 B5. 📞 272 3662. Ⓜ Chernyshevskaya. 🚌 46, K-15, K-76. 🚎 3, 8, 15. 🚎 90. 🕐 8am–8pm daily.

DESPITE ITS monumental Neo-Classicism, and the surrounding fence made of guns captured during the Russo-Turkish wars (*see p22*), Vasiliy Stasov's church has an intimate air as it nestles in its leafy square. The original church on this site was built by Tsarina Elizabeth to honour the Preobrazhenskiy Guards, but it was rebuilt after a fire in 1825. Today, the church is famous for its excellent choir, which is second only to that in the Alexander Nevsky Monastery (*see pp130–31*).

Dolls in 17th–19th century Russian folk costumes, in front of the Terem Room, Stieglitz Museum

Tauride Palace ❻
Таврический дворец
Tavricheskiy dvorets

Shpalernaya ulitsa 47. **Map** 4 D4.
Ⓜ *Chernyshevskaya.*
🚌 *46, 136.* ⚫ *to public.*

THIS FINELY proportioned palace by Ivan Starov was built in 1783–9 as a present from Catherine the Great to her influential lover Prince Grigoriy Potemkin *(see p25)*. Potemkin had successfully annexed the Crimea (Tauris) to Russia in 1783 and was given the title of Prince of Tauris, hence the palace's name.

Uncompromising in its lack of external ornamentation, the long, yellow building with its distinctive six-columned portico was one of Russia's first Neo-Classical designs. Sadly, the magnificent interiors have been badly damaged both by Catherine's son, Paul I, who turned the palace into a barracks, and by the many reconstructions undertaken.

The palace has played a vital role in 20th-century cultural and political life. In 1905, the impresario Sergey Diaghilev *(see p43)* organized the first ever exhibition of Russian 18th-century portraiture here. The following year the palace hosted Russia's first parliament, the State Duma. After the February Revolution of 1917 it became the seat of the Provisional Government, then the Petrograd Soviet of Workers' and Soldiers' Deputies. Today it is still a government building.

The lovely gardens, with winding streams, bridges and an artificial lake, are among the city's most popular parks.

Façade of the Smolnyy Cathedral with adjacent convent buildings

Smolnyy Convent ❼
Смольный монастырь
Smolnyy monastyr

Ploshchad Rastrelli 3/1. **Map** 4 F4.
📞 *271 9421.* 🚌 *46, 136.*
🕐 *11am–5pm Fri–Wed.* 📷 ♿ ✅
English.

THE CROWNING GLORY of this architectural ensemble is the stunning cathedral with its dome and four supporting cupolas topped by golden orbs.

As a symbol of her majesty, Tsarina Elizabeth founded the convent where many young noblewomen were to be educated. It was designed in 1748 by Bartolomeo Rastrelli *(see p93)*, who conceived a brilliant fusion of Russian and Western Baroque styles. Work advanced extremely slowly; 50,000 wooden piles were used to secure the foundations in the marshy soil and the architect's model alone, now in the Academy of Arts *(see p63)*, took seven years to build.

Catherine the Great disliked Rastrelli's work and had little sympathy for the late Elizabeth. When she came to power in 1762, funding for the project

stopped. It was only in 1835 that Nicholas I commissioned the Neo-Classical architect Vasiliy Stasov to complete the cathedral. His austere white interior contrasts dramatically with the luxuriant exterior.

Exhibitions are now held here, as well as regular weekly concerts of church music *(see p194)*. There are spectacular views of the city from the cathedral tower.

Smolnyy Institute ❽
Смольный Институт
Smolnyy Institut

Ploshchad Proletarskoy Diktatury.
Map 4 F4. 📞 *276 1461.* 🚌 *22, 46, 136, K-15, K-129, K-136, K-147.* 🚋
5, 7, 15, 16, 49. **Smolnyy Museum**
🕐 *11am–4pm Mon–Fri by appt only.*
📷 ♿ ✅ *English.*

BUILT IN 1806–8 to house a school for young noblewomen which had outgrown its premises at the Smolnyy Convent, Giacomo Quarenghi considered this Neo-Classical building to be his masterpiece.

It was from here, on 25 October 1917, that Lenin directed the Bolshevik *coup d'état* while the second All-Russian Congress of Soviets was convening in the Assembly Hall. The Congress confirmed Lenin in power and this was his seat of government until March 1918. With the Germans advancing and the outbreak of civil war *(see p27)*, the government left for Moscow. The Institute was taken over by the Leningrad Communist Party. On 1 December 1934, the First Secretary of the party, Sergey Kirov *(see p72)*, was murdered here, an event that was to

View of Tauride Gardens and the Tauride Palace beyond the lake

Isaak Brodskiy's 1927 painting of Lenin, Smolnyy Institute Assembly Hall

provide cover for the purges of the late 1930s *(see p27).*

The rooms where Lenin lived and worked can be viewed by appointment. The rest of the institute is now the Mayor's Office. The imperial eagle has replaced the hammer and sickle, but the statue of Lenin has survived.

Sheremetev Palace ❾
Шереметевский дворец
Sheremetevskiy dvorets

Naberezhnaya reki Fontanki 34. **Map 7 A1. Anna Akhmatova Museum** ☎ 272 2211. Ⓜ *Mayakovskaya.* 🚋 *3, 8, 15.* 🚎 *12, 28, 54, 90.* ⭘ *10am–6pm Mon–Fri.* 🎟 excursions. **Museum of Musical Life** ☎ 272 4441. Ⓜ *Gostinyy Dvor.* 🚋 *3, 8, 15.* 🚎 *12, 28, 54, 90.* ⭘ *noon–6pm Wed–Sun.* 🎟 🎫

T HE SHEREMETEV family lived on this site from 1712 – when the first palace was built here by Field Marshal Boris

Sheremetev – until the Revolution. The palace is also known as the Fountain House, or *Fontannyy dom*, because of the many fountains that once adorned its grounds. The existing Baroque building dates essentially from the 1750s when it was designed by Savva Chevakinskiy and Fyodor Argunov, although numerous later alterations were made.

Field Marshal Sheremetev's descendants were fabulously wealthy, at one time owning some 200,000 serfs. They were also among Russia's leading artistic patrons and the palace is now home to the Museum of Musical Life, which charts the family's contribution to the musical life of the city. In the 18th and 19th centuries, serf composers, musicians and actors from rural estates owned by the family performed in many concerts and plays at the palace. Among those to praise the fine Sheremetev choir was the composer Franz Liszt.

The museum's exhibits include a variety of period instruments and a number of scores, some of which are compositions by the Sheremetevs themselves.

One of Russia's greatest 20th-century poets, Anna Akhmatova, lived in one of the service blocks of the palace from 1933 to 1941 and then again between 1944 and 1954. Her flat is open to the public as the Anna Akhmatova Museum (*Muzey Anny Akhmatovoy*) and is reached through the courtyard of No. 53 Liteynyy prospekt. By the time she moved into the palace, it had been divided into dingy communal apartments. The rooms where she lived and worked display some of her personal possessions, which trace her intriguing life. Recordings of the poetess reading her own poems can also be heard.

ANNA AKHMATOVA

By 1914 Anna Akhmatova (1889–1966) was a leading light of Russia's "Silver Age" of poetry *(see p44).* Tragedy gave her work a new dimension when first her husband was shot by the Bolsheviks, and then, in the 1930s, her son and her lover were arrested in Stalin's purges. Anna herself was placed under police surveillance and officially silenced for more than 15 years. Her most famous poem, *Requiem* (1935–61), inspired by her son's arrest, was written in fragments and distributed amongst friends to memorize. Anna was partially rehabilitated late in her life and received honorary awards abroad in 1965.

Pilastered façade of Sheremetev Palace on the Fontanka embankment

Dostoevsky House-Museum ❿
Музей Достоевского
Muzey Dostoevskovo

Kuznechnyy pereulok 5/2. **Map** 7 B3.
📞 *311 4031.* Ⓜ *Vladimirskaya.*
🚃 *3, 8, 15.* 🚎 *2, 49, 90.* ⏰ *11am–6pm Tue–Sun.* 📷 🎧 *English.*

THIS EVOCATIVE museum was the final home of the famous Russian writer, Fyodor Dostoevsky *(see p44)*, who lived here from 1878 until his death in 1881. Dostoevsky was then at the height of his fame, and it was here that he completed his last great novel, *The Brothers Karamazov,* in 1880. Gambling and debts, however, confined him to a fairly modest lifestyle in this five-roomed apartment.

Although Dostoevsky's public persona was dour and humourless, he was a devoted and affectionate husband and father. The delightful nursery contains a rocking horse, silhouettes of his children and the book of fairy tales which he read aloud to them. In Dostoevsky's study are his writing desk and a reproduction of his favourite painting, Raphael's *Sistine Madonna.*

Chesma Church (1777–80), a very early example of Neo-Gothic in Russia

Chesma Church ⓬
Чесменская церковь
Chesmenskaya tserkov

Ulitsa Lensoveta 12. Ⓜ *Moskovskaya.*
🚃 *16.* 🚎 *29, 45.* ⏰ *10am–7pm daily.*

THERE IS LITTLE Russian about the highly unusual Chesma Church, which was designed by Yuriy Velten in 1777–80. Its fanciful terracotta-coloured façade is decorated with thin vertical stripes of white moulding which direct the eye upwards to its zig-zagged crown and Neo-Gothic cupolas.

The name commemorates the great Russian naval victory over the Turks at Chesma in the Aegean in 1770. During the Communist era the church became a museum to the battle, but today the building is once again used as a church.

On the opposite side of ulitsa Lensoveta is the Neo-Gothic Chesma Palace (1774–77), formerly *Kekerekeksinen,* or Frog Marsh Palace. Also designed by Velten, it served as a staging post for Catherine the Great en route to Tsarskoe Selo *(see pp150–53).* Wedgwood's famous dinner service with its frog emblem, now in the Hermitage *(see p91),* was designed specially for the Chesma Palace.

The palace achieved notoriety when Rasputin's body lay in state here after his murder in 1916 *(see p121).* Now substantially altered, it serves as a home for the elderly.

Alexander Nevsky Monastery ⓫
Александро-Невская лавра
Aleksandro-Nevskaya lavra

Ploshchad Aleksandra Nevskovo.
Map 8 E4. 📞 *274 1612 or 274 1124.* Ⓜ *Ploshchad Aleksandra Nevskovo.* 🚃 *8, 27, 46.* 🚎 *1, 14, 16, 22.* 🚎 *7, 65.* **Cemeteries** ⏰ *10am–7pm Fri–Wed (10am–4pm Dec–Apr).* **Church of the Annunciation** ⏰ *11am–5pm daily.* 📷 *cemeteries and Church of the Annunciation.* 🎫

FOUNDED BY Peter the Great in 1710, this monastery is named after Alexander Nevsky, the prince of Novgorod, who defeated the Swedes in 1240. Peter himself defeated them again in 1709 *(see p18).*

From the entrance, a path runs between two large, walled cemeteries, then across

Reliquary with Alexander Nevsky's remains, Trinity Cathedral

Dostoevsky's tombstone

a stream and into the main monastic complex. The oldest building is the Church of the Annunciation (1717–22), designed by Domenico Trezzini. The church, its ground floor recently opened to the public, was the burial place for non-ruling members of the Russian royal family. A series of red and white, mid-18th-century monastic buildings, including the Metropolitan's House (1755–8), surround the courtyard. Among the trees in the courtyard lie the graves of atheist Soviet scholars and leading Communists. Dominating the essentially Baroque complex is the twin-towered and domed Neo-Classical Holy Trinity Cathedral, constructed by architect Ivan Starov in 1776–90. The wide nave inside is flanked by Corinthian columns with statues by Fedot Shubin. This leads to the impressive red agate and white marble iconostasis, which features copies of works by Van Dyck, Rubens and others. To the right of the iconostasis is a silver reliquary that contains the remains of Alexander Nevsky, transferred

Victory Monument 🔢

Монумент Защитникам
Ленинграда

*Monument Zashchitnikam
Leningrada*

Ploshchad Pobedy. 📞 *373 6563.*
Ⓜ *Moskovskaya.* **Memorial Hall**
🕐 *10am–6pm Thu & Sat–Mon,
10am–5pm Tue & Fri.* ♿

Erected in 1975 to coincide
with the 30th anniversary
of the end of World War II, this
is on the site of a temporary
triumphal arch built to greet
the returning troops. Named
the Monument to the Heroic
Defenders of Leningrad, it
commemorates the victims of
the Siege *(see p27)*, and its
survivors. It was designed by
Sergey Speranskiy and Valentin
Kamenskiy and sculpted by
Mikhail Anikushin. A 48-m
(157-ft) high obelisk of red
granite is near a vast, circular
enclosure which symbolizes
the vice-like grip of the siege.
Sculptures of soldiers, sailors
and grieving mothers
surround the monument.

An underpass on Moskovskiy
prospekt leads to the gloomy,
subterranean Memorial Hall.
Here solemn music gives way
to the persistent beat of a
metronome, the wartime radio
signal, intended to represent
the city's defiant heartbeat.
The subdued lighting com-
prises 900 dim, orange lamps,
one for each day of the Siege.
On the marble walls are tablets
inscribed with the names of
the 650 Heroes of the Soviet
Union who were awarded the
title after the war, while, on
the far wall, a mosaic depicts
the women of the city greeting their soldier menfolk at
the end of the grim conflict.

Around the hall a small
display of artifacts, including
Shostakovich's violin *(see p43)*,
records the contribution of
different sections of the community to the war effort, while
an illuminated relief map
illustrates the battle lines.
Most disturbing is the tiny
piece of bread, which was
many people's daily ration.

Heroic partisans facing south towards the enemy during the Siege of Leningrad, detail of Victory Monument

to the previous church on
this site in 1724. Behind the
reliquary hangs a painting of
Nevsky, who has been venerated as a saint in Russia since
the mid-16th century.

Many of the nation's leading
cultural figures are buried in
the two monastic cemeteries
near the main entrance. The
city's oldest graveyard, the
Lazarus Cemetery, to the east,
contains the graves of the
polymath Mikhail Lomonosov
(see p45) and a number of
prominent architects, including
Andrey Zakharov, Thomas de
Thomon, Giacomo Quarenghi,
Carlo Rossi *(see p110)* and
Andrey Voronikhin. Clustered
together along the northern
wall of the Tikhvin Cemetery
(to the west) are the tombs of
some of Russia's most famous
composers. Many of their
tombs are inscribed with musical motifs. Fyodor Dostoevsky
(see p44) is also buried here,
to the right of the entrance.

TOMBS OF INTEREST AT TIKHVIN CEMETERY

1 Mikhail Glinka
(Composer, 1804–57)
2 Ivan Krylov
(Poet, 1768–1844)
3 Marius Petipa
(Choreographer, 1818–1910)
4 Pyotr Klodt
(Sculptor, 1805–67)
5 Ivan Kramskoy
(Painter, 1837–87)
6 Pyotr Tchaikovsky
(Composer, 1840–93)
7 Modest Mussorgsky
(Composer, 1839–81)
8 Nikolai Rimsky-Korsakov
(Composer, 1844–1908)
9 Fyodor Dostoevsky
(Writer, 1821–81)

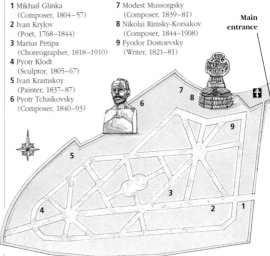

KEY

✝ Gate church

| 0 metres | 50 |
| 0 yards | 50 |

Two Guided Walks

S<small>T PETERSBURG IS</small> a very manageable city to explore on foot, and many of its sights are best appreciated in this way. The two walks chosen present different sides of the city's character. However, since St Petersburg is dominated by its location on a group of islands at the mouth of the Neva river, water plays a central part in both.

The first walk follows two of the many waterways, the Moyka river and the Griboedov canal, which criss-cross the heart of the city presenting the magnificent scale of St Petersburg as it was built in the 18th and 19th centuries. It shows the contrasts of rich palaces and overcrowded apartment blocks, gilded bridges and the dilapidation of the area around Sennaya

19th-century urn on the steps of Yelagin Palace

ploshchad. An alternative way to appreciate the canals is to take a boat trip *(see pp218–19)*, which delivers another perspective on the city's glorious historical buildings.

The second walk explores the world where Petersburgers have spent much of their free time since the 18th century. The Yelagin and Kamennyy islands, to the north of the centre, were once the preserve of the rich, who spent the hot summers in the cool of their *dachas*, the marvellously varied architecture of which can still be admired today. Now the islands offer a calm retreat for all. Locals come to walk and row boats in summer, collect leaves in autumn, ski and skate in winter, or simply to breathe the fresh air in spring.

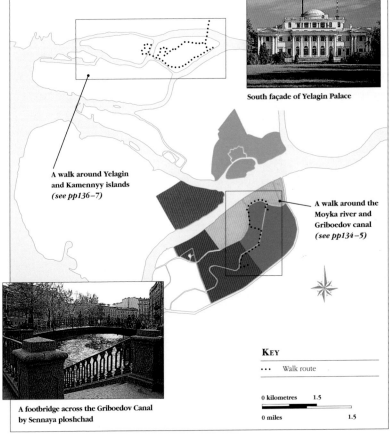

South façade of Yelagin Palace

A walk around Yelagin and Kamennyy islands *(see pp136–7)*

A walk around the Moyka river and Griboedov canal *(see pp134–5)*

KEY

••• Walk route

0 kilometres   1.5

0 miles   1.5

A footbridge across the Griboedov Canal by Sennaya ploshchad

◁ **Peace and tranquillity enjoyed on one of the lakes of Yelagin Island**

A Walk along St Petersburg's Waterways

A STROLL ALONG the embankments of the Moyka river and the Griboedov canal is a chance to appreciate the history and splendid architecture of this beautiful city. The two waterways present interesting contrasts. The Moyka winds past the Imperial Summer and Winter Palaces and the lavish mansions of the aristocracy, while the Griboedov is lined with 19th-century apartments, once home to merchants, civil servants and, towards Sennaya Ploshchad (see p122), the working class. The walk also includes a short stretch of the majestic Nevskiy prospekt.

> **TIPS FOR WALKERS**
>
> **Starting point:** Church on Spilled Blood. **Length:** 5.8 km (3 miles). **Getting there:** Nevskiy Prospekt metro. **Stopping-off points:** Café Minutka, Nevskiy prospekt 20; Bistro Layma, nab kanala Griboedova 16.

View of the Church on Spilled Blood and the Griboedov canal

The Moyka River

Begin the walk at the recently restored Church on Spilled Blood ① (see p100), built over the spot where Alexander II was assassinated in 1881 (see p26). From here, walk around the church beside the park, crossing the canal bridge to Konyushennaya ploshchad. The square is embraced by the elongated façade of the former Imperial Stables ② (see p113). Straddling the junction of the Griboedov canal and the Moyka river are two ingeniously linked bridges, the Malo-Konyushennyy most (Little Stable Bridge) and Teatralnyy most (Theatre Bridge) (see p37). Cross over these bridges to the north bank of the Moyka and the expansive façade of the Adamini House ③, designed by Domenico Adamini in 1823–7. Between 1916 and 1919 the basement was used

by an artists' and writers' club known as "The Bivouac of the Comedians". Visitors included the avant-garde theatre director Vsevolod Meyerhold and the poets Aleksandr Blok and Anna Akhmatova (see p44).

Turn left onto naberezhnaya reki Moyki and walk past the Round Market ④ built in 1790 by Giacomo Quarenghi, who had shopping arcades as one of his specialities. Continue along the embankment, passing Adam's Bolshoy Konyushennyy most (Great Stables Bridge) to Prince Abamelek-Lazarev's former mansion ⑤ built in 1913–15. The handsome façade, with Corinthian pilasters and graceful reliefs of dancing figures, is by Ivan Fomin. On the opposite bank is the 17th-century apartment block where Pushkin spent the last few months of his life. His flat is now a museum ⑥ (see p113).

At the intersection of Millionaya ulitsa and the beautiful Winter Canal (Zimnyaya Kanavka) are the former barracks of the elite First Regiment of the Preobrazhenskiy Life-Guards. This prestigious corps was formed by Peter the Great in the 1690s.

General Staff Building

Quarenghi's arcaded Round Market (1790), overlooking the Moyka river

0 metres   300
0 yards   300

KEY

*** Tour route

Ⓜ Metro station

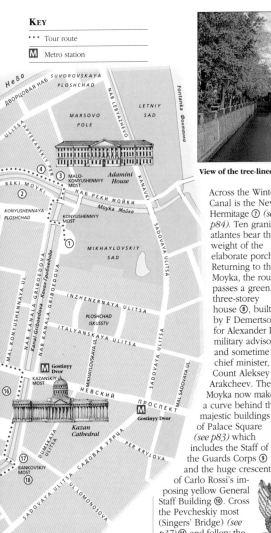

View of the tree-lined Griboedov canal

Across the Winter Canal is the New Hermitage ⑦ (see p84). Ten granite atlantes bear the weight of the elaborate porch. Returning to the Moyka, the route passes a green, three-storey house ⑧, built by F Demertsov for Alexander I's military advisor and sometime chief minister, Count Aleksey Arakcheev. The Moyka now makes a curve behind the majestic buildings of Palace Square (see p83) which includes the Staff of the Guards Corps ⑨ and the huge crescent of Carlo Rossi's imposing yellow General Staff Building ⑩. Cross the Pevcheskiy most (Singers' Bridge) (see p37) ⑪ and follow the Moyka down to the Politseyskiy most (Police Bridge). The yellow building on the other side of the Moyka is the Literary Café ⑫, renowned as a meeting-place for writers in Pushkin's day (see p83).

Nevskiy Prospekt

Turn left onto St Petersburg's main street, where a range of architectural styles can be seen. On the left, the elegant façade of Paul Jacot's Dutch Church building ⑬ (see p47) hides a series of shops. Across the road, the superb façade of the Baroque Stroganov Palace ⑭ (see p112) contrasts starkly with the triple-arched glass frontage of the Style-Moderne Fashion House ⑮ (see p47). The colonnaded forecourt of the Cathedral of Our Lady of Kazan ⑯ (see p111) can be seen further along.

The Griboedov Canal

Cross Nevskiy prospekt by the attractive Dom Knigi (see p47) and follow the Griboedov south. When you reach Georg von Traitteur's Bankovskiy most (see p35) ⑰, decorated with golden griffons, cross the canal and continue past the wrought-iron railings to the rear of the former Assignment Bank ⑱ (now occupied by an Economics University). Further south the humped Kamennyy most (Stone Bridge) has survived since 1776 despite an attempt by the revolutionary group, Peoples' Will, to blow it up as Tsar Alexander II passed in his carriage. Across the Demidov most, on the corner of Kaznacheyskaya ulitsa ⑲ (No.1), is the apartment where Dostoevsky wrote *Notes from the House of the Dead* (1861). He was living on the same street when he wrote *Crime and Punishment*. Also with literary associations, the former Zverkov House ⑳ was where the novelist and dramatist Nikolai Gogol (see p44) lived in the 1830s.

The walk ends in Sennaya ploshchad (see p122), where there are two metro stations.

Griffons on Bank Bridge (1826), Griboedov canal

Apartment block where Dostoevsky lived, on the Griboedov canal

A Walk around Kamennyy and Yelagin Islands

AN AREA OF ROLLING parkland, birch and lime groves and fine river views, the northern islands of the Neva delta offer a retreat from city life. The imperial family built palaces on Kamennyy and Yelagin islands at the end of the 18th century and were soon joined by wealthy aristocratic families. Before the Revolution, many government ministers, industrial magnates and celebrities built themselves a *dacha* here. Today these neglected houses, some intimate, some palatial, in styles ranging from Neo-Gothic to Neo-Classical and Style Moderne, are being returned to their former glory by the new business elite.

Wooden façade of Dolgorukov Mansion

the fashionable architect, Vladimir Apyshkov, to build this splendid Style-Moderne mansion in 1913–14.

Continue west, and cross the canal bridge to reach the wooden Kamennoostrovskiy Theatre ⑥ which took only 40 days to erect in 1827. Though in need of a coat of paint, its Neo-Classical portico, rebuilt by Albert Kavos in 1844, is still impressive. The banks of the Krestovka river, with views across to the boat-yards of Krestovskiy Island, are ideal for a picnic. Return to the path and cross 1-y Yelagin most to Yelagin Island.

Yelagin Island
This island is an oasis of calm, popular with Petersburgers wishing to escape the city. A tollgate marks the entrance to the grounds of Carlo Rossi's

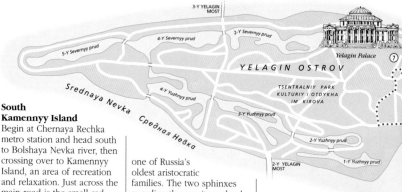

South
Kamennyy Island
Begin at Chernaya Rechka metro station and head south to Bolshaya Nevka river, then crossing over to Kamennyy Island, an area of recreation and relaxation. Just across the main road is the small red-brick Church of St John the Baptist ①, designed in Neo-Gothic style by Yuriy Velten in 1776–8. Nearby a yellow gateway leads to the grounds of Kamennoostrovskiy Palace ② (now a retirement home) from where Alexander I led the Russian campaign of 1812 against Napoleon *(see p26).*

Follow Kamennoostrovskiy prospekt to the Malaya Nevka river, then turn right on to naberezhnaya Maloy Nevki where there is an imposing wooden mansion ③ at No. 11 with a white-columned portico. The Dolgorukov Mansion was built in 1831–2 by Smaragd Shustov for the Dolgorukovs,

one of Russia's oldest aristocratic families. The two sphinxes guarding the granite embankment date to 1824. From this point you can see across to Aptekarskiy or Apothecary's Island, named after the medicinal herb gardens founded by Peter the Great. St Petersburg's Botanical Gardens are still located there. Continue along the path, which turns into naberezhnaya reki Krestovki. Standing in the middle of the path are the remains of Peter the Great's oak tree ④, said to have been planted by the tsar in 1718. The house on the left, towards the Malo-krestovskiy most, is the former home of Sergey Chaev ⑤, the chief engineer of the Trans-Siberian railway. Chaev commissioned

The tower of the Church of St John the Baptist (1776–8)

Kamennoostrovskiy Theatre (1827)

graceful Yelagin Palace ⑦ *(see p126)*. The western spit of the island is ideal for viewing the often spectacular sunsets over the Gulf of Finland, especially during the White Nights *(see p51)*. Across 2-y Yelagin most, leading south to Krestovskiy Island, are Petrovskiy Stadium and the Maritime Victory Park, while to the north, 3-y Yelagin most leads to Primorskiy prospekt and the Buddhist Temple, erected by Gavriil Baranovskiy in 1909–15 and inspired by traditional Tibetan architecture.

North Kamennyy Island

Return to Kamennyy Island across 1-y Yelagin most, taking the left fork on to Teatralnaya alleya from where you can see the former mansion of Aleksandr Polovtsov ⑧, minister of foreign affairs under Nicholas II. This splendid Neo-Classical mansion with Style-Moderne touches was built by Ivan Fomin in 1911–13. Leave Teatralnaya alleya and cut through the quiet and restful park, passing between the ponds and the canal. Near the junction with Bolshaya alleya are two more early 20th-century mansions. Follenveider's mansion ⑨ on the left, with its distinctive

Early 20th-century Polovtsov Mansion

tented tower, was designed by Roman Meltzer in 1904 and now belongs to the Danish consulate. Yevgeniya Gausvald's dacha ⑩ dates from 1898 and stands as one of the earliest Style-Moderne buildings in St Petersburg. It was designed by Vasiliy Schöne and Vladimir Chagin.

Finally, the last stage of the walk leads along the 2-ya Berezovaya alleya, back to the starting point at Ushakovskiy most and Chernaya Rechka metro.

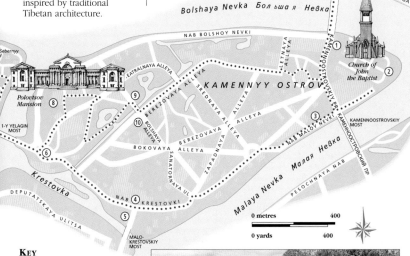

The tree-shrouded grassy banks of the Krestovka river

KEY

••• Walk route

Ⓜ Metro station

TIPS FOR WALKERS

Starting point: Chernaya Rechka metro station (see p215).
Length: 6 km (3.5 miles).
Stopping-off points: Café in former stables of Yelagin Palace (summer only) and plenty of places to picnic.

BEYOND
ST PETERSBURG

BEYOND ST PETERSBURG

THE COUNTRYSIDE *around St Petersburg is typical of northwest Russia. Among its flat sweeps of land, pine forests and lakes there are sights of cultural interest, including the imperial palaces and the walled medieval city of Novgorod. Venturing away from St Petersburg allows a richer and deeper insight into this splendid land.*

Before St Petersburg was founded in 1703, the surrounding landscape was a marshy and inhospitable wilderness, inhabited by wolves. Nevertheless, the area from the Gulf of Finland to Lake Ladoga was of strategic importance for trading and thus one of the reasons for continuous wars between Sweden and Russia. At the time the only city of importance here was Novgorod, an independent and quite wealthy principality *(see p17).* It has retained its medieval atmosphere, so different from the imperial palaces adorning the countryside south of St Petersburg. They each reflect the tastes of their owners. Peter the Great's fine residence, Peterhof, is dominated by water; the Gulf and the fountains mirror his maritime interest. Elizabeth wanted vibrant colour and excess to

Muse of love and poetry, Pavlovsk

accommodate her extravagant balls, hence the grand Baroque palace at Tsarskoe Selo. Catherine the Great's love of intimacy led her to add private apartments to Tsarskoe Selo, and the exquisite Chinese Palace at Oranienbaum. Paul I's military mania made him turn Gatchina into a castle, while his wife Maria Fyodorovna created a feminine, elegant residence at Pavlovsk. All the palaces except Oranienbaum suffered devastating damage during World War II *(see p27).* A great deal of effort has been made to restore them painstakingly over the last 50 years.

While the aristocracy indulged in their extravagances, the middle classes had more modest country houses. The comfortable *dacha* of the artist Repin, northwest of the city, gives visitors a feel of his more bohemian lifestyle.

The Novgorod Kremlin with the Cathedral of St Sophia and its belfry

◁ The gilded maze of the main staircase at Peterhof's Grand Palace

Exploring St Petersburg's Surroundings

MOST ST PETERSBURGERS leave the city to spend time at their *dacha* or country house for weekends and holidays. But there are several ways of experiencing the countryside around St Petersburg. There are many stunning imperial palaces, spread out like pearls in a necklace south of the city. Each one of them offers splendid interiors as well as beautifully laid out parks and gardens with lakes. Around the artist's studio at Repino is a more typical Baltic landscape, with pine and fir trees stretching down to the pebbly beaches of the Gulf of Finland.

Further away to the south, the medieval town of Novgorod is a great representative of an old Russian city, complete with a walled kremlin and onion-domed churches.

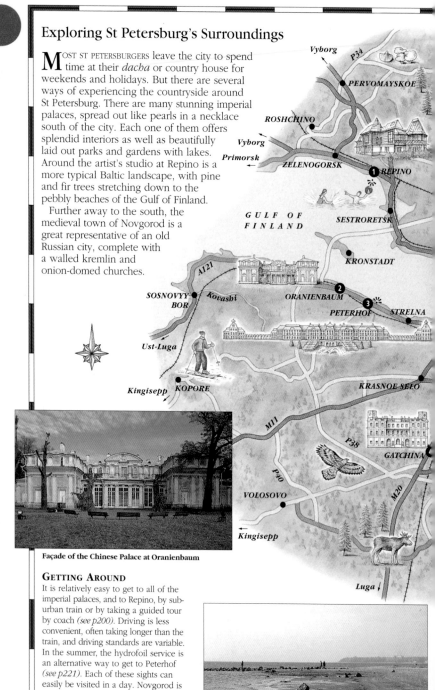

Façade of the Chinese Palace at Oranienbaum

GETTING AROUND

It is relatively easy to get to all of the imperial palaces, and to Repino, by suburban train or by taking a guided tour by coach (*see p200*). Driving is less convenient, often taking longer than the train, and driving standards are variable. In the summer, the hydrofoil service is an alternative way to get to Peterhof (*see p221*). Each of these sights can easily be visited in a day. Novgorod is situated further away, however, and so it makes sense to spend longer there. Mainline trains depart from Moscow railway station (*see p221*) for Novgorod.

Coastal landscape along the Gulf of Finland

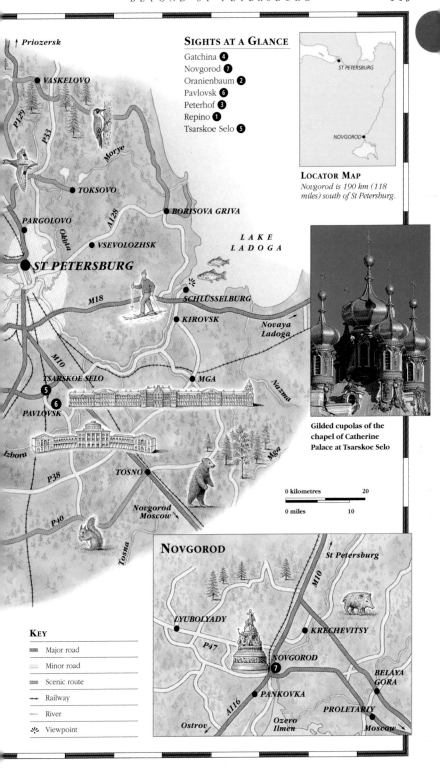

↑ *Priozersk*

• **VASKELOVO**

P129

P33

Morye

• **TOKSOVO**

PARGOLOVO

A128

Okhta

• **VSEVOLOZHSK**

ST PETERSBURG

• **BORISOVA GRIVA**

L A K E
L A D O G A

M18

SCHLÜSSELBURG

• **KIROVSK**

Novaya
Ladoga →

M10

TSARSKOE SELO
⑤
⑥

PAVLOVSK

Izhora

P38

• **MGA**

Nazma

Mga

TOSNO •

Novgorod
Moscow →

P40

Tosna

SIGHTS AT A GLANCE

Gatchina **④**
Novgorod **⑦**
Oranienbaum **②**
Pavlovsk **⑥**
Peterhof **③**
Repino **①**
Tsarskoe Selo **⑤**

LOCATOR MAP
Novgorod is 190 km (118 miles) south of St Petersburg.

ST PETERSBURG

NOVGOROD

Gilded cupolas of the
chapel of Catherine
Palace at Tsarskoe Selo

0 kilometres   20

0 miles   10

NOVGOROD

St Petersburg

M10

LYUBOLYADY •

P47

KRECHEVITSY •

NOVGOROD
⑦

BELAYA
GORA

A116

PANKOVKA •

Ozero
Ilmen

PROLETARIY

Moscow →

Ostrov ↙

KEY

▬▬ Major road

▭▭ Minor road

▬▬ Scenic route

+—+ Railway

— River

☼ Viewpoint

Repino ❶
Репино
Repino

47 km (29 miles) NW of St Petersburg.
🚊 *from Finland Station.* 🚌 *411 from
Chernaya Rechka metro.* **Penaty,**
Primorskoe shosse 411. 📞 *231 6828.*
🕙 *10:30am–5pm Wed–Mon.* 🌐
♿ *ground floor.*

Only about an hour's drive
from St Petersburg on
Primorskoe shosse, the northern coastal road, is a region
of lakes, pine-scented forests
and sandy beaches. Among
the green-painted *dachas* and
sanatoria is Repino, a resort
named after one of Russia's
greatest artists, Ilya Repin
(see p106–7), who lived here
for over 30 years until his
death in 1930 at the age of 86.
His extraordinary *dacha,* with
its steeply pitched glass roof
and angled windows, was
restored after damage in
World War II and is now open
as a museum.

Named Penaty in honor of
the Roman household gods,
penates, the house was redesigned by Repin himself to
accommodate all that an artist
might need, including a glass-
panelled veranda downstairs,
which was used as a winter
studio. On display in the first
floor studio are the artist's
brushes and a number of his
works, including an unfinished
portrait of Pushkin *(see p44)*
and Repin's last self-portrait.

Works by the artist adorn the
dining room, including portraits
of the singer Fyodor Chalyapin
and writer Maksim Gorky who
were among Repin's many visitors. A revolving dining table
enabled guests to serve themselves and to store away their

Studio of the eminent artist Ilya Repin at his home in Repino

used dishes, since there were
no servants. Anyone failing to
obey this household rule had
to give an impromptu speech
from the lectern in the corner.

In the garden, two small
wooden follies are hidden
among the trees, and Repin's
grave is marked by a simple
cross on the top of a hillock.

Oranienbaum ❷
Ораниенбаум
Oranienbaum

Oranienbaum, 40 km (25 miles) W of
St Petersburg. 📞 *422 3753 or 423
1627.* 🚊 *from Baltic station.* **Grounds**
🕙 *9am–7pm.* **Palaces & Sliding Hill
Pavilion** 🕙 *11am–5pm Mon, Wed–
Sun (times vary slightly for individual
buildings).* **Chinese Palace and Sliding
Hill Pavilion** ⬛ *Oct–Apr.* 🌐 📷

As the extravagant project of
Peter the Great's closest
friend and main political advisor, Aleksandr Menshikov *(see
p62),* Oranienbaum was far
more ambitious in conception
than Peter's palace at Peterhof
(see pp146–9), which lies just
12 km (7 miles) to the west.
The grandiose plan bankrupted

Menshikov and, when he fell
from grace in 1727, the estate
entered the state treasury.

The Baroque appearance of
Oranienbaum's Great Palace
has changed little since it was
constructed in 1710–25. Built
by Gottfried Schädel and
Giovanni-Maria Fontana, its
sweeping wings culminate in
two remarkable pavilions.
Parts of the palace and the
east (Japanese) pavilion are
now open to the public.

From 1743 to 1761 the estate
became the residence of the
heir to the throne, the future
Peter III, who built himself a
miniature fortress with a small
lake for his "navy" and a
parade ground where he was
fond of playing war games
with soldiers. Peter also commissioned Antonio Rinaldi to
build him a modest palace.

Peter's wife, Catherine (later
Catherine the Great), abhorred
her isolated existence here,
but after Peter's murder *(see
p22)* she recovered her spirits
and created what she described
as her "personal *dacha*". Built
by Rinaldi in the 1760s and
known as the Chinese Palace,
it is famous for its fabulous
Rococo interiors and voguish
displays of chinoiserie.

The most unusual building
at Oranienbaum is Rinaldi's
Sliding Hill Pavilion, built in
1762 on Catherine's initiative.
Wooden sledging hills were a
common source of amusement
among the Russian nobility.
Catherine's visitors would climb
the blue and white pavilion
before descending at top
speed by sledge or toboggan
along a roller coaster run. The
track, 500 m (1,640 ft) long,
was originally flanked by a

Façade of Menshikov's Great Palace (1710–25), Oranienbaum

colonnade. Sadly, this structure collapsed in 1813 but there is a model in the pavilion.

A pleasant few hours can be spent in the grounds with their secluded paths, pine woods, ponds and bridges.

Oranienbaum was the only local palace to escape German occupation during World War II (see p27). In 1948, the estate was renamed Lomonosov after the famous 18th-century physicist (see p45) who laid many of the foundations of modern Russian science. The complex has now reverted to its original name, an allusion to the exotic orange trees planted here by Menshikov.

Austere central section of Gatchina palace

to her son and heir Paul (later Paul I). Paul asked his favourite architect Vincenzo Brenna to re-fashion the palace to match his pronounced martial tastes. Brenna's large-scale alterations included the construction of an additional storey and a moat with a drawbridge.

The next Romanov to spend any time here was Alexander III who made it his permanent family residence in the late 19th century. The estate provided a safe and remote haven from the sporadic social unrest which was threatening the capital (see p26). The imperial family led a simple and secluded existence here. In keeping with the increasingly bourgeois tastes of the nobility in the whole of Europe, they scorned the state rooms, confining themselves instead to the cosy and more intimate servants' quarters.

In 1917, immediately after the Bolshevik party had

seized power, the proclaimed leader of the Provisional Government, Aleksandr Kerensky, fled to Gatchina where he made a last ditch attempt to rally his supporters. After a week, he deserted his troops and slipped away into exile.

After World War II, in which the palace was badly damaged, Gatchina was used for many years as a military academy. The lengthy and thorough restoration process is still under way. Of the restored rooms, the three most impressive are the Marble Dining Room, Paul I's gloomy bedroom at the top of one of Brenna's towers and the magnificent White Ballroom. There is also a display of weaponry on the ground floor.

The delightful grounds are the wildest of all the palace parks. Among the attractions are the circular Temple of Venus (1792–3) on the secluded Island of Love and the Birch House (1790s). At first glance the latter appears to be nothing more than a pile of logs, but it actually conceals a suite of exquisite rooms.

The lake has boats for hire and its clean water makes it an ideal spot for swimming in the summer.

Chinoiserie decorations in Catherine the Great's Chinese Palace, Oranienbaum

Peterhof ❸

See pp146–49.

Gatchina ❹
Гатчина
Gatchina

45 km (28 miles) SW of St Petersburg. 🚉 *from Baltic Station.* 🚌 *431 from pl Pobedy.* 📞 *8 271 13492.* ⏰ *10am– 5pm Tue–Sun.* 📷 ✏ *English (phone to book).* 🚻

I N 1765, Catherine the Great presented the village of Gatchina to her lover, Prince Grigoriy Orlov. He commissioned Antonio Rinaldi to build a Neo-Classical palace which was completed in 1781. When Orlov died, two years later, Catherine transferred the estate

Tsarskoe Selo ❺

See pp150–53.

Gatchina's sumptuous White Ballroom with its pseudo-Egyptian statues

Peterhof ❸
Петергоф
Petergof

WITH ITS COMMANDING views of the Baltic, Peterhof is a perfect expression of triumphalism. Originally designed by Jean Baptiste Le Blond, the Great Palace (1714–21) was transformed during the reign of Tsarina Elizabeth when Bartolomeo Rastrelli added a third storey and wings with pavilions at either end. He tried to preserve Le Blond's early Baroque exterior, but redesigned the interiors, indulging his love for gilded Baroque decoration. Peterhof stands at the centre of a magnificent landscaped park, with both French and English gardens.

View from palace of Grand Cascade leading down to the Gulf of Finland

Neptune Fountain

Oak Fountain

Mezheumnyy Fountain

The Upper Gardens are framed by borders and hedges and punctuated with ornamental ponds.

The Imperial Suite
The imperial suite lies in the palace's east wing. Peter's Oak Study is one of the few rooms to have survived unaltered from Le Blond's design. Some of the oak panel designs are originals (1718–21) by Nicholas Pineau.

Cottage Palace

Orangery

Roman Fountain

Pyramid Fountain

Monplaisir

Adam Fountain

★ **The Grand Cascade**
The dazzling cascade (1715–24) is a sequence of 37 gilded bronze sculptures, 64 fountains and 142 water jets (see p149), descending from the terraces of the Great Palace to the Marine Canal and the sea.

0 metres   25
0 yards   25

PETER THE GREAT'S PALACE

After his victory over the Swedes at Poltava in 1709, Peter the Great decided to build a palace "befitting to the very highest of monarchs". A visit to Versailles in 1717 furthered Peter's ambitions and he employed more than 5,000 labourers, serfs and soldiers, supported by architects, water-engineers, land-scape gardeners and sculptors. Work proceeded at a frenetic pace from 1714 until Peterhof was officially opened in 1723.

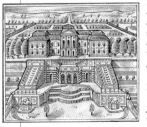

Le Blond's Great Palace was completed in 1721 and has changed considerably over the decades. Catherine the Great commissioned Yuriy Velten to redecorate some of Rastrelli's interiors in the 1770s, including the Throne Room and the Chesma Room.

Jean Baptiste Le Blond's original two-storey Great Palace

VISITORS' CHECKLIST

Petrodvorets, 30 km (19 miles) W of St Petersburg. ▮ *420 0073.*
▯ from Baltic station (see p220) to Novvy Petergof. ▯ *Hermitage (May–Oct) (see p220).* **Great Palace** ◯ *11am–5pm Tue–Sun.* **Other pavilions** ◯ *May–Sep: 11am–5pm Tue–Sun; Oct–Apr: 11am–5pm Sat & Sun.* **Fountains** ◯ *May–early Oct: 11am–5pm.* ▮▮▮▮▮▮

★ Main Staircase

Caryatids and gilded carvings adorn Rastrelli's glittering staircase. The ceiling fresco depicts Aurora and Genius chasing away the night.

Golden Hill Cascade

Marly and Hermitage

Eve Fountain

STAR FEATURES

★ Grand Cascade

★ Main Staircase

★ The State Rooms

Hydrofoil and Gulf of Finland

The Marine Canal
enabled the tsars to sail from the Gulf of Finland up to the Great Palace.

★ The State Rooms

The highlight of the State Rooms is the opulent Throne Room, redesigned by Yuriy Velten in 1770. The relatively restrained stucco ornament-ation, red velvet hangings and parquet floor provide an exquisite setting for portraits of Russia's imperial family.

Exploring Peterhof Park

THE GROUNDS AT PETERHOF include the Upper, Lower and Alexandria parks, covering an area of around 607 hectares (1,500 acres). As well as the numerous palaces and fountains, there are tree-lined avenues, wooded paths and the Baltic shore. Le Blond designed the grounds next to the Great Palace to be laid out in the formal French style with geometrically arranged flower beds, sculptures, summerhouses and pergolas. The trees and shrubs, including limes, elms, maples and roses, were imported from all over Russia and abroad.

Cottage Palace in Alexandria Park

Monplaisir palace (1714–22), overlooking the Gulf of Finland

Monplaisir
This delightfully unpretentious palace was designed in 1714 by Johann Braunstein. Even after the Great Palace was built, Peter continued to live and entertain at Monplaisir where his guests were usually subjected to a punishing regime of heavy drinking. At breakfast the coffee cups were filled with brandy and by nightfall guests were often discovered wandering drunk in the park.

While not as lavish as those of the Great Palace the interiors are still impressive, in particular the wood-panelled Ceremonial Hall. A painting on its vaulted ceiling depicts Apollo surrounded by characters from a masque. Russian icon painters skilfully carried out the decoration of the exquisite Lacquered Study in the Chinese style then in vogue. Peter's collection of canvases by Dutch and Flemish artists hang in the rooms and there are wonderful views of the gulf from the tsar's Naval Study.

Adjoining Monplaisir is the Catherine Wing, which was built for Tsarina Elizabeth by Rastrelli in 1747–54. Catherine

the Great was staying here in 1762 when her lover, Count Orlov, arrived with news of the coup which was to bring her to the throne (*see p24*).

Marly Palace
Named after Marly-le-Rois, the king of France's hunting lodge which Peter the Great visited on a tour of Europe in 1717, this beautifully proportioned country residence was built for the tsar's guests. The rooms open to the public

Elaborate tiled kitchen in the Marly Palace (1720–3)

include the Oak and Plane Tree studies, Peter's bedroom and the Dining Room. It is set in its own formal garden with sculptures, fountains, a large pond and Niccolò Michetti's Golden Hill Cascade, which was added in 1731–7.

The Hermitage
Standing in splendid isolation on the shores of the gulf, this elegant pavilion (1721–5), by Braunstein, was conceived as a private dining venue for the tsar and his friends. To highlight the need for solitude, the building was raised on a plinth and surrounded by a moat that was crossed by a small drawbridge. The stuccoed façade is decorated with Corinthian pilasters, elaborate wrought-iron balconies and enlarged windows. All the servants were confined to the ground floor and a mechanical device took meals up from the kitchen.

Cottage Palace
The romantic landscaped grounds of Alexandria Park, named after Alexandra, wife of Nicholas I, provide a perfect setting for the Cottage Palace. The Neo-Gothic house is more imposing than the term cottage suggests. The Scottish architect, Adam Menelaws, designed it in 1826–9 for Nicholas I and his wife, who wanted a domestic environment in keeping with their bourgeois tastes.

The Gothic theme is pursued throughout, most effectively in the Great Drawing Room with the rose window motif in the carpet and the lace-like tracery of the stuccoed ceiling. The exquisite 5,200-piece crystal and porcelain dinner service in the Dining Room was made for the royal couple at the Imperial Porcelain factory.

The Fountains at Peterhof

JEAN-BAPTISTE LE BLOND submitted his "water plan" to Peter the Great in 1717, by which time the tsar had begun sketching his own ideas. The centrepiece is the Grand Cascade, fed by the underground springs of the Ropsha Hills about 22 km (14 miles) away. The cascade is a celebration of the triumph of Russia over Sweden *(see p19)*, symbolized by Mikhail Kozlovskiy's glorious

Detail of the Mezheumnyy Fountain

sculpture of Samson rending the jaws of a lion. An imaginative variety of fountains, mostly concentrated in the Lower Park, includes triton and lion fountains, dragon fountains with checker-board steps, and smaller fountains with fish-tailed boys blowing sprays of water through conches. Most playful are trick fountains such as the Umbrella which "rains" on those who come too close.

The Adam Fountain, sculpted by Giovanni Bonazza, was commissioned by Peter in 1718, along with a similar statue of Eve. The two fountains suggest the earthly paradise the tsar had recreated at Peterhof.

The Neptune Fountain predates Peterhof by more than 50 years. The Baroque sculpture was erected in 1658 in Nuremberg to mark the end of the Thirty Years War and was sold to Tsar Paul I in 1782 because there was not enough water to make it work.

The Roman Fountains *were designed by Ivan Blank and Ivan Davydov in 1738–9. The two-tiered marble fountains were inspired by one in St Peter's Square in Rome.*

The Grand Cascade *was originally adorned with lead statues which weathered badly and were recast in bronze and gilded after 1799. Shubin, Martos and other noted sculptors worked to create this stunning cascade.*

The Pyramid Fountain *(1720s) is one of a number of fountains whose jets create a special shape. Over 500 jets of water rise in seven tiers to create an "obelisk" commemorating the Russian victory over Sweden.*

Tsarskoe Selo ❺

Царское Село
Tsarskoe Selo

THE LAVISH imperial palace at Tsarskoe Selo was designed by Rastrelli *(see p93)* in 1752 for Tsarina Elizabeth. She named it the Catherine Palace in honour of her mother, Catherine I, who originally owned the estate. The next ruler to leave her mark on the palace was Catherine the Great, and during her reign she commissioned the Scotsman Charles Cameron to redesign the Baroque interiors according to her more Neo-Classical taste. Cameron also built the ensemble for taking traditional Russian cold and warm baths, containing the Agate Rooms, and the Cameron Gallery. Post-war restoration of the palace continues and 20 state rooms are now open, as well as the beautiful park.

★ **The Great Hall**
Light streams into Rastrelli's glittering hall illuminating the mirrors, gilded carvings and the vast ceiling painting, The Triumph of Russia *(c.1755), by Giuseppe Valeriani.*

The Great Staircase (1860), by Ippolito Monighetti, ascends to the state rooms on the first floor.

Entrance

Atlantes
The stunning 300-m (980-ft) long Baroque façade is adorned with a profusion of atlantes, columns, pilasters and ornamented window framings.

0 metres   25
0 yards   25

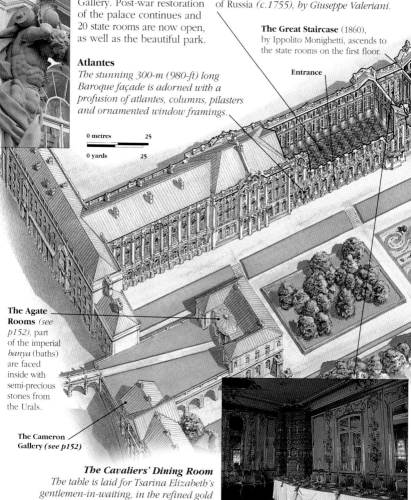

The Agate Rooms *(see p152),* part of the imperial *banya* (baths) are faced inside with semi-precious stones from the Urals.

The Cameron Gallery *(see p152)*

The Cavaliers' Dining Room
The table is laid for Tsarina Elizabeth's gentlemen-in-waiting, in the refined gold and white room created by Rastrelli.

The Royal Chapel is richly decorated in dark blue and gold. Built by Chevakinskiy in the 1740s, it contains an elaborate six-tiered iconostasis.

VISITORS' CHECKLIST

Tsarskoe Selo, 25 km (16 miles) S of St Petersburg. ▢ *from Vitebsk station to Detskoe Selo, then* ▭ *371 or 382.* **Palace** 〔 *465 5308.* ▢ *10am– 5pm Wed–Mon.* ● *last Mon of month.* ▨ ✔ ▯ ▢ **Agate Rooms** ▢ *10am– 4:30pm (to 5:30pm in summer) Thu–Mon.* ● *last Wed of month.* **Cameron Gallery** ▢ *10am–5pm Wed–Mon.* **Park** ▢ *daily.* ▨ *mid-May–Sep.*

★ Amber Room
The original amber panels (1709) by Andreas Schlüter were a gift from Friedrich Wilhelm I of Prussia to Peter the Great. The room has been recreated from photos, complete with carved reliefs and panels in Florentine mosaic.

The Blue Drawing Room is characterized by blue floral motifs painted on silk. Among the royal portraits hanging here is a painting of Peter the Great by Ivan Nikitin, dating from around 1720.

To the Lycée and the Church of the Sign (see p153)

The Picture Gallery displays canvases by Italian, French, Dutch and Flemish masters of the 17th and 18th centuries.

★ Green Dining Room
Cameron's restrained Neo-Classical style contrasts with the Baroque flamboyance of Rastrelli's work. The exquisite stucco bas-reliefs, sculpted by Ivan Martos, were based on motifs from frescoes discovered in Pompeii.

The French-style formal gardens were laid out in the 1740s. Their formality and symmetry contrasts with the naturalistic English-style landscaping of the park (see p152), created in 1768.

Small Enfilade
A varied selection of furniture and objets d'art *make up the exhibition in these unrestored rooms. Chinese lacquer furniture and Oriental rugs were among the treasures used to furnish the palace in the 19th century.*

STAR FEATURES

★ **The Great Hall**

★ **Amber Room**

★ **Green Dining Room**

Exploring Tsarskoe Selo

THE MAGNIFICENT PARKS and gardens of Tsarskoe Selo (the Tsar's Village) were created out of dense forest by thousands of soldiers and labourers. Work began on the formal gardens in 1744 but later, in 1768, Catherine the Great commissioned one of Russia's first landscaped parks. The 567 hectares (1,400 acres) of grounds are dotted with captivating pavilions set around the central lake. The grounds and the town of Tsarskoe Selo, to the northeast of the palace, are also a delight to explore.

Formal gardens in front of Catherine Palace, Catherine Park

Catherine Park

The formal gardens to the southeast of the palace are laid out geometrically with radiating avenues, parterres and terraces, decorous ponds, hedges, elegant pavilions and Classical statuary. Nearest to the palace are Cameron's sumptuous **Agate Rooms** (1780–87). Their heavily rusticated lower storey contrasts with the upper tier, modelled on a Renaissance villa. The building takes its name from the agate, jasper, malachite and other semi-precious stones covering the interior.

Girl with a Pitcher by Pavel Sokolov (1816)

The impressive **Cameron Gallery**, built in 1783–7, has a rusticated stone ground floor, surmounted by a Neo-Classical peristyle of 44 Ionic columns. Ranged along the colonnade are bronze busts of ancient philosophers, poets and rulers. In 1792–4 Cameron added a long stone ramp to facilitate access to the gardens for the ageing Catherine the Great.

The Neo-Classical **Lower and Upper Baths** were built by Ilya Neyelov in 1777–80. The domed Lower Baths were for the use of courtiers while the exquisite Upper Baths were reserved for members of the imperial family.

Construction work on Rastrelli's **Grotto** began in 1749, but the original decoration of the interior with more than 250,000 shells continued well into the 1770s.

The gardens' main avenue leads to the **Hermitage** (1756), a Baroque pavilion built by Rastrelli, where Elizabeth would entertain small groups of guests for dinner.

The romantic landscaped area of the lower park was begun in 1768 by master gardeners such as John Bush, who worked under the overall supervision of the architect, Vasiliy Neyelov. A 16-km (10-mile) waterway was built to feed the numerous canals, cascades and man-made lakes,

including the *pièce de résistance*, the **Great Pond**. From Giacomo Quarenghi's pavilion (1786) on the island, musicians would serenade Catherine and her courtiers as they floated by in gilded gondolas.

A naval theme links Vasiliy Neyelov's Dutch, Neo-Gothic **Admiralty** (1773–7) with the 25-m (82-ft) high **Chesma Column** which is decorated with ships' prows. The column, designed by Antonio Rinaldi in 1771, commemorates the Russian victory over the Turks in the Aegean.

The reflection of the pink dome and minaret of the **Turkish Bath** shimmers in the placid waters on the far side of the lake. Nearby is Neyelov's colonnaded **Marble Bridge** (1770–76). Perched on a rock overlooking the pond is the **Girl with a Pitcher**, a statue by Pavel Sokolov. The figure inspired Pushkin to write his memorable poem, *Fountain at Tsarskoe Selo*, in which he muses on the girl who has broken her urn and now "sits timelessly sad over the timeless stream".

Evidence of the 18th-century craze for chinoiserie can be found on the border with the wilder Alexander Park where Cameron built his **Chinese Village** in 1782–96. Other examples are Yuriy Velten's **Creaking Pavilion**, so-called because it was designed to creak when visitors entered, and Neyelov's **Great Caprice** (1770s), a hump-backed bridge surmounted by a pagoda-like columned structure.

The Moorish-style Turkish Baths (1852) by Ippolito Monighetti

Creaking Pavilion (1778–86)

The Town of Tsarskoe Selo

This town of some 80,000 inhabitants was developed in the 19th century as a summer resort for the aristocracy. In 1937, it was renamed after the poet Alexander Pushkin *(see p43)* who was educated at the local **Lycée** in 1811–17, in room No. 14. One of Russia's most prestigious schools, it was founded by Alexander I

in 1811 to educate members of the nobility. In 1998 the town took back its original name.

The attractive **Church of the Sign**, dating to 1734, is one of the town's oldest buildings. In a garden next door a statue by Roman Bach depicts Pushkin dressed in the Lycée uniform.

Pushkin and his new bride, Natalya, spent the summer of 1831 in the delightful wooden house, now named **Pushkin's Dacha**. The writer, Nikolai Gogol, was amongst the many friends they entertained here.

On the town's western edge is the **Alexander Palace**, commissioned by Catherine for her grandson, the future Alexander I. Designed in 1792 by Giacomo Quarenghi, the austere, Neo-Classical building has a colonnaded façade and protruding wings. It was the residence of Russia's last tsar, Nicholas II, and his family who lived here from 1904 until they were placed under house arrest

in 1917 *(see p28)*. The exhibition inside includes Nicholas' magnificent Style-Moderne study, designed by Meltzer.

Lycée
  10:30am–4:30pm Wed–Mon.

Pushkin's Dacha
  10:30am–4:30pm Wed–Sun.

Alexander Palace
  10am–5pm Wed–Mon.

Alexander Pushkin's statue (1900), by Roman Bach

TSARSKOE SELO PARK

Admiralty ⑦
Agate Rooms ②
Alexander Palace ⑰
Cameron Gallery ③
Catherine Palace pp150–51 ①
Chesma Column ⑧
Church of the Sign ⑮
Creaking Pavilion ⑫
Girl with a Pitcher ⑪
Great Caprice ⑬
Grotto ⑥
Hermitage ⑤
Lower and Upper Baths ④
Lycée ⑭
Marble Bridge ⑩
Pushkin's Dacha ⑯
Turkish Bath ⑨

Imperial standard of the Romanovs flying at the Catherine Palace ▷

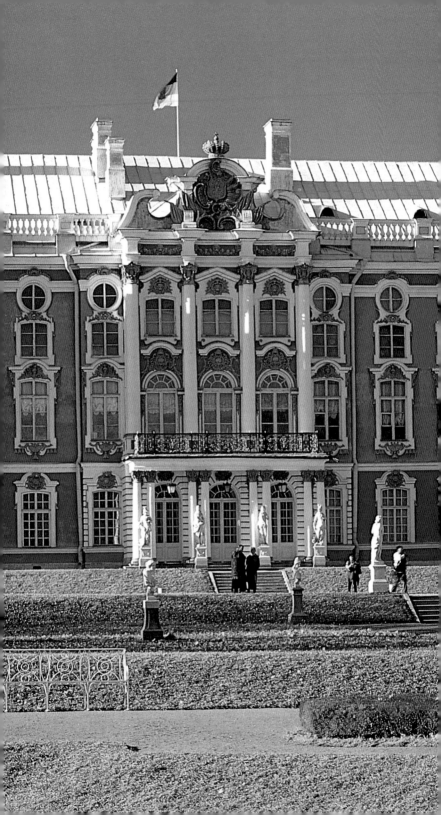

Pavlovsk ❻

Павловск
Pavlovsk

To CELEBRATE THE BIRTH of his heir, Catherine the Great presented her son, the Grand Duke Paul, with these lands in 1777. She also "gave" him her favourite architect, Charles Cameron, to design both palace and park. Work at Pavlovsk (from "Pavel" or Paul) began in 1780 and was continued by Paul's grieving widow, Maria Fyodorovna, long after his death. "English gardens" were at the height of fashion and inspired Cameron's design of a seemingly natural landscape dotted with pavilions (used for informal parties), romantic ruins and attractive vistas around the Slavyanka river.

Cold Baths
This austere pavilion was built by Cameron in 1799 as a summer swimming pool, complete with elegant vestibule, paintings, furniture and rich wall upholstery.

The Apollo Colonnade
Cameron's colonnade (1782–83) encircles a copy of the Apollo Belvedere, above a romantically dilapidated cascade.

Three Graces Pavilion

The Centaur Bridge by Voronikhin (1805) nestles on a bend of the Slavyanka river.

Aviary

Cameron's Dairy (1782) housed both a milking shed and a stylish salon.

★ **Pavlovsk Palace**
Cameron's elegant Palladian mansion (1782–6) forms the central block of today's palace (see pp158–9), with wings added in 1789 by Paul's favoured architect, Vincenzo Brenna.

★ **Temple of Friendship**
This Doric temple (1780) was the first use of Greek forms in Russia.

Green Woman Alley

Pavlovsk Railway Station

Visconti Bridge
One of the most famous bridges which cross the winding Slavyanka, it was designed by Andrey Voronikhin in 1807.

The Étoile
The Étoile, the earliest landscaped area in the park, was laid out by Cameron in 1780. The circle of statues represents the nine Muses, protectresses of the arts and sciences.

The Beautiful Valley was the favourite spot of Elizabeth, wife of Alexander I.

0 metres	200
0 yards	200

Paul's Mausoleum (1808–9) bears the inscription "To my beneficient consort".

The Rose Pavilion was the favourite haunt of Maria Fyodorovna from 1812. She held many concerts and literary evenings in this cottage.

STAR FEATURES

★ **Temple of Friendship**

★ **Great Palace**

Pil Tower and Bridge
Brenna's tower (1795–97) contained a spiral staircase, lounge and library. The bridge was a later addition made in 1808.

Exploring Pavlovsk Palace

Late 18th-century clock, Grecian Hall

CATHERINE COMMISSIONED Charles Cameron to build the Great Palace (1782–86) whilst Paul and his wife Maria Fyodorovna travelled around Europe incognito as the Comte and Comtesse du Nord. They, meanwhile, bought up everything they saw including French clocks, Sèvres porcelain, tapestries and furniture, to fill their new home. Once back in Russia, they brought in Brenna to add taller, more elaborate wings to Cameron's elegant Palladian mansion, turning it into a true palace.

West façade of the Palladian mansion

PLAN OF PAVLOVSK PALACE, FIRST FLOOR

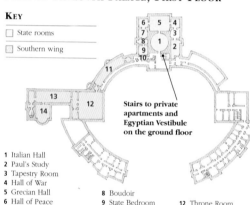

KEY

☐ State rooms

☐ Southern wing

Stairs to private apartments and Egyptian Vestibule on the ground floor

1 Italian Hall
2 Paul's Study
3 Tapestry Room
4 Hall of War
5 Grecian Hall
6 Hall of Peace
7 Maria Fyodorovna's Library
8 Boudoir
9 State Bedroom
10 Dressing Room
11 Picture Gallery
12 Throne Room
13 Hall of Knights
14 Chapel

STATE ROOMS

The Italian Hall, originally by Cameron and Brenna, 1789

NEARLY ALL OF the palace apartments at Pavlovsk, including the official ones, are relatively modest in scale. They reflect Maria Fyodorovna's intensely feminine tastes which have given Pavlovsk a distinct charm rather than grandeur.

A fire in 1803 necessitated some remodelling of the palace interiors by Andrey Voronikhin. The entrance hall, or Egyptian Vestibule, gained its present appearance after he added the painted bronze figures and zodiac medallions. At the top of the stairs is Brenna's State Vestibule, where the bas-reliefs reflected Paul's passion for all things military. It leads onto the Italian Hall, situated beneath the central cupola, with lantern windows and heavy doors of rosewood and mahogany.

The northern row of rooms on this floor were for Paul, the southern ones for Maria. Paul's Study is dominated by Johann Lampi's fine portrait of Maria (1794), who holds a drawing of six of their children. Beneath it is a model temple of amber,

ivory and gilded bronze, made by Maria's herself. Next door, the Tapestry Room is named after the Don Quixote tapestries made by Gobelin and presented to Paul by Louis XVI. The mahogany writing table was actually made for the new Engineers' Castle *(see p101)* but, after Paul's murder there in 1801 *(see p22)*, Maria moved much of the specially-designed furniture to Pavlovsk Palace.

The corner rooms are a Hall of War for Paul and Maria's contrasting Hall of Peace, both richly adorned with bas-reliefs and heavy gilding. Between the two lies the magnificent Grecian Hall, Cameron's Neo-Classical masterpiece.

Maria Fyodorovna's rooms commence with a small, comfortable library. The chair at the desk was designed for her by Voronikhin; note the pots built into the spine for flowers. Her Boudoir has pilasters painted with motifs copied from the Raphael Loggias in the Vatican, and a porphyry fireplace. The State Bedroom was reputedly never slept in, but was part of court ceremony. Opposite the

Maria Fyodorovna's Boudoir, designed by Brenna, 1789

Brenna's Picture Gallery (1789), with chandeliers by Johann Zeck

bed is a 64-piece Sèvres toilet set, complete with a coffee cup and an eye bath, which was a gift from Marie Antoinette.

Another present dominates the Dressing Room, a superb set of steel furniture including dressing table, chair, vases and ink stand made by the renowned gun-makers of Tula (1789). This was presented to Maria by Catherine the Great.

SOUTHERN WING

FROM THE ELEGANTLY curved picture gallery, built in 1798, there are excellent views. Only a few of the paintings, mostly purchased during the young couple's trip to France, are worthy of special notice, as their taste was for applied art.

The largest room in the palace is the Throne Room, designed by Brenna (1797) after Paul became tsar. Despite its name it was generally used for balls and state dinners. The tables are now laid with part of a 606-piece gilded dinner service. Vast blue Sèvres vases

stand on plinths, bought directly from the factory (Paul and Maria spent huge sums on porcelain there alone). The ceiling was painted during restoration after World War II (see p26), and is taken from an original design which was never used.

The Knights of St John chose Paul as Grand Master when they fled Napoleon's occupation of Malta in 1798. This suited Paul's military taste and he commissioned vast lamps, thrones and decorative items (now in the Hermitage), as well as the Hall of Knights, for ceremonies of the Order. The pale green room is adorned with Classical statues, saved from the Germans in World War II by being buried in the grounds.

The suite of rooms ends with the Imperial Chapel of SS Peter and Paul, a very un-Orthodox church by Brenna (1797–98), decorated with copies of European paintings.

PRIVATE APARTMENTS

LOCATED ON THE ground floor are the private apartments. The Pilaster Room (1800), with its golden pilasters, is furnished with a dark mahogany suite. The Lantern Study, designed a few years later by Voronikhin, is named after its apsed bay window forming the "lantern".

Maria Fyodorovna's Dressing Room leads into the Bedroom (1805) she actually used (as opposed to the State Bedroom upstairs). Pieces of the original silk were saved in the war and used to edge the new curtains.

The small pink and blue Ballroom was for private parties and hung with paintings by the most fashionable artist of the day, Hubert Robert. The General Study, used as a family sitting room, is decorated with portraits of the family. The Raspberry Room, Paul's private study, contains paintings with views of Gatchina Palace, made for the Engineers' Castle.

The Lantern Study, one of Voronikhin's most successfully designed interiors, 1804

MARIA FYODOROVNA (1759–1828)

Paul's wife, Maria Fyodorovna, bore 10 children, and Pavlovsk was considered her 11th child. Paul himself preferred Gatchina (see p145) and in 1788 Maria was given Pavlovsk entirely. She devoted all her energy to adorning both palace and park, giving precise directions to designers and architects, who bemoaned their lack of independence. Born Sophia of Württemberg-Stuttgart, Maria had a practical German upbringing which she put to good use. Pieces of her own work, from furniture to family portraits, are throughout the palace.

Inkstand (1795) created from initial design by Maria Fyodorovna

Novgorod ❼

T HE ANCIENT TOWN of Novgorod (New Town) was founded in 859 by the Varangian (Viking) Prince Rurik *(see p17)*. The city's proud tradition of self-government began in the 11th century and lasted until 1478, when Ivan III subjugated the city. Favourably sited on the River Volkhov with convenient connections from Scandinavia to the Aegean, the city of Novgorod became a powerful trading community during this period. In 1570, Ivan the Terrible put Novgorod to the sword, torturing and massacring thousands of its inhabitants when the city plotted against him. It was, however, the rise of St Petersburg which finally set the seal on Novgorod's decline. Much of the city's splendid cultural heritage, damaged in World War II, is now being restored and can be appreciated in the many medieval churches and picturesque streets of the old town.

Detail of bronze door on Cathedral of St Sophia

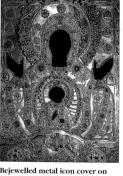

Bejewelled metal icon cover on display in the Chamber of Facets

The Kremlin

Situated on the left bank, or Sofiskaya Storona (Sophia side), of the River Volkhov, the formidable red-brick walls and cone-topped towers of the oval-shaped Detinets, or Kremlin, date from the 11th to the 17th centuries. According to the prevailing practice at the time, the first stone of the original walls was laid on the body of a living child.

Of the many towers, the 17th-century Kukui is the most remarkable, and also the tallest at 32m (105ft). The lower floors once contained a wine cellar and treasury chamber, while the octagonal room beneath the cupola was used, according to chronicles, "for surveying the whole town".

Kremlin walls, with the silver dome of St Sophia's Belfry (15th century)

At the heart of the fortress is Novgorod's oldest and largest church, the strongly Byzantine **Cathedral of St Sophia** (1045–62). It was modelled on the cathedral of the same name in Kiev, but the tendencies of the Novgorod school already appear in the lack of ornament and the scarcity of windows, necessary because of the cold. On the north wall a section of whitewash has been removed to reveal the original mosaic effect of the grey-yellow stone and brick façade.

The exquisitely sculpted and extremely rare bronze doors adorning the west side were seized as booty in 1187 from the Swedish town of Sigtuna. In the lower left hand corner there are portraits of the craftsmen, named in the Latin inscription as Riquin and Weissmut. The interior is divided by piers into five aisles, three ending in altar apses. Fragments of early frescoes survive, but the iconostasis is one of the oldest in Russia and contains icons from the 11th–17th centuries.

East of the cathedral is **St Sophia's Belfry**, much altered since it was first built in 1439. The bells, now displayed below, were cast in the late 16th and early 17th centuries.

The northwest corner of the Kremlin is occupied by the **Archbishops' Court**, in its heyday a powerful body with its own treasury, police force and military guard. Beneath the 15th-century clock tower an attractive staircase leads to the **Library**, housing magnificent medieval religious manuscripts. Backing onto the cathedral, the **Chamber of Facets** is the most famous part of this ensemble. A superb star-vaulted reception hall dates from 1433 and displays treasures from the cathedral, including goblets, jewelled mitres and icon covers in precious metals.

The 11th-century Cathedral of St Sophia, the landmark of Novgorod

Within the Kremlin is the **Museum of History, Architecture and Art**, which houses a magnificent collection of 12th–17th-century icons of the Novgorod school. One of the most remarkable is the 12th-century portable icon of the Virgin of the Sign, whose miraculous image is said to have saved Novgorod from the armies of Prince Andrey Bogolyubskiy of Suzdal in 1169. Scenes from the battle are depicted on a vibrant 15th-century icon *(see p163).* There are also works by leading 18th- and 19th-century artists, including Dmitriy Levitskiy, Karl Bryullov and Vasiliy Serov *(see p106).* The museum has a number of precious public documents and private letters written on birch bark, some of which date from the 11th century. These give details of ordinary, everyday life and are evidence of the unusually widespread literacy among the city's inhabitants.

In the Kremlin's central square, the huge, bell-shaped **Millennium Monument** was sculpted by Mikhail Mikeshin. The monument was unveiled in 1862, a thousand years after Rurik's arrival in Novgorod. The figure kneeling before the Orthodox cross personifies Mother Russia while, below, the decorative frieze depicts Rurik, Ivan III, Mikhail (the first Romanov tsar), Peter the Great and many others. The frieze around the base shows over 100 figures: heroes, statesmen, artists, composers, princes and chroniclers.

The carved Royal Gates of an iconostasis in the Museum of History, Architecture and Art

Cathedral of St Sophia
(81622) 73556. ◻ 8am–8pm daily.
Chamber of Facets
(81622) 73608 or 73770.
◻ 10am–6pm Thu–Tue. 🖾 🖌
English by appt.
Museum of History, Architecture and Art
(81622) 73608 or 73770.
◻ 10am–6pm Wed–Mon. 🖾 🖌
English by appt.

Yaroslav's Court
Across the River Volkhov was the official seat of the princes, known as Yaroslav's Court. The palace of Yaroslav the Wise (1019–54) has since disappeared but several churches have survived. The area adjacent to the Court is Novgorod's

VISITORS' CHECKLIST

190 km (118 miles) S of St Petersburg. 🚂 240,000. 🚌 from Moscow Station. 🚌 from Coach Station (see p221). 🛈 Intourist Hotel, ul Dmitrevskaya 16, (81622) 73074. 🎫 by appt (tel: 73770).

commercial centre, once the site of the medieval market, part of whose wall still stands.

The oldest church on this side of the river, **St Nicholas' Cathedral** (1113–36), was built by Prince Mstislav. It dominates the area and once symbolized the prince's power.

Novgorod's merchants were keen to show their recognition of God's hand in their prosperity, and so funded many of the city's churches. **St Paraskeva Pyatnitsa**, erected in 1207 and then rebuilt in 1345, was dedicated to the patron saint of commerce. The more decorative **Church of the Holy Women** and **Church of St Procopius**, both 16th century, were financed by wealthy Moscow merchants. The fanciful tastes of the Muscovite patrons mark a departure from Novgorod's austere style.

Millennium Monument, celebrating Novgorod's 1,000 years of history

Yuriev Monastery walls and bell tower with the silvery domes of the Cathedral of St George in the background

Beyond Yaroslav's Court
In the 12th century, Novgorod boasted over 200 churches, while there are only 30 today. Many of these are hidden away in the quiet hinterland of 19th-century streets to the east of Yaroslav's Court. On Ilyina ulitsa, the arrangement of windows, niches and inset crosses on the **Church of the Saviour of the Transfiguration** façade (1374) is almost whimsical. Inside, there are original frescoes by one of Russia's greatest medieval artists, Theophanes the Greek (1335–c.1410), who came from Constantinople and decorated 40 Russian churches. Andrey Rublev (1360–1430), Russia's most famous icon painter, worked under Theophanes at the beginning of his career.

On the same street, the five-domed **Znamenskiy Cathedral**, or Cathedral of the Sign (1682–8), has an attractive gateway and faded frescoes on the outer walls. The beautiful interior was decorated in 1702 by Ivan Bakhmatov.

The **Church of Theodore Stratilates** on Mstinskaya ulitsa to the north was built in 1360–61 by the widow of a wealthy Novgorod merchant. The delicate purple and pink

Fresco inside Znamenskiy Cathedral

frescoes contrast with the harsher colours found in most 14th-century Novgorod frescoes. *The Annunciation*, for example, combines sensitivity and charm with religious intensity.

Further Afield
A pleasant stroll 3 km (2 miles) south along the river bank leads to the **Yuriev Monastery**. This is the largest and most important monastery in the area, founded in 1030 and built on the orders of Prince Vsevolod. Its imposing Cathedral of St George was built in 1119–30 by "Master Peter", the first named architect in Russian chronicles. This beautifully proportioned church with its

three asymmetrical cupolas was restored in the 19th century, and unfortunately most of the interior murals were lost. There were once 20 monastic buildings in the complex, dating mainly from the 19th century.

In the woods across the road lies the fascinating open-air **Museum of Wooden Architecture**, which displays churches and peasant huts moved from local villages. Of particular interest are the 17th-century two-tiered Kuritsko Church of the Dormition and the tiny wooden church of St Nicholas from Tukhel village.

⛪ Yuriev Monastery
Yurevskaya nab. **【** (81622) 73020.
◯ 8am–8pm daily.

🏛 Museum of Wooden Architecture
Yurevo. **【** (81622) 73770. **◯** 24 hrs.
Exhibitions: 10am–6pm (mid-Oct–mid-Apr: 10am–4:30pm) daily. 🖼 📷

Rebuilt 19th-century peasant hut (*izba*), Museum of Wooden Architecture

Russian Icon Painting

THE RUSSIAN ORTHODOX Church uses icons for both worship and teaching, but never for mere ornament, and there are strict rules for the creation of each image. Icons were believed to be imbued with the force of the saint depicted, and were therefore invoked for protection during wars. Because the content was considered more important than the style, old, revered icons were often repainted again and again.

Early stone icon found in Novgorod

The first icons were brought to Russia from Byzantium. Greek masters came too, to train local painters. The northern schools which developed during the 13th–15th centuries were less restricted by Byzantine canons and have an earthy style linked to Russian peasant life. Novgorod, never under the Mongol yoke and with a thriving economy, was the source of many of the finest icons made for the northern monasteries.

Virgin of Vladimir
The most venerated icon in Russia, this 12th-century work was made in Constantinople. Its huge influence on Russian icon painting cannot be overstated.

Battle of Novgorod and Suzdal
This mid-15th-century work of the Novgorod School is thought to be Russia's earliest historical painting. Icons could have a political purpose – in this case to use Novgorod's great past as a justification for its independence from Moscow. Note the multiple touches of red – a colour central to everyday Russian life and typical for icons of the Novgorod School.

Old Testament Trinity by Rublev
Andrey Rublev was one of the greatest artists of the Moscow School. He was strongly influenced by recent developments in Byzantine painting, brought to Russia by Greek masters in the late 14th century. His Trinity icon dates from the early 15th century.

THE ICONOSTASIS

The iconostasis screens off the sanctuary from the main part of the church, as if it were a boundary between heaven and earth. In Russian practice it is covered with icons strictly arranged in up to six tiers, each with its own dogmatic purpose.

The Festival Tier shows the 12 major church festivals, such as the Entry into Jerusalem and the Crucifixion. Such pictorial representation aided the faith of the illiterate.

The Royal Gates represent the entrance from the temporal world to the spiritual, between which the priests pass during the service.

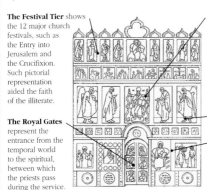

Christ Enthroned

The Deesis Tier, above the Royal Gates, contains Christ Enthroned, flanked by the Virgin and St John interceding on behalf of mortal sinners.

The Local Tier is for local saints, those the church is dedicated to and patron saints of major donors.

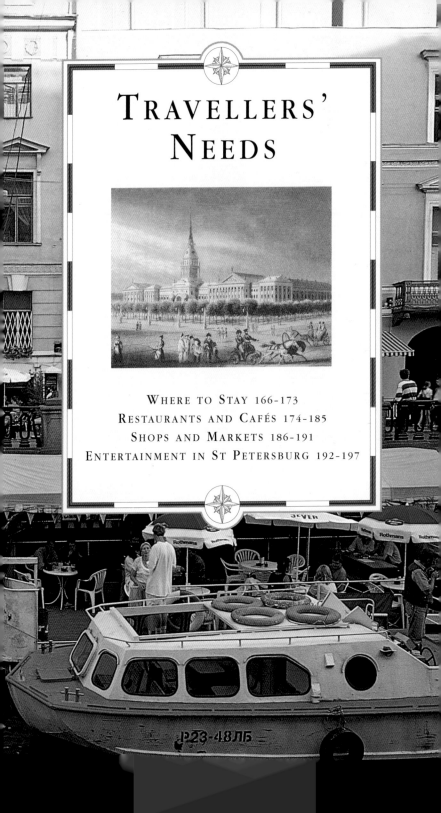

TRAVELLERS' NEEDS

WHERE TO STAY

THERE IS A SERIOUS dearth of good accommodation in St Petersburg, particularly in the city centre and in the lower price bracket. The majority of tourists visiting St Petersburg arrive with a package tour and are housed in one of the large, modern hotels formerly managed by the State Tourist Agency, Intourist. These are anonymous and rarely central but, on the whole, provide a reasonably good service with many amenities such as restaurants, bars and sports facilities. The would-be individual tourist is no longer compelled to travel on a package tour,

Doorman at Hotel Europe

as was the case during the Soviet era. Nowadays visas and hotel bookings can be made independently and hotels can be reserved directly or through a booking agency. For the summer months, particularly during the White Nights, it is recommended to make bookings well in advance for the city's most prestigious and centrally located hotels.

Those on a tight budget with no knowledge of Russian are advised to make arrangements in advance. Rooms are limited and visitors with no reservations may be refused. There is a selection of hotels on *pp172–73*.

Pribaltiyskaya, a popular hotel for package tours

WHERE TO LOOK

VERY FEW hotels are located in central St Petersburg and the hotels listed in this chapter are scattered around the city, often at a distance from the centre. Visitors on a package tour usually find they are staying in a former Intourist hotel such as the Pribaltiyskaya or Pulkovskaya situated in modern high-rise areas on the city's outskirts. It is important for the independent traveller to decide at the start what your priorities are going to be: location, price or service.

HOW TO BOOK

HOTEL RESERVATIONS for the White Nights *(see p51)* should be made up to six months in advance. The best way to book independently is by fax. The larger hotels will require a credit card number and money will be debited if a cancellation is made less

than 24 hours in advance. Most hotels are able to provide the necessary documentation for a visa application *(see p202)*.

The **St Petersburg International Youth Hostel** can now take bookings by e-mail, a convenient service which is increasingly being provided by other hotels. For a choice of accommodation, two reliable booking organizations in St Petersburg are **Cosmos** and the **MIR Travel Company** which also offer guide and transport bookings *(see p200)*.

FACILITIES

ALL THE HOTELS listed include at least a shower and a television and usually an individual telephone. Most hotels have a luggage room for storing baggage after the midday check-out time.

Ex-Intourist hotels are all very similar, with a vast lobby, several restaurants and cafés, bars, discos and usually a

sauna. These were built at the height of the Soviet tourist boom with the aim of keeping foreign tourists in restricted areas, generally situated away from the centre of the city. Formerly, the lack of access to public transport in these areas did cause a problem for those tourists who wanted to be more independent. However, the transport infrastructure has been greatly improved, providing routes to all parts of the city, and there are also numerous taxis.

PRICE

LACK OF sufficient competition is the main reason for prices still being relatively high for hotel accommodation in St Petersburg. Middle range hotels ($90–120 per person) are all located outside the centre with encumbent public

Fitness Centre, one of many facilities at the Grand Hotel Europe

transport problems. To stay in the city centre with all facilities your only choice is to opt for top range hotels, such as the Grand Hotel Europe, which can offer anything from an exclusive single room to imperial suites costing several thousand dollars a day.

Prices are rarely on display, and, in most hotels, rates increase during the high season, late May until late September.

Entrance to the luxurious, modern Nevskij Palace Hotel

HIDDEN EXTRAS

MOST HOTELS include local taxes in their prices, with the notable exception of the exclusive Grand Hotel Europe. Breakfast is generally included in the room rate. If it is not, it can be a significant addition to your final bill in the larger hotels. The biggest shock, however, is likely to be the cost of international or even local phone calls from your hotel room. The larger hotels have their own satellite lines which make all calls easy but very expensive. Bear in mind that calls which use the local network are relatively cheap and phonecards can be purchased to make international calls from street booths *(see p208)*. Even BCL satellite lines in hotel and restaurant lobbies are cheaper than calling through the hotel operator.

The Pribaltiyskaya adds a hefty booking charge for an individual booking, which can radically affect the cost of a short stay. Most hotels charge a small extra sum for registering your passport which is in any case obligatory *(see p202).*

SECURITY

SECURITY IN HOTELS has become stricter in recent years, with the top range establishments using metal-detectors and selective bag searches at entrances. Smaller hotels have a doorman, who may ask to see a visitor's card or identification. Since this is simply a precaution for your protection, there is no reason to object.

Many hotels have safes in the rooms, and security deposit boxes at the front desk. Large sums of money and valuables should always be left in one of these places.

DISABLED TRAVELLERS

DUE TO THE thick snow in winter, most buildings in St Petersburg have steps up to their entrances, making access extremely difficult for disabled visitors. The Grand Hotel Europe and Nevskij Palace, St Petersburg's two most elite hotels, are the only places which are fully wheelchair accessible and where the staff have been trained to be

Room in the Grand Hotel Europe

of assistance. However, more and more hotels are adding ramps, widening doors and trying to adapt to meet the needs of disabled travellers.

CHILDREN

ST PETERSBURG has never been vaunted as a great children's destination and very few of the hotels cater specifically for them. It is possible to arrange babysitters in the Grand Hotel Europe or the Nevskij Palace, and increasingly in many smaller hotels.

The elegant Winter Garden restaurant in the Astoria Hotel

BUDGET HOTELS

ACCOMMODATION in St Petersburg is not cheap by any means and anyone on a low budget should be prepared for prices corresponding to around $40 or more per person per night for one of the cheaper hotels. The lower-price hotels such as Oktyabrskaya and Rus offer some of the best locations, but also tend to be rather run down. Mir, further from the centre, offers more pleasant surroundings, while Matisov Domik, which is undoubtedly the best of the few hotels in the lower price bracket, combines personal service and attractive location.

Lobby of the small, family-run Matisov Domik

HOSTELS

FOR THE BUDGET traveller seeking comfortable accommodation in a reasonably central location, the functional **St Petersburg International Youth Hostel** is, by any standard, the cream of the

Efficient and helpful travel bureau service at the St Petersburg International Youth Hostel

crop. The hostel, which is often booked up a long time in advance, provides a travel bureau, English-language videos every evening and excellent advice on St Petersburg.

The slightly larger and less polished **Holiday Hostel**, just behind Finland Station (see p126), tends to be a popular choice with Russian visitors, making it ideal for those

wishing to get into the swing of local life. The most centrally located hostel, right behind the Kazan Cathedral (see p111), is **Hertzen University Hostel**. You can book with the hostels direct, but, unlike most hotels, they do not provide visa support.

An excellent alternative for those seeking a novel experience is to stay at the quaint **Petrodvorets Sanatorium**, housed in the former stables of Peterhof's magnificent palace (see pp146–9). At very low prices for a double room, and with the hydrofoil (see p221) running every hour from the palace to the city centre during the summer months,

Petrodvorets Sanatorium, occupying the stables at Peterhof

DIRECTORY

ACCOMMODATION RESERVATIONS

Cosmos
Vasilevskiy Island, 2-ya Liniya 35. **Map** 1 A5.
(327 7256.
W www.guide.spb.ru

HOFA Host Families Association
Tavricheskaya ulitsa 5–25. **Map** 4 D5.
(FAX 275 1992.
W www.hofa.us

MIR Travel Company
Nevskiy pr. 11. **Map** 6 D1.
(325 7122.
W www.mirtc.ru

Canongate Books Limited
(People to People Russia – introductions to Russians)
14 High Street, Edinburgh EH1 1TE.
((0131) 557 5111.

HOSTELS

Herzen University Hostel
Общежитие Гос. Педагогического Университета имени Герцена
Obshchezhitie Gos. Pedagogicheskovo Universiteta im. Gertsena
Kazanskaya ulitsa 6.

Map 6 E2.
(314 7472.
FAX 314 7659.

Holiday Hostel
Хостел Холидей
Khostel Kholidey
Ulitsa Mikhaylova 1.
Map 4 C3.
(327 1033.
FAX 327 1070.

Petrodvorets Sanatorium
Санаторий Петродворец
Sanatoriy Petrodvorets
Ulitsa Avrova 2, Noviy Peterhof.
(427 5098.
FAX 427 5021.

St Petersburg International Youth Hostel
3-ya Sovetskaya ulitsa 28. **Map** 7 C2.
(329 8018.
FAX 329 8019.
W www.ryh.ru

CAMPING

Retur Camping
Retur Ретур
Retur
26 km (16 miles) NW of St Petersburg, Sestroretsk, Bolshaya Kupalnaya str. 28.
(434 5022.
FAX 437 7533.

Impressive façade of the Oktyabrskaya Hotel, dating from 1847

the sanatorium offers a marvellous opportunity to enjoy a leafy country setting within easy reach of St Petersburg. The food is undeniably poor at the sanatorium, but Peterhof has a number of pleasant cafés.

STAYING WITH FAMILIES

FOR A REALLY good insight into Russian life, staying with a family can be an interesting and cheap option. The system works very much like any bed and breakfast in Europe with prices including breakfast but no other meals, although extra meals can usually be provided at a cost.

HOFA (Host Families Association) has a wide range of families on its books and a particularly good reputation in this area. Each family is checked out personally by the organizations who will then do their best to suit the accommodation to your needs.

Your hosts are likely to be extremely hospitable and will tend to overfeed you rather than otherwise. In many cases they will be keen to talk to you about their life in Russia and Western perceptions of their country. Many Russian apartments are reached through scruffy entrance halls or courtyards, but don't let this put you off as it gives little indication of the quality of the accommodation inside.

Canongate Books Limited publishes *Russia* in their *People to People* series, with introductions to over 1,000 Russians willing to offer hospitality and assistance to visitors. You will, of course, be expected to cover your own expenses.

RENTING A DACHA

FOR THOSE spending some time in and around St Petersburg, renting a *dacha* or country house can be an attractive and much more tranquil alternative to staying in the city. One of the most pleasant times of the year to do this is in April, when the snows have thawed and spring has really set in.

Dachas come in a wide range of specifications: the basic wooden chalet has electric light, a wood fire and an outside toilet, while more luxurious, and far more expensive, models come with gas-heated hot water and a telephone.

One of the best places to rent a *dacha* is in the beautiful and richly-forested district around the small town of Komarovo on the Gulf of Finland. Direct trains take one hour to St Petersburg from nearby Zelenogorsk, a six-kilometre (three-mile) train ride from Komarovo.

There are many summer attractions, including the famously clean Komarovo lake, while in winter, cross-country skiing is popular.

Dacha in pine forest near Repino on the Gulf of Finland (*see p144*)

CAMPING

ST PETERSBURG'S cold winter weather does not make it ideal for camping. Summer visitors, however, now have an excellent option in **Retur**, which offers chalets and camping places, a swimming pool, sauna and tennis courts, all set in the peaceful woods along the Gulf of Finland. Horse riding is on offer here and mushroom picking is popular in the autumn.

USING THE LISTINGS

The hotels on pages 172–3 are listed according to area and price category. The symbols summarize the facilities at each hotel.

⛨ all rooms have bath and/or shower unless otherwise indicated
1️⃣ single-rate rooms available
👫 rooms for more than two people available, or an extra bed can be put in a double room
24 24-hour room service
TV television in all rooms
Y mini-bar in all rooms
▤ air conditioning in all rooms
🏋 gym/fitness facilities
🏊 swimming pool
🖥 business facilities: message-taking service, fax service, meeting room
👶 babysitting service
♿ wheelchair access
🛗 lift
P car parking available
Y bar
🍴 restaurant
💳 credit and charge cards accepted:
AE American Express
DC Diners Club
MC Mastercard
V VISA
JCB Japanese Credit Bureau

Price categories are based on a standard double room in high season, including breakfast, tax and service.
⑤ under US$75
⑤⑤ US$75–125
⑤⑤⑤ US$125–200
⑤⑤⑤⑤ US$200–300
⑤⑤⑤⑤⑤ over US$300

Popular Hotels in St Petersburg

Accommodation in st petersburg has improved in recent years, but there is still really only a handful of hotels from which to choose. Unfortunately few of these are conveniently situated for the city centre and it is important to decide on your priorities, be it location, price, character, service or amenities. This selection represents the city's most popular hotels.

Pribaltiyskaya
The dark, sedate interiors of this popular package-tour hotel contrast with the stunning views over the Gulf of Finland.

Matisov Domik
The intimate, friendly ambience of this small hotel makes it one of St Petersburg's most welcoming and pleasant retreats.

Sovetskaya
This 1970s hotel offers wonderful views of the city centre from its rotunda bar. At sunset or during White Nights the vista is particularly magical.

Astoria Hotel
One of the city's most luxurious and centrally located hotels, the Astoria is perfect for exploring St Petersburg on foot. The attractive building overlooks St Isaac's Square and Cathedral.

St Petersburg
The package-holiday tourists usually housed in the St Petersburg get one of the city's most beautiful views over the Neva and Palace Embankment from the Bel-Etage café.

Grand Hotel Europe
Situated in the heart of the city, this historic hotel is the finest place to stay in St Petersburg. Elegant decor and refined service are complemented by many facilities.

Corinthia Nevskij Palace
Spotless, well-run and efficient, this hotel is characterized by sparse, modern interiors.
It is well-located on Nevskiy prospekt and has excellent restaurants and business facilities.

Pulkovskaya
Comfortable and clean, this vast modern hotel has many business facilities, including an auditorium. The hotel's main advantage is its proximity to the airport.

0 kilometres   2

0 miles   2

Choosing a Hotel

THIS LIST of hotels covers all areas and price categories with additional information to help you choose a hotel that best meets your needs. All these hotels welcome children and all have at least a café offering often quite substantial meals. Hotels within the same price category are listed alphabetically. For map references see pages 230–7.

Column headings: Credit Cards · Walking Distance from Centre · Sauna · Number of Rooms

ST PETERSBURG

MATISOV DOMIK Матисов домик — $ · MC V · Sauna · 24
Nab reki Pryazhki 3/1, 190121. **Map** 5 A3. (318 5445. FAX 318 7419.
A real getaway location overlooking a tree-lined waterway. A compact modern building offering friendly service. Transport to the centre is by tram only, and it can be difficult to catch a taxi.

MIR Мир — $ · Sauna · 120
Ul Gastello 17, 196135. (108 4910. FAX 108 5165.
This 1970s hotel is popular with budget travellers, and in the high season it can be difficult to get a room. Moskovskaya metro station and some wonderful examples of Stalinist architecture are reasonably close by.

NEVA Нева — $ · MC V · Walking distance · 90
Ul Chaikovskogo 17, 191187. **Map** 3 A4. (278 0500. FAX 273 2593.
The Neva is an old Soviet-style hotel. The ladies on duty are proud of their hotel and polite and friendly to their guests, even if the facilities are a little limited. Just a short walk from the Summer Gardens.

RUS Русь — $ · AE DC MC V · Walking distance · Sauna · 163
Artilleriyskaya ul 1, 191104. **Map** 3 B5. (273 4683. FAX 279 3600.
Just 15 minutes' walk from Nevskiy prospekt, this is the cheapest hotel in the centre, but the service and small rooms leave something to be desired. No restaurant but there are good cafés and restaurants close by.

OKHTINSKAYA-VICTORIA Охтинская-Виктория — $$ · AE DC MC V · Sauna · 290
Bolsheokhtinskiy pr 4, 195027. (227 4438. FAX 227 2618. W www.okhtinskaya.spb.ru
Clean, bright rooms at reasonable prices, many overlooking the river. The hotel is a short walk from various bus, tram and trolleybus routes, which take just under half an hour to reach the centre.

OKTYABRSKAYA Октябрьская — $$ · AE DC MC V · Walking distance · Sauna · 672
Ligovskiy pr 10, 193172. **Map** 7 C2. (277 6255. FAX 315 7501.
Favoured by regular visitors who feel that they are staying in a truly Russian hotel. Room security is poor, but its dark, brooding corridors, traditional Russian cakes in the café and remnants of former glory add to its character. Guests should avoid rooms located in the extension opposite Moscow Station.

SOVETSKAYA Советская — $$ · AE DC MC V · Sauna · 976
Lermontovskiy pr 43/1, 198103. (140 2640. W www.sovetskaya.com
The Riga or Fontanka buildings have superb views of the Fontanka river and the city centre. Rooms are modern and sparsely furnished, but service is pleasant, and several nearby trams run to the city centre or to the metro.

HOTEL DESON-LADOGA Отель Десон-Ладога — $$ · AE DC MC V · Sauna · 96
Shaumiana ul 26, 195213. (528 5628. FAX 528 5220. W www.deson.lek.ru
This hotel is ideal for those looking for a high standard of service at a moderate price. All staff speak English, while the rooms are bright and spacious. The room price includes breakfast and a morning sauna.

MOSKVA Москва — $$ · AE DC MC V · Sauna · 770
Aleksandra Nevskovo pr 2, 193317. **Map** 8 E3. (274 0022. FAX 274 2130.
This enormous, curving 1970s block is intended to cater for large groups. It has more personal touches than other Intourist hotels, such as the traditional Soviet-style key lady sitting by the lifts on each floor, available to help with anything from ironing and emergency clothing repairs to making tea.

NEPTUNE Нептун — $$ · AE DC MC V · Sauna · 70
Nab Obvodnovo kanala 93-a, 191 119. **Map** 6 F5. (324 4610. @ hotel@neptun.spb.ru
Popular with business travellers, Neptune offers efficiency and cleanliness. Close to Ligovskiy prospekt and Pushkinskaya metro, this modern building is located on the Obvodnyy Canal.

	CREDIT CARDS	WALKING DISTANCE FROM CENTRE	SAUNA	NUMBER OF ROOMS

Price categories are based on a standard double room in high season, including breakfast, tax and service:

Ⓢ under US$75
ⓈⓈ US$75–125
ⓈⓈⓈ US$125–200
ⓈⓈⓈⓈ US$200–300
ⓈⓈⓈⓈⓈ over US$300.

CREDIT CARDS
The following credit cards are accepted: AE American Express; DC Diners Club; MC Master Card/Access; V Visa; Japanese Credit Bureau JCB.

WALKING DISTANCE FROM CENTRE
The hotel is within easy walking distance (20 minutes) of the centre and the main sights.

SAUNA
The hotel has a sauna or *banya* for the use of hotel guests that can be booked for individuals or small groups by the hour.

ST PETERSBURG Санкт-Петербург ⓈⓈⓈ
Pirogovskaya nab 5/2, 194175. **Map 3 A2.** ☏ 380 1909. ℻ 380 1920. 🌐 www.hotel-spb.ru
The atmosphere in this 1960s hotel is curiously provincial. The rooms at the front have magnificent views of the Neva, however during White Nights *(see p51)* the sun shines into them for most of the night. The Bel-Etage, where you can take tea or beer, affords the same views. 🚗 1 🏨 24 📺 🅿 🍸

AE DC MC V — 410

PRIBALTIYSKAYA Прибалтийская ⓈⓈⓈ
Korablestroiteley ul 14, 199226. ☏ 356 3001. ℻ 356 0094. 🌐 www.travel.spb.ru/pribalt
The Pribaltiyskaya offers stunning views of the Gulf of Finland. The hotel itself, a vast, 1980s rabbit warren with five restaurants and a bowling alley, is characterized by dark furniture and dim lighting. Pribaltiyskaya metro is a bus ride or a bracing 20-minute walk away. 🚗 1 24 📺 🍸 🖥 🍽 🛁 ⛱ 🅿 🍸

AE DC MC V JCB ● 1200

PULKOVSKAYA Пулковская ⓈⓈⓈ
Pl Pobedy 1, 196240. ☏ 123 5122. ℻ 264 6396. 🌐 www.pulkovskaya.com
Another large, anonymous tourist hotel much used by package tours. Its restaurants have been revamped, and the small cafés are pleasant. 🚗 1 📺 🖥 🛁 ⛱ 🅿 🍸

AE DC MC V ● 840

ANGLETERRE Англетер ⓈⓈⓈⓈ
Bolshaya Morskaya ul 39, 190000. **Map 6 D2.** ☏ 313 5666. 🌐 http://angleterre.hotels.spb.ru
Twinned with the Astoria, with which it shares facilities, this modern hotel offers a nightclub and casino and an outstanding location at the very heart of historic St Petersburg. 🚗 1 🏨 24 📺 🍸 🖥 🍽 🛁 ⛱ 🅿 🍸

AE DC MC V JCB ■ ● 232

ASTORIA Астория ⓈⓈⓈⓈⓈ
Bolshaya Morskaya ul 39, 190000. **Map 6 D2.** ☏ 313 5757. 🌐 www.astoria.hotels.spb.ru
Same location and facilities as the Angleterre but with a historic interior and the calm and grace of a hotel with a history. Outstanding view from front rooms over St Isaac's Cathedral. 🚗 1 🏨 24 📺 🍸 🖥 🍽 🛁 ⛱ 🅿 🍸

AE DC MC V JCB ■ ● 193

CORINTHIA NEVSKIJ PALACE HOTEL Коринтия Невский палас отель ⓈⓈⓈⓈⓈ
Nevskiy pr 57, 191025. **Map 7 B2.** ☏ 380 2001. ℻ 380 1937. 🌐 www.corinthia.ru
This top-class modern hotel has fine restaurants and a patisserie, the Vienna Café, patronized by expatriates and locals alike. Its good facilities make it popular with business people. 🚗 1 🏨 24 📺 🍸 🖥 🍽 🛁 ⛱ 🅿 🍸

AE DC MC V JCB ■ ● 283

GRAND HOTEL EUROPE Гранд Отель Европа ⓈⓈⓈⓈⓈ
Mikhaylovskaya ul 1/7, 191011. ☏ 329 6000. **Map 6 F1.** 🌐 http://europe.hotels.spb.ru
The most luxurious hotel in the city. The impeccable service combines old-fashioned discretion with up-to-date quality. The light and airy atrium café of the internal yard serves coffee and cakes all day in an atmosphere of civilized utopian serenity. 🚗 1 🏨 24 📺 🍸 🖥 🍽 🛁 ⛱ 🅿 🍸

AE DC MC V JCB ■ ● 301

RADISSON SAS ROYAL HOTEL Рэдиссон САС Ройял Отель ⓈⓈⓈⓈⓈ
Nevskiy prospekt 49/2, 191025. **Map 6 D1.** ☏ 322 500. @ StPetersburg@RadissonSAS.com
The newest of the top hotels is a relatively small, bustling hive of activity downstairs, its bars and cafes all with large windows looking out onto Nevskiy prospekt, and more spacious calm upstairs. 🚗 1 🏨 24 📺 🍸 🖥 🍽 🛁 ⛱ 🅿 🍸

AE DC MC V JCB ■ ● 164

NOVGOROD

VOLKHOV Волхов Ⓢ
Predtechenskaya ul. 24. ☏ 8162 115548. ℻ 8162 115526. 🌐 www.novtour.ru
An inexpensive and comfortable option, run by the same pepele as the Beresta but more modest in price and less bland in its warm service. 🚗 1 🏨 24 📺 🖥 🍽 🛁 ⛱ 🅿 🍸

AE DC MC V ● 132

BERESTA PALACE HOTEL Береста Палас Отель ⓈⓈ
Studencheskaya ul 2a, 173014. ☏ 8162 158010. ℻ 8162 158025. 🌐 www.novtour.ru
Great river views, good food and efficient service. The hotel offers cheap weekend deals, often with transport from St Petersburg. 🚗 1 🏨 24 📺 🍸 🖥 🛁 ⛱ 🅿 🍸

AE DC MC V ● 226

For key to symbols *see p169*

RESTAURANTS AND CAFÉS

THE RESTAURANT SCENE is changing rapidly in St Petersburg, as specialist eateries, cafés and bars spring up all over town. Eating out may still not be as exciting as in many European cities, but the options are increasing.

In recent years the "business lunch", with an inexpensive fixed price menu, has become widespread, and not only at the big hotel restaurants but also at smaller establishments. Since the hotel restaurants are also catering for the local community, they liven things up with regular special events, such as festivals of foreign

Sign for Tbilisi

cuisine or traditional Russian fare. These are advertised in the English-language press *(see p209)*. Ethnic food, from the former Soviet republics as well as from abroad, is a growing trend which provides more variety and a wider selection of vegetarian dishes. Small cafés offer reasonable food at reasonable prices and are the most convenient place to eat away from Nevskiy prospekt *(see p108)*. Getting a plain green salad used to be a big problem for visitors, but now most restaurants and a number of good quality cafés offer a wide range of fresh salads.

Interior of the family-run Staraya Derevnya restaurant

WHERE TO EAT

RESTAURANTS and cafés are scattered all over town, but it is possible to find good food without straying far from Nevskiy prospekt *(see pp46–9)*. Since restaurants in this area cater mainly for foreigners, they tend to be more expensive and accept credit cards. Cheaper eateries, such as Pirosmani *(see p181)*, Staraya Derevnya *(see p182)* and Staroe Kafe *(see p185)*, which have an enjoyable atmosphere and reasonable food, are often in more inconvenient locations. The moderate outlay on food easily allows for the taxi fare.

TYPES OF RESTAURANT

THE TOP RANGE restaurants largely serve European food with a few select Russian dishes. Smaller, more intimate

venues like 1913 Goda *(see p180)* and Staraya Derevnya pride themselves on serving specifically Russian cuisine. This is generally uncomplicated food such as fried meat or fish with a selection of vegetables and pickles. The increasing

Outdoor café in the arcade of Gostinyy dvor *(see p108)*

number of ethnic and regional restaurants provides a touch of variety. The former Soviet republics, Georgia and Armenia, have both left their mark on Russian cuisine with *lobio* (spicy beans), *shashlyk (see p176)* and *tolma* (stuffed vine leaves). A full range of these can be found at the Georgian Pirosmani *(see p181)* and Armenian Krunk *(see p183)*.

Indian, Chinese, themed and "traditional American" eateries are also popular.

All restaurants require smart dress, although a suit and tie are rarely obligatory.

READING THE MENU

MOST RESTAURANTS, as well as some cafés, have a summary of their menu in English. The disadvantage of this is that in smaller places the menu may change daily, but only in its Russian version. Thus the English menus are often misleading. Most waiters will make some effort to overcome language difficulties. In restaurants accepting credit cards there is usually at least one English-speaking waiter.

PAYMENT AND TIPPING

MAJOR RESTAURANTS are likely to accept some credit cards, but check beforehand. This guide gives an indication of price range in dollars, but restaurants cannot accept foreign currency in payment *(see p207)*, although some may have their own exchange office. Tips are 10–15 per cent unless service is already included. To ensure the waiter receives the tip, it is best to give it in cash, rather than including it on a credit card.

OPENING TIMES

ALTHOUGH lunching out is not such an accepted habit among Russians, most restaurants open at midday and stay open until around 11pm or midnight. In rare cases, when for example there is an adjoining casino or nightclub, they may stay open until 1am.

Cafés close early, usually around 10pm at the latest, while bars, particularly those with live music *(see p196)*, usually stay open until around 2 or 3am.

Last food orders are rarely taken after 11pm, but there are a number of bars offering food well into the small hours.

Street sign for Pirosmani

MAKING A RESERVATION

NEARLY ALL restaurants require reservations to be made. Some establishments, notably Pirosmani, refuse to accept casual guests without a reservation, even if they are not fully booked. Some English will be spoken in all major restaurants, but your hotel concierge will be able to make bookings for you.

Apart from in the hotel restaurants, it is usually only possible to reserve a table a few days in advance. The majority of upmarket restaurants, however, start taking bookings earlier during the

The beautifully decorated interior of the Russian Room in the Ambassador *(see p182)*

White Nights *(see p51)*. The city's most popular eateries can then be fully booked up to two weeks in advance so it is wise to plan ahead.

Cafés do not generally require reservations. Since they rely heavily on special events, they may sometimes be unexpectedly closed to the public.

CHILDREN

ALTHOUGH few restaurants or cafés cater directly for children, establishments will rarely refuse entry to them. The only places likely to turn children away are those more geared towards entertainment.

Russians are slowly acquiring the habit of taking their children out to dine with them. The fast food outlets are obviously a good option and Bistro Sadko's *(see p183)* can also be accommodating.

On the whole Russians love children and staff can often be persuaded to adjust a dish to suit a child's special requests.

VEGETARIANS

TRADITIONAL RUSSIAN food is very much meat oriented, and vegetarian food is limited. The main hotel restaurants all offer several vegetarian dishes while ethnic food, particularly Georgian and Armenian, Indian and Mexican, may also offer a higher proportion of vegetarian dishes. A small

number of vegetarian cafés now operate, making life easier, but those who eat seafood will find the choice considerably broader.

SMOKING

NEARLY ALL restaurants will allow smoking, and smoking during meals is considered acceptable. Few places except the hotel restaurants have separate non-smoking areas. In smaller cafés serving food, smoking is often prohibited and desperate smokers may be forced outside.

DISABLED ACCESS

WAITERS and doormen in most restaurants are helpful to those in wheelchairs but cafés and bars prove more problematic. Not only are there usually stairs either up or down, but the doorways are narrow. The disabled are on the whole limited to the most expensive eateries and bars in the Nevskij Palace Hotel *(see p173)* and Grand Hotel Europe *(see p173)*.

USING THE LISTINGS

Key to symbols in the listings on pages 180–82.

🍽 fixed price lunch
V vegetarian dishes
🚼 suitable for children
♿ wheelchair access
T formal dress
🗐 air conditioning
▦ outdoor eating
🎜 live entertainment
🍷 recommended wine list
★ highly recommended
🄯 credit cards accepted:
AE American Express
DC Diners Club
MC Mastercard
V VISA
JCB Japanese Credit Bureau

Price categories for a three-course meal for one, including service and tax (excluding wine):
⑤ under US$25
⑤⑤ US$25–40
⑤⑤⑤ US$40–50
⑤⑤⑤⑤ over US$50

What to Eat in St Petersburg

RUSSIA'S VAST RANGE of climates and cultures has produced a diverse culinary repertoire. Traditionally each region has its own cuisine, but dishes such as *shashlyk*, from Georgia, are now popular throughout Russia. Influences from Europe and the Middle East have also

Sprig of dill added specialities to the Russian table. Despite this diversity, some ingredients, such as sour cream (*smetana*), curd cheese (*tvorog*), cucumbers, beetroot and dill, are still fundamental to the Russian taste.

Khachapuri
Originally from Georgia, these cheese-filled breads come in various shapes and sizes. The traditional filling is sulguni, a cheese made from sheep's milk.

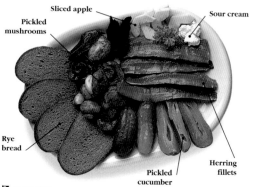

Sliced apple

Pickled mushrooms

Sour cream

Rye bread

Herring fillets

Pickled cucumber

ZAKUSKI

Comprising a variety of hors d'oeuvres, *zakuski* are served as starters for lunch or dinner. The robust spicy and salty flavours stimulate the appetite. Caviar, *kolbasa* (smoked sausages), pickles and cheese are also typical.

Rassolnik
There are many versions of this classic soup, including recipes using chicken, fish or kidney. Pickled cucumbers are a vital ingredient in all of them.

Solyanka
Made from either meat or fish, this soup has a distinctive rich, spicy taste. The meat version has a strong tomato flavour.

Borshch
Borshch gets its colour from beetroot and tastes sour and sweet. It is served hot in winter and chilled in summer.

Shashlyk
This version of a kebab is made from marinated mutton or lamb. The pieces of meat may be interspersed with vegetables such as onions and tomatoes.

RUSSIAN CAVIAR (*IKRA*)

Black caviar is sturgeon roe. It is produced by three species of sturgeon all found in the Caspian sea. Beluga caviar is the rarest and has a distinctive nutty taste. Osetrova has a creamy flavour, often compared to brie, while sevruga tastes of sea salt. Red caviar is salmon roe, often from Siberian wild salmon (*keta*). Caviar is often served with pancakes (*blini*) and sour cream (*smetana*).

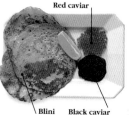

Red caviar

Sour cream

Blini

Black caviar

Red caviar jar

Black caviar jar

Osetrina
The sturgeon is renowned for its roe (caviar), but the fish itself is also eaten in a variety of ways, such as salted or smoked.

Savoury Pirozhki
Pirozhki can be stuffed with a variety of fillings such as meat and rice, fried cabbage, curd cheese or mushrooms.

Kotlety po-Kievskiy
Chicken breasts are filled with garlic butter, coated in breadcrumbs and deep fried. This is called Chicken Kiev in English.

Pelmeny
Originally a Siberian dish, these meat or fish dumplings are typically served in broth or with sour cream, butter or vinegar.

Kulebiaka
Puff or yeast pastry encloses a filling of salmon, rice, hard-boiled eggs and mushrooms. The pie is sliced and served cold.

Golubtsy
Minced meat and rice rolled in cabbage leaves, golubtsy are boiled or baked and served with a tomato sauce or sour cream.

DESSERTS

An important part of any Russian meal, most desserts are uncompromisingly rich. Russian cuisine has a wide variety of cakes, pies, tarts, pastries and ice cream.

Bef Stroganov and Kasha
This dish of sautéed strips of beef in a sour cream, onion and mushroom sauce is often served with boiled buckwheat (grechnevaya kasha).

Vatrushki are sweet curd cheese tartlets.

Vareniki are boiled sweet dumplings, with various fruit fillings.

Khvorost are deep-fried biscuits, with honey and sugar.

Sweet Pirozhki
Made with yeast dough, sweet piroshki can have a variety of fillings, including fruit or jam, and may be served with cream.

Sharlotka
Devised for Tsar Alexander I by French chef Antoine Carême, this sponge cake is filled with pieces of apple.

Morozhenoe
Ice cream is traditionally a favourite dessert in Russia. Look out for local brands.

What to Drink in St Petersburg

Shot of Starka

RUSSIAN VODKA is famous throughout the world and the Liviz distillery in St Petersburg is Russia's second largest distillery, the largest being in Moscow. Vodka first appeared in Russia sometime in the 14th or 15th century. Peter the Great *(see p18)* was particularly fond of anise- or pepper-flavoured vodkas and devised modifications to the distillation process which greatly improved the quality of the finished drink.

Tea is Russia's other national drink. Traditionally made using a samovar and served black, tea has been popular in Russia since the end of the 18th century, when it was first imported from China.

A 19th-century Russian peasant family drinking vodka and tea

CLEAR VODKA

Smirnov   **Sinopskaya**   **Sankt-Peterburg**

VODKA IS PRODUCED from grain, usually wheat, although some rye is also used in Russia. St Petersburg's Liviz distillery produces some excellent vodkas using the renowned pure waters from Lake Ladoga. From the cheaper Sankt Peterburg to the top quality, smooth-tasting Sinopskaya and Diplomat, Liviz dominates the vodka market in northern Russia. They also make Russia's most famous vodka, Stolichnaya (meaning "from the capital city") under licence, but mainly for export. A recent and excellent arrival on the market is the Russian Smirnov, made just outside Novgorod *(see pp160–63)* and not to be confused with the Western Smirnoff.

Kubanskaya

Vodka is always served with food in Russia, often with a traditional range of richly-flavoured accompaniments called *zakuski (see p176)*.

FLAVOURED VODKA

THE PRACTICE OF flavouring vodka has entirely practical origins. When vodka was first produced commercially in the Middle Ages, the techniques and equipment were so primitive

Pepper vodka

that it was impossible to remove all the impurities. This left un-pleasant aromas and flavours, which were disguised by adding honey together with aromatic oils and spices. As distillation techniques improved, flavoured vodkas became a speciality in their own right. Limonnaya, its taste deriving from lemon zest, is one of the most traditional, as is Pertsovka, flavoured with red chilli pepper pods. Okhotnichya (hunter's vodka) has a wider range of flavourings including juniper, ginger and cloves. Starka (old vodka) is a mix-ture of vodka, brandy, port and an infusion of apple and pear leaves, aged in oak barrels.

Limonnaya   **Okhotnichya**   **Starka**

MAJOR WINE REGIONS

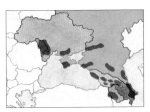

■ Wine growing region	■ Russia
■ Moldova	■ Georgia
■ Ukraine	■ Armenia
	■ Azerbaijan
	— International boundaries

**White
and red Georgian wine**   **Shampanskoe**

WINE

THE SOVIET UNION was one of the world's largest producers of wine (*vino*), but many of the major wine regions are now republics in their own right. Several indigenous types of grape are cultivated in the different regions, along with many of the more familiar international varieties.

Georgia is considered the best wine-making area. Its wines include those made from the Rkatsiteli grape, characterized by a floral aroma and subtle, fruity flavour, and the Gurdzhaani which gives a unique, slightly bitter touch. Among its best red wines is the smooth Mukuzani. Moldova produces white, sparkling wines in the south and central regions, while the south is also known for its red wines. Since 1799, Moldova also produces a sweet, champagne-like wine called Shampanskoe.

OTHER ALCOHOLIC DRINKS

BRANDY (KONYAK) WAS ORIGINALLY a by-product of wine-making and commercial production only began in Russia in the 19th century. Armenian brandy is one of the finest with a distinctive vanilla fragrance, resulting from its ageing in 70–100-year-old oak barrels. Georgia and Daghestan also produce good brandies. St Petersburg beer (*pivo*) is amongst the best in Russia. Baltika, Vena and Stepan Razin make a full range of beers in bottles and on draught. In addition, Tver beers such as Afanasy are well-worth trying. Various imported beers are also available.

**Baltika
Beer**   **Armenian
brandy**

OTHER DRINKS

KVAS IS A LIGHTLY FERMENTED DRINK made from rye and barley, consumed by adults and children alike. Russia's vast range of mineral waters (*mineralnaya voda*) includes many with unusually high mineral contents. Mineral waters from the Caucasus are particularly prized. Also widely available are fruit juices (*sok, mors* or *kompot*), including cranberry (*klyukva*). Look out for traditional Russian *shiten*, made from honey and herbs.

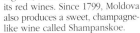

**Mineral water   Kvas   Cranberry
juice**

TEA

RUSSIAN TEA IS SERVED BLACK with a slice of lemon and may be drunk from tall glasses or cups. Sweetened with jam instead of sugar, tea (*chay*) is an ideal accompaniment to rich cakes and pastries. The boiling water for tea traditionally comes from a samovar. The water is used to brew a pot of tea, from which a little is poured into a cup and is then diluted with more hot water.

**A glass of tea, with jam
(varenye) to sweeten it**

THE SAMOVAR

Made from brass or copper and heated by coals in the central chimney, samovars traditionally provided boiling water for a wide variety of domestic purposes and were an essential wedding gift. Modern electric ones are made of stainless steel and are used mainly for boiling water to make tea. The word samovar comes from *samo* meaning "it-self" and *varit* meaning "to boil".

Choosing a Restaurant

THE RESTAURANTS in this guide have been selected across a wide price range for their exceptional food, interesting location and good value. The chart below lists restaurants in St Petersburg by area; those in the *Beyond St Petersburg* section are arranged by town. Most welcome children at lunchtime, but some are less receptive in the evening. For map references, see pages 230–7.

	CREDIT CARDS	RUSSIAN CUISINE	LIVE ENTERTAINMENT	FIXED PRICE LUNCH
VASILEVSKIY ISLAND				
CSARDAS Ксардас Makarova naberezhnaya 22. **Map** 1 B4. ☏ *323 8588.* One of the few restaurants on the north side of Vasilevskiy Island, Csardas offers an excellent Hungarian menu in a pseudo-rural Hungarian setting. ● *Thu.* Ⅴ ⚐	$$		■	●
THE OLD CUSTOMS HOUSE Старая Таможня 1 Tamozhenny pereulok. **Map** 1 C5. ☏ *327 8980.* Retaining its popularity even amongst St Petersburg's highly fickle clientele, The Old Customs House has a strongly French orientation in its wines and *haute cuisine* menu. The open kitchen is popular with those who like to see their food being prepared. ⚐ ▤ ⚑	$$	AE DC MC V		■ ●
RESTORAN Ресторан Ресторан Tamozhennyy pereulok 2. **Map** 1 C5. ☏ *327 8979.* Highly fashionable, stylishly minimalist restaurant, the name of which is a pun on the Russian word for 'restaurant'. Smart food too, and foreigners tend to get good service.	$$	AE DC MC V	●	
RUSSIAN KITSCH Русский китч Universitetskaya naberezhnaya 25. **Map** 5 B1. ☏ *325 1122.* For those who remember the Soviet and *perestroika* periods, this is a deliberately nostalgic look backwards. With six rooms, a café and dancehall, Russian Kitsch offers utterly un-Soviet and highly fashionable fusion cuisine. ⚐ ⚑	$$$	AE DC MC V	●	■ ●
NEW ISLAND Rumyantsevskiy spusk. **Map** 5 C2. ☏ *963 6765.* On a boat moored on the southern embankment, the New Island runs up and down the river every two hours (departures at midday, 2pm, 4pm, 6pm, etc) for as long as the Neva is not frozen. Enjoy eating caviar as you sail past the Winter Palace and the Summer Gardens. ⚐ ⚑ ★	$$$$	AE DC MC V	●	■
PETROGRADSKAYA				
DEMYANOVA UKHA Демянова уха Kronverkskiy prospekt 53. **Map** 1 C3. ☏ *232 8090.* For fish lovers – they do other dishes, but 90 per cent of the menu consists of fish. In May try *voblya*, a local delicacy that smells of fresh cucumbers when raw. Children are more than welcome here. ⚐ ★	$		●	■ ●
AUSTERIA Аустерия Peter and Paul Fortress. **Map** 2 E3. ☏ *238 4262.* Inside the fortress which Peter the Great built when he founded the city (*see p18*), Austeria seeks to imitate the hearty eating and drinking he also encouraged, with a strong emphasis on meat. ⚐ ⚏	$$	AE MC V	●	●
AQUAREL Акварель By Birzhevoy Bridge. **Map** 1 C4. ☏ *320 8600.* Located near the Strelka, the panoramic views over the River Neva and the French chef's fusion cuisine recently made this St Petersburg's restaurant of the year, among both critics and the public. There are three areas: the restaurant proper, a grill bar and a dessert café. ⚐ ⚑ ★	$$$	AE MC V		●
PALACE EMBANKMENT				
KALIF Калиф Millionnaya ulitsa 21/6. **Map** 2 E5. ☏ *312 2265.* Uzbek (Central Asian) interior and cuisine, with live music and even belly dancing in the evenings. Fall exhausted out of the Hermitage and into Kalif – just three minutes' walk away. Ⅴ ⚐	$	MC V		■

<table>
<tr><td>

Price categories for a three-course meal for one, including service and tax (excluding wine and other drinks):

$ under US$25
$$ US$25–$40
$$$ US$40–50
$$$$ Over US$50.

</td><td>

CREDIT CARDS
Indicates which credit cards are accepted: AE American Express; DC Diners Club; MC Master Card/Access; V Visa; JCB Japanese Credit Bureau.

RUSSIAN CUISINE
Traditional Russian fare is served.

LIVE ENTERTAINMENT
Live music and/or dancing on occasions.

FIXED-PRICE LUNCH
A good-value lunch menu is offered, usually described as a 'Business Lunch'.

</td></tr>
</table>

	CREDIT CARDS	RUSSIAN CUISINE	LIVE ENTERTAINMENT	FIXED PRICE LUNCH
LITERARY CAFÉ Литературное кафе $ Nevskiy prospekt 18. **Map** 6 E1. 312 6057. More of a historical than a gourmet experience, the Literary Café retains its popularity with tourists and lovers of Russian literature: this is the former Wolff and Beranger Café, from where the idolized Russian poet Alexander Pushkin set off for his fatal duel.	AE DC MC V	●	■	●
DAVIDOV'S $$ Hotel Astoria, Bolshaya Morskaya ulitsa 39. **Map** 6 D2. 313 5815. Although Davidov's concentrates on Russian cuisine, with Russian music in the evenings, it also arranges striking seasonal food festivals throughout the year – watch the English-language press. _evening._	AE DC MC V	●	■	●
SENAT Сенат $$$ Galernaya ulitsa 1. **Map** 5 C1. 314 9253. A restaurant-bar offering not only fine cuisine but also one of the city's most extensive range of drinks. There is a good wine shop attached.	AE DC MC V	●		
TALEON Талеон $$$ Naberezhnaya reki Moyki 59. **Map** 6 D2. 312 5373. Very busy complex with a restaurant, exclusive casino and three bars. The restaurant offers a good Sunday brunch (with childcare) and an economic business lunch. Popular with the local business community of all nationalities. _evening._	AE DC MC V	●		●
GOSTINYY DVOR				
PUSHKA INN Пушка инн $ Naberezhnaya reki Moyki 14. **Map** 2 E5. 314 0663. Right next door to the Pushkin Museum (hence the pun of the name). About a three-minute walk from the Hermitage, at the heart of historic St Petersburg, this is an ideal place for lunch. In the evenings it tends to fill with the foreign crowd.	AE DC MC V	●		●
SADKO'S $ Mikhaylovskaya ulitsa 1/7. **Map** 6 F1. 329 6000. Grand for sitting and watching the bustle of Nevskiy prospekt. During White Nights the streetside tables allow you to see the world go by until it finally gets darkish – after midnight.	AE DC MC V	●	■	●
LA STRADA $$ Bolshaya Konyushennaya ulitsa 27. **Map** 6 E1. 312 4700. Has to be one of the best places to take children for lunch or dinner, with a special children's menu and even a crèche. Standard Italian fare with the occasional innovation in the menu to keep you on your toes.	AE DC MC V			●
COUNT SUVOROV Граф Суворов $$$ Lomonosova ulitsa 6. **Map** 6 F2. 315 4328. Superb for a candlelit dinner for two (or more if you wish), with the best of Russian cuisine and romantic Russian songs to aid digestion.	AE DC MC V	●	■	●
KAVKAZ BAR Кавказ бар $$$ Karavannaya ulitsa 19. **Map** 7 A1. 312 1665. Russians love the food of the Caucasus – Georgia and Armenia. Try the _shashlik_ of lamb or vegetables, spicy beans (_lobio_), or the chicken in yoghurt and spices. The restaurant also has a more modestly priced café attached. ★	AE DC MC V	●	■	
CAVIAR BAR $$$$ Mikhaylovskaya ulitsa 1/7. **Map** 6 F1. 329 6000. Although you can get caviar cheaper elsewhere, it will be served with less variety and originality. Small, elegant portions, presented with finesse. ★	AE DC MC V	●	■	●

For key to symbols *see p175*

<table>
<tr><td colspan="2">

Price categories for a three-course meal for one, including service and tax (excluding wine and other drinks):

$ under US$25
$$ US$25–$40
$$$ US$40–50
$$$$ Over US$50.
</td><td colspan="6">

CREDIT CARDS
Indicates which credit cards are accepted: AE American Express; DC Diners Club; MC Master Card/Access; V Visa; JCB Japanese Credit Bureau.

REGIONAL CUISINE
Traditional Russian fare is served.

LIVE ENTERTAINMENT
Live music and/or dancing on occasions.

FIXED-PRICE LUNCH
A good-value lunch menu is offered, usually described as a 'Business Lunch'.
</td></tr>
</table>

	CREDIT CARDS	RUSSIAN CUISINE	LIVE ENTERTAINMENT	FIXED PRICE LUNCH
EUROPE Европа $$$$ Grand Hotel Europe, Mikhaylovskaya ulitsa 1/7. **Map** 6 F1. 📞 329 6000. *Haute cuisine* in a magnificent Art Nouveau interior. Book a box if you prefer cosiness to vast open space. For a cheaper option try the Sunday brunch which includes caviar, oysters, vodka and a choice of 20 desserts – the large portions will last you for a week. 🅥 🏃 ♿ 🍴 📋 🍷 ★	AE DC MC V		▣	●

SENNAYA PLOSHCHAD

	CREDIT CARDS	RUSSIAN CUISINE	LIVE ENTERTAINMENT	FIXED PRICE LUNCH
1913 1913 Год $ Voznesenskiy prospekt 13. **Map** 5 C3. 📞 315 5148. Generous portions and outstanding rural Russian dishes such as *draniki* (potato pancakes) with bacon and mushrooms, and international dishes such as lobster fricassée. Bland interior but warm atmosphere. 🅥 🏃 🍴 🍷 ★	AE DC MC V	●	▣	●
KROKODIL Крокодил $ Galernaya ulitsa 18. **Map** 5 C1. 📞 314 9437. Dark basement café-restaurant, extremely relaxed and cosmopolitan in atmosphere. All freshly-made food, excellent salads and soups, with one of the city's most consistently good lunch menus. 🅥 🏃 ★	AE DC MC V		▣	
KOCHUBEY Кочубей $$ Konnogvardeyskiy bulvar 7. **Map** 5 C2. 📞 312 8934. In the restored Kochubey Palace this is true aristocratic dining, albeit of the heavier, late-19th-century style (lots of wooden panelling and some rather heavy dishes on the menu too). 🅥 🏃 🍷	AE DC MC V	●	▣	●
LE FRANÇAIS $$$ Galernaya ulitsa 20. **Map** 5 C1. 📞 315 2465. Live piano music accompanies your candlelit dinner in this truly French restaurant, with attached bistro-bar. A grandiose French wine list. 🏃 🍴 🍷	AE DC MC V		▣	●
THE NOBLE NEST Дворянское гнездо $$$$ Dekabristov ulitsa 21. **Map** 5 C3. 📞 312 3205. Authentic early 19th-century interiors in the summer pavilion standing in the garden of the Yusupov Palace, perfect for elegant dining before or after the Mariinskiy Theatre. 🅥 🏃 🍴 🍷 ★	AE DC MC V	●	▣	●

FURTHER AFIELD

	CREDIT CARDS	RUSSIAN CUISINE	LIVE ENTERTAINMENT	FIXED PRICE LUNCH
KRUNK Крунк $ Solyanoy pereulok 14. **Map** 3 A5. 📞 273 4523. Exquisite Armenian food in a vaulted basement space with excellent service. Next door is Mukha-Tsokotukha, offering the same menu but with live jazz most evenings. 🅥 🏃 ★				
RIONI Риони $ Shpalernaya ulitsa 24. **Map** 3 A4. 📞 273 3261. Plain interior, but outstanding selection of freshly cooked Georgian dishes with highly personal service. Includes some rarely available Georgian specialities and you can ask them to adapt any dish to suit you personally. 🅥 🏃 ★	AE DC MC V			
SUNDUK Сундук $ Furshtatskaya ulitsa 42. **Map** 3 C4. 📞 311 5575. Defining itself as an "art café", with live jazz most nights, Sunduk is nonetheless definitely food-oriented. The excellent food is true Russian (it tends to be a little heavy) and the atmosphere relaxed. Book the only cabin if you want to dine alone… 🅥 🎵 ★	AE DC MC V	●	▣	
7-40 $$ Bolshoy Sampsonievskiy prospekt 108. 📞 246 3444. 7-40 is a well-known Jewish song and dance, and this restaurant offers a wide range of traditional Jewish dishes in a typical Jewish interior. Good for vegetarians. 🅥 🏃	DC MC V		▣	

....

BAGRATIONI Багратиони   ⓢⓢ | AE DC MC V
Liteynyy prospekt 5/19. **Map** 3 A4. 【 272 7448.
Named for a Georgian aristocrat and military hero of the Napoleonic wars, Bagrationi serves a meat-oriented range of Caucasian (Georgian and Armenian) food, complete with spit roast in the middle of the restaurant to cook your *shashlik* while you watch. 🔥 🍷

MATROSSKAYA TISHINA Матросская тишина   ⓢⓢ | MC V
Marata ulitsa 54/34. **Map** 7 B3. 【 164 4413.
Matrosskaya tishina has French chefs and offers a refined French menu, with a strong emphasis on seafood. 🔥 *lunch.* 🍷

SHINOK Шинок   ⓢⓢ | AE DC MC V
Zagorodniy prospekt 13. **Map** 7 A3. 【 311 8262.
Typical rural Ukrainian food is on offer here. The salted pork belly (*salo*) is an ideal accompaniment to vodka and Shinok offers a range of *salo* and some wonderful sour cabbage soup (*shchi*), in addition to more familiar foods. 🅥 🔥 ♿ 🍽 📋 📶 🍷 ★

STARAYA DEREVNYA Старая деревня   ⓢⓢ | AE DC MC V
Savushkina ulitsa 72. 【 431 0000.
Twelve years on and still a great restaurant list and a striking experience. It is a long way from the centre, but the interior is comfortable (rather than elegant), the service personal and the Russian/Jewish food is fresh. ● *Mon.* 🅥 🔥

TROIKA Тройка   ⓢⓢ | AE DC MC V
Zagorodnyy prospekt 27. **Map** 6 F4. 【 113 2999.
Not just live music but a tacky, wild and wonderful variety show, with circus acts and lots of dyed feathers while you dine. Or try the reasonable business lunch, without entertainment. ● *Sun.* 🔥 *lunch.* 🍽 *evening.* 🍷

BARBAZAN Барбазан   ⓢⓢⓢ | AE DC MC V
Radisson SAS Royal Hotel, Nevskiy prospekt 49/2. **Map** 7 A2. 【 322 5000.
Divided into two sections, one more formal than the other, Barbazan allows you to watch the crowds go by on the Nevskiy prospekt while you sit in luxury and pass the time with excellent food and elegant service. 🅥 🔥 ♿ 🍽 📋 🍷

DEMIDOV Демидов   ⓢⓢⓢ | AE DC MC V
Naberezhnaya reki Fontanki 14. **Map** 2 F5. 【 272 9181.
Priding itself on using often long-forgotten traditional Russian recipes such as venison with cherries, Demidov also offers gorgeous views over the River Fontanka and the Mikhail Fortress. 🔥 🍽 🍷

LANDSKRONA Ландскрона   ⓢⓢⓢ | AE DC MC V
Corinthia Nevskij Palace Hotel, Nevskiy prospekt 57. **Map** 7 B2. 【 380 2001.
Open in the evenings only, this silver service restaurant offers panoramic views over the city and the best in European cuisine. 🅥 🔥 ♿ 🍽 📋 🍷

BEYOND ST PETERSBURG

NOVGOROD: DETINETS Детинец   ⓢ
In the Pokrovskaya Tower, Detinets (Novgorod Kremlin). 【 (8162) 274624.
Still the best restaurant in town, with outstanding traditional food (cooked from fresh so you might have to wait), right inside the Detinets. 🅥 🔥 📶 ★

PAVLOVSK: PODVORIE Подворье   ⓢⓢ | AE DC MC V
16 Filtrovskoe Shosse. 【 470 6952.
Nobody does Russian folk music and kitsch better than this – even the Russians love it. Set in a reproduction 17th-century Russian wooden palace, five minutes walk from Pavlovsk station. 🅥 🔥 📶 ★

PETERHOF: TRAPEZA Трапеза   ⓢ
Kalininskaya ulitsa 9. 【 465 1399.
Very small, very comfortable, very friendly and well hidden in a small pavilion to right of the palace as you approach from the road. Excellent traditional food and drinks (try the *shiten'* or the more alcoholic *medovukha* – a honey drink). ● *Mon.* 🔥 ★

TSARSKOE SELO: STARAYA BASHNYA Старая башня   ⓢⓢ | MC V
Akademicheskiy prospekt 14. 【 466 6698.
Tiny restaurant with bare brick walls and low ceilings and a vast menu. There are not many such cosy restaurants in and around St Petersburg. 🅥 🔥 🍷 ★

Light Meals and Snacks

THE DECOR of a café gives little indication of what is on offer, making it difficult to recognize a good establishment at first glance. Many of the newer places have Western-style names and offer foreign cuisine, but are often expensive. Russian and ethnic cafés, however, can serve tasty food ranging from a sandwich to a reasonably priced three-course meal. These cafés are scattered all over the city, and you can generally rely on most of them for a good unpretentious meal. In most places, meat dominates the menu.

The distinction between bars and other establishments is often blurred. Even small cafés and cake shops offer beer and spirits all day, and many are open past midnight.

RUSSIAN

TRADITIONAL RUSSIAN dishes such as *borshch*, *pelmeny* (dumplings filled with meat), and *draniki* (potato pancakes, a rural dish) are widely offered.

Priboy is well located just behind the Hermitage (*see pp84–93*). **Krokodil** has a bohemian crowd and hosts special events as well as offering traditional food. **Stroganovsky Dvor**, situated near Nevskiy prospekt (*see p108*), serves 20 kinds of salad and a changing menu. **Zhili-byli** and **Khlebosolye** are nearby. Just off St Isaac's Square (*see p79*) is the **Idiot**, which has literary and culinary pretensions as well as offering books for sale. It offers some of the best vegetarian food in town. Further east, with outdoor tables on the Griboedova canal is **Restaurant Sankt-Peterburg**.

For those wanting to eat Russian *blini* (pancakes) in savoury and sweet varieties try **Russkiye bliny**. These can also be purchased from stalls (*Teremok*) around town.

GEORGIAN AND ARMENIAN

GEORGIAN AND Armenian food is much loved in St Petersburg. Both **Metekhi** and **Tbilisi** offer a selection of *lobio* (spicy beans), *Satsivi* (chicken in a spicy walnut sauce), *kharcho* (heavy meat soup) and the ubiquitous *shashlyk* (kebab). The tiny basement café **Lesnoy** offers 25 kinds of *shashlyk*, whilst a variety of dishes is offered at **Rioni** but check it is open before visiting.

FAST FOOD, PIZZA AND PASTA

IN ADDITION to the standard chains, St Petersburg has good local options. **Green Crest** serves salads, while **Gushe** has vegetarian food. Popular with clubbers, **Layma** is open 24 hours, serving *pirozhki*, steak, soups, beer and fresh juice.

Russian fast food is an open sandwich with cheese or salami, or alternatively *pirozhki* filled with rice, egg and cabbage, or something sweet like apple. Avoid the fried *pirozhki* with meat sold on Nevskiy prospekt.

Pizza and pasta houses are popular and provide easy meals. **Patio Pizza** make their own speciality pizzas that are well worth trying. **Ottolina** is a cheap and cheerful option.

GERMAN

THE FIRST GERMAN (and non-state-owned) bar to open in St Petersburg was **Tschaika**, which is still busy offering huge portions of wurst and chips or Baltic herring. **Antwerpen** is a similar establishment. **Schwabskiy domik** and **Bierstube** have a more traditional menu.

NORTH AMERICAN

FOR THOSE craving big juicy steaks, try **Daddy's Steak Room** for reliable food. **Bistro Sadko** is an American bar offering a varied menu of hamburgers, vegetarian dishes and tempting desserts.

PASTRIES AND SWEETS

RUSSIANS ARE notoriously sweet-toothed and tea is never offered without biscuits or cakes in private homes. Cakes and pastries are sold in most of the city's cafés, and ice cream is eaten with relish year round. **Sladkoezhka** sells almost entirely fresh cream desserts. Delicious pastries can be taken out at **Denisov-Nikolaev**, or eaten in at St Petersburg's renowned **Sever/Nord**. More luxurious European-style cheesecakes and cakes are the fare at **Ontromes**. For a unique St Petersburg experience, visit the **Idealnaya Chashka**, a chain of coffee-houses each with an individual style, selling a variety of coffees and pastries. Alternatively, try **Mokko Club**.

PUBS

A COMBINATION OF English and Irish pubs and German bars, the city's "pubs" are often run by foreigners. Although the interiors and the food tend to be a little unadventurous, the beer is generally good. Reflecting the ever-growing popularity of Irish drinking culture, draught Guinness is available at two Irish bars, **Mollie's Irish Bar** and **Shamrock**. **Korsar** and **James Cook** provide a varied programme of live music and themed entertainment, but probably the liveliest spot of all is **Tribunal**: the sort of place to acquire a hangover.

EATING OUT ON DAY TRIPS

FINDING A PLACE for lunch outside the city can be difficult. Pavlovsk (*see pp156–9*) and Peterhof (*see pp146–9*) have reasonable restaurants in the palaces, although space is limited in summer.

Oranienbaum (*see p144*) is a gastronomic desert, so take a picnic. Most hotels and some cafés in St Petersburg, such as **La Chandeleur**, will provide packed meals.

Novgorod (*see pp160–63*) has more to offer. The **Aziya** restaurant serves good Korean food, or snatch a quick pizza at **Kafe Charodeyka**.

DIRECTORY

RUSSIAN

Idiot
Идиот
Nab reki Moyki 82.
Map 5 C2.
C 315 1675.

Khlebosolye
Клебосолье
Bolshaya Konyushennaya
ulitska 1. **Map** 2 E5.
C 312 9554.

Kreatyur
Креатюр
Bolshaya Morskaya ulitsa 6.
Map 6 D1.
C 318 6132.

Krokodil
See p182.

Priboy
Прибой
Nab reki Moyki 19.
Map 2 E5. *C* 311 8285.

**Restaurant Sankt-
Petersburg**
Ресоран Санкт-
Петербург
Nab kanala Griboedova 5.
Map 6 E1.
C 314 4947.

Russkiye bliny
Русские блины
Ul Gagarinskaya 13.
Map 3 A4.
C 279 0559.

Staroe kafe
Старое кафе
Nab reki Fontanki 108.
Map 6 E4.
C 316 5111.

Stroganovsky Dvor
Строгановский Двор
Nevskiy prospekt 17.
Map 6 E1.
C 315 2315.

Teremok
Теремок
Around the city. Also
Sennaya ploschad.
Map 6 D3.

Zhili-byli
Жили-Были
Nevskiy prospekt 52.
Map 6 F1. *C* 314 6230.

GEORGIAN AND
ARMENIAN

Lesnoy
Лесной
Lesnoy prospekt 48.
C 245 6357.

Metekhi
Метехи
Ul Belinskovo 3.
Map 7 A1. *C* 272 3361.

Rioni
See p182.

Tbilisi
Тбилиси
Sytnynskaya ul 10.
Map 2 D2.
C 232 9391.

U Mimino
У Мимино
Karavannaya ul 24.
Map 7 A1.
C 315 3800.

FAST FOOD, PIZZA
AND PASTA

Green Crest
Грин крест
Vladimirskiy pr 7.
Map 7 A2.
C 113 1380.

Gushe
Гуше
Vladimirskyy pr 1.
Map 7 A2.

Layma
Лайма
Nab kanala Griboedova 16.
Map 6 E1.
C 318 9219.

McDonalds
Kamennoostrovskiy pr 39.
Sennaya pl 4.
Map 6 E3.

Ottolina
Оттолина
Marata ul 33.
Map 7 B3.
C 164 5686.

Patio Pizza
Патио-Пицца
Nevskiy prospekt 30.
Map 6 E1.
C 314 8215.
Nevskiy prospekt 182.
Map 6 E1.
C 271 3177.

GERMAN

Antwerpen
Антверпен
Kronverkskiy pr 13/2.
Map 2 E2. *C* 233 9746.

Bierstube
Nevskij Palace Hotel,
Nevskiy pr 57. **Map** 7 B2.
C 380 2001.

Schwabskiy domik
Швабский домик
Novocherkasskiy pr 28/19.
C 528 2211.

Tschaika
Чайка
Nab kanala Griboedova 14.
Map 6 E1. *C* 312 4631.

NORTH AMERICAN

Bistro Sadko
Бистро Садко
Mikhaylovskaya ulitsa 1/7.
Map 6 F1. *C* 329 6000.

Daddy's Steak Room
Moskovskiy pr 73.
Map 6 D3.
C 252 7744.

PASTRIES AND
SWEETS

**Denisov-Nikolaev
Confectionery**
Кондитерская Денисов-
Николаев
Bolshaya Pushkarskaya ul
34. **Map** 1 C2.

Idealnaya Chashka
Nevskiy prospekt 15.
Map 6 D1. *C* 315 0927.
Nevskiy prospekt 112.
Map 7 B2. *C* 275 7140

Mokko Club
Мокко Клуб
Nevskiy prospekt 27.
Map 6 E1.
C 312 1080

Ontromes
Онтроме
Nab. Kanala Griboedova
58. **Map** 6 D3.
C 310 7339

Republic of Coffee
Республика Кофе
Nevskiy prospekt 106.
Map 7 B2.
C 272 7650

Sever/Nord

Север
Nevskiy prospekt 22.
Map 6 E1.

Sladkoezhka
Сладоежка
Marata ul 2. **Map** 7 B2.
C 311 1420.
Sadovaya ul 60.
Map 5 C4.
C 310 8144

Vienna Café
Кафе Вена
Nevskiy pr 57.
Map 7 B2.
C 380 2001.

PUBS

James Cook
See p197.

Korsar
See p197.

Mollie's Irish Bar
See p197.

Shamrock
See p197.

Tribunal
See p197.

DAY TRIPS

Aziya
Азия
Shteikova ul 22, Novgorod.
C (81622) 722 27.

La Chandeleur
Bolshaya Konyushennaya
ulitsa 1. **Map** 2 E5.
C 314 8380.

Detinets
See p183.

Kafe Charodeyka
Кафе Чародейка
Volosova ul 1/1, Novgorod.
C (81622) 751 54.

Podvorie
See p183.

Trapeza
See p183.

Tsarskoe Selo
Царское Село
Detskoe Selo Railway
Station, Tsarskoe Selo.
C 470 1349.

SHOPS AND MARKETS

Matryoshka doll

ATRIP ROUND St Petersburg's shops, markets and large department stores provides an intriguing insight into local life. In addition to the many traditional stores, the city is dotted with street-sellers trading in an eclectic miscellany of goods.

Shopping in Russia requires a certain amount of spontaneity, flexibility and even a sense of adventure since you never quite know when and where you will find what is needed. As a rule, shop windows reveal surprisingly little about what might be found within. In recent years, imported goods (sold at inflated prices) have sadly pushed out many local products. Vodka, caviar and time-honoured Russian crafts and toys, however, make wonderful gifts.

Most shops tend to be concentrated around the city's main streets such as Nevskiy, Kamennoostrovskiy and Bolshoy (Petrogradskaya) prospekts.

Clothes in showroom of local designer Tatyana Parfyonova

OPENING HOURS

OPENING HOURS vary, but shops are usually open from around 10am until 7pm or later. Most close for an hour at lunch, food shops generally between 1–2pm and consumer goods stores between 2–3pm. On Sunday, the large department stores are open between 11am–6pm, and each area has food shops and a chemist open all day.

HOW TO PAY

CASH PAYMENTS can only be made in roubles. Occasionally prices may be in "y.e." or units (usually around one US dollar). Paying in non-Russian currency is a criminal offence. The only place you might be able to pay in foreign currency is at a tourist market. Between 10am and 6pm, there is no shortage of exchange

offices (*see p206*), some in the shops themselves, where you can get roubles for cash or on credit card. Few stores, even those selling imported goods, will accept credit card payments. The larger antique shops are the exception to this rule and nearly all now accept Visa and Mastercard.

In most shops, customers are forced to peer at goods stacked behind the counter. If you would like a closer look, just point to what you want and say "*mozhno*" ("may I?"). To purchase something, pay for it at the cash desk and then return to collect the item from the counter. Shop assistants will usually realise if you do not speak Russian and will write down the prices for you to hand to the cashier. In theory, defective goods can be taken back if you keep the receipt.

BARGAINING ETIQUETTE

IF A SET PRICE is displayed at markets, this indicates no bargaining. In all other cases you can usually get some reduction if you haggle, especially since visitors are often likely to be quoted a higher price than locals. Haggling in Russia, however, is not to be treated as a pleasant pastime. It is a serious matter, so do not bother unless you genuinely intend to buy.

Second-hand bookshop sign

BUYING ART AND ANTIQUES

UNDER RUSSIAN law, all objects made before 1956, and all objects made from valuable materials such as gold, silver, precious stones and fur, are subject to strict export controls. Works of art, including contemporary water-colours, also fall under this ruling and likewise books published before 1946.

All suitcases are thoroughly x-rayed at the air-port check-in, so it is pointless to try to hide, for instance, an icon with a metal cover. In practice, customs officials generally turn a blind eye to prints and watercolours without frames, and, likewise, unless a book is extremely rare you are likely to be able to export it without authorization. Permission to export both books and art objects can be obtained from a department of the **Ministry of Culture**. This process can be very slow and complicated, depending on the date and value of your acquisition. It is much better if the gallery or

Russian box-camera (1920s)

EXPORT PERMISSIONS

Ministry of Culture
Министерство культуры
Ministerstvo kultury
Malaya Morskaya Ulitsa 17.
Map 6 D1. ☎ *311 5196.*
○ *Mon–Fri 11am–5pm.*

DLT department store

artist from whom you are purchasing assists you with the process, as this often speeds things up considerably.

If you have not obviously tried to cheat customs, any objects not allowed through can simply be handed over to someone who is remaining in St Petersburg. If, however, there is any hint of foul play, the item will be placed in storage at the airport, for which, if you wish to reclaim it later, there will be a charge. Any objects that remain unclaimed after a year will be confiscated, as will objects which have obviously been hidden to avoid detection. Valuable pieces will generally be donated to a museum.

DEPARTMENT STORES

KNOWN AS "univermag" or universal shop, Russian department stores generally evolved from the old trading rows, which were literally rows of kiosks owned by different traders. Present-day department stores have altered a great deal and now operate as a complex of boutiques and distinct sections. Every visitor to St Petersburg should explore **Gostinyy dvor** *(see p108)*, the oldest and largest shopping centre in the city, and **Passazh** *(see p48)*, a smaller and more elite department store. Although they now have a large proportion of imported goods, and prices for local goods are relatively high, it is worthwhile observing

what the locals are buying. **DLT**, also in the city centre, is more Western in layout and is in itself an interesting piece of Style-Moderne architecture. To empty your pockets of any surplus roubles after a visit to St Petersburg, a good place to stop off en route to the airport is **Moskovskiy univermag**.

MARKETS AND BAZAARS

MANY LOCALS shop for food in one of the eleven farmers' markets (*rynoks*) dotted around the city. The most centrally located market is **Kuznechnyy**, just off Nevskiy prospekt, which sells flowers, fruit, vegetables, delicious home-made cream cheese and wonderful natural honey which you can sample. In front of the main entrance old ladies sell mushrooms in autumn, woollen socks in winter, flowers in summer and a hundred other odds and ends from pickled cucumbers and dried fish to old shoes and the family crystal ware. Note that prices at these markets tend to be higher than the supermarkets but you do have the option of haggling.

These days the yard inside **Apraksin market** *(see p95)* is best known for wholesale and retail sales of liquor, cigarettes, and clothes, especially Turkish leather jackets.

Flea markets, thought by the local administration to reflect badly on the city's image, are perpetually being moved on. Yet sellers continue to pop up relentlessly at the city's main fruit and vegetable markets.

Souvenir watercolours and prints are sold throughout the

Souvenirs sold at the tourist market opposite the Church on Spilled Blood

year at the open-air market, **Vernisazh**, which takes place outside St Catherine's Church *(see p48)*. **Rynok suvenirov**, a small tourist market near the Church on Spilled Blood *(see p100)*, sells both the best and cheapest selection of *matryoshka* dolls *(see p189)*. You are also likely to find handmade chess sets, watches, fur hats, old cameras, t-shirts and military paraphernalia.

Women selling a variety of goods outside Kuznechnyy market

MUSEUM SHOPS

SOME of the best quality souvenirs, whether it be jewellery, *matryoshka* dolls, prints or books, are usually found in the museums. The main shop in the **Hermitage** *(see pp84–93)* offers reproduction prints and objects, and books on the city and its art. The **Russian Museum** *(see pp104–107)* produces a good range of souvenirs such as jewellery, textiles and reproduction posters, to accompany special exhibitions. The shops, of which there are several in the main building as well as branches in the Stroganov Palace *(see p112)* and the Mikhaylovskiy Castle *(see p101)*, also have a large stock of beautiful art books. Other large museum shops are found in the **Peter and Paul Fortress** *(see pp66–7)* and in the palaces at **Pavlovsk**, **Peterhof** and **Tsarskoe Selo** *(see pp146–59)*.

What to Buy in St Petersburg

IT IS EASY to find interesting and beautiful souvenirs in St Petersburg. They range in price from small, enamelled badges, which sell for very little, through to hand-painted Palekh boxes and samovars which can be very expensive. Traditional crafts were encouraged by the state in the old Soviet Union and many

Decorative box

items, such as lacquered boxes and bowls, matryoshka dolls, wooden toys and chess sets, are still made by craftsmen and women using age-old methods. Memorabilia from the Soviet era also make good souvenirs and Russia is definitely the best place to buy the national specialities, vodka and caviar.

Vodka and Caviar

An enormous variety of both clear and flavoured vodkas (such as lemon and pepper) is available (see p178). They make excellent accompaniments to black and red caviar (ikra), which are often served with blini (see p176).

Clear vodka

Flavoured vodka

Red caviar

Black caviar

Samovar
Used to boil water to make tea, samovars come in all shapes and sizes (see p179). A permit is needed to export a pre-1945 samovar.

Malachite egg

Amber ring

Semi-precious Stones
Malachite, amber, jasper and a variety of marbles from the Ural mountains are used to make a wide range of items – everything from jewellery and chess sets to inlaid table tops.

Wooden Toy
These crudely carved wooden toys often have moving parts. They are known as Bogorodskiye toys and make charming gifts.

Matryoshka Dolls
These dolls fit one inside the other and come in a huge variety of styles. The traditional dolls are the prettiest, but those painted as Russian, Soviet and world leaders are also very popular.

Chess Sets
Attractive chess sets made from all kinds of beautiful materials, including malachite, are widely available. This wooden chess set is painted in the same style as the matryoshka dolls.

LACQUERED ARTIFACTS

Painted wooden or papier-mâché artifacts make popular souvenirs and are sold all over the city. The exquisite hand-painted, lacquered Palekh boxes can be very costly, but the eggs decorated with icons and the typical red, black and gold bowls are more affordable.

Palekh Box

The art of miniature painting on papier-mâché items originated in the late 18th century. Artists in the four villages of Palekh, Fedoskino, Mstera and Kholui still produce these hand-painted marvels. The images are based on Russian fairytales and legends.

Painted wooden egg

Bowl with Spoon

The brightly painted bowls and spoons, usually known as "Khokhloma", have a lacquer coating, forming a surface which is durable, but not resistant to boiling liquids.

Russian hand-painted tray

Tuners

Strings

Musical Instruments

Russian folk music uses a wide range of musical instruments. This gusli is similar to the Western psaltery and is played by plucking the strings with both hands. Also available are the brightly painted balalaika and the bayan (accordion).

Russian Scarf

These brilliantly coloured traditional woollen shawls are good for keeping out the cold of a Russian winter. Mass-produced polyester versions are also available, mostly in big department stores, but these are not as warm.

Soviet Memorabilia

An eclectic array of memorabilia from the Soviet era is on sale. Old banknotes, coins, pocket watches and Red Army kits, including belt buckles, badges and other items of uniform, can be found along- side watches with cartoons of KGB agents on their faces.

Gzhel Vase

Ceramics with a distinctive blue and white pattern are produced in Gzhel, an area near Moscow. Ranging from figurines to household crockery, they are popular with Russians and visitors alike.

Pocket watch

Badge with Soviet symbols

Red Army leather belt

Where to Shop in St Petersburg

THE MAIN DEPARTMENT stores in the city centre stock everything from souvenirs to vodka and furs, all of a high quality. Some of the smaller shops on and around Nevskiy prospekt, however, give you more chance to avoid the crowds; they also tend to be cheaper. In a city which prides itself on its native intellectuals, books and art are appropriately St Petersburg's other main exports. Soviet memorabilia have also become very popular.

VODKA AND CAVIAR

BUYING VODKA from anywhere other than a reputable shop is not advisable. Cheaper brands can be fairly potent and a certain amount of illegal vodka still makes its way into the smaller outlets. **Gostinyy dvor** department store and **Yeliseev's** are the most central and reliable places for vodka. Alternatively, the **Liviz** outlets normally stock a good range. The better local brands of clear vodka are the Russian Smirnov and Sinopskaya (see p178).

For good quality caviar, Yeliseev's fish department and **Ryba** are the best places to go, and on occasions they have fresh caviar, for which you bring your own jar. Another good supermarket in the centre is in **Passazh** department store.

Kuznechnyy and **Apraksin dvor** markets have the cheapest food products in the city, but check the date on caviar tins. In the summer it is best to buy only from shops with refrigerators.

SOUVENIRS AND CRAFTS

DURING THE summer months when traders set up stalls by all the major tourist spots, St Petersburg is flooded with *matryoshka* dolls, shawls and painted lacquerware. In the winter, by contrast, it often seems as if everything has gone into hibernation. **Rynok suvenirov** and **Vernisazh** markets, however, operate all year round. Museum shops also stock souvenirs and crafts, and some (such as in the Hermitage) also sell art books.

Probably the smallest souvenir shop, **Rossiysky Yuvelirnyy Dom** is also one of the best, but places such as **Khudozhestvennyye**

promysly have a larger variety. The city's porcelain factory makes some fine china, particularly coffee cups, and you can buy its products from its own outlet, **Farfor**. Locally made porcelain, glass and crystal is also sold at **Farfor, Khrustal, Steklo**.

SOVIET MEMORABILIA

ARTIFACTS from the Soviet era are now produced specifically for the tourist market. For original blatant propaganda material, **Sekunda** has one of the best stocks. The **Rynok suvenirov** market also has a wide range of military paraphernalia. Soviet badges are compact and easily transportable. A little shop on the first floor of the military bookshop **Dom voyennoy knigi** usually has a cheap selection. They and **Antikvariat** sell cameras, from the 1920s to the 1970s.

ANTIQUES AND ART

BEARING IN MIND all the restrictions on antiques and art, it is still worth seeing what might fall outside the export rules, whether it be a small watercolour, a modern print or a quaint 1960s tea service from stalls at **Apraksin dvor**. Shops such as **Russkaya Starina, Tertsiya** and **Rapso-diya** are mainly for the tourist trade, while **Peterburg Antikvariat** caters for all, but is at the top of the price range. Only buy an expensive object subject to customs regulations if you are sure the relevant paperwork and export applications can be obtained (see p202).

Paintings all require export licences, but galleries generally do this themselves, so it is worth dropping in to **Anna**

or the **Soyuz khudozhnikov** and see what they have. The most original and exciting gallery is **Borey** which has rapidly changing exhibitions and performance art to watch.

BOOKS

ST PETERSBURGERS perceive their city as an intellectual focal point, with a great literary and artistic past. The centre has many new and second-hand bookshops, which also tend to sell prints and often antiques. The best, and most famous, are the magnificent **Dom knigi** (see p47) and **Knizhnaya lavka pisateley**. Art books, both new and old, can be found at **Iskusstvo**, **The Art Shop** and **Bukvoed**, while if you are looking for English-language literature, **Anglia** sells fiction and reference works. Rummaging around antiquarian shops, such as **Staraya kniga** and **Na Liteynom**, can turn up interesting old prints, literature and travel guides, but foreign language publications tend to be heavily overpriced. **Severnaya lira** sells sheet music, ranging from classical to folk songs, as well as instruments, CDs and books.

FASHION AND ACCESSORIES

CLOTHES, SHOES and other accessories are generally imported nowadays, and the big names in fashion shopping are all foreign. Many local designers have their own boutiques, notably **Tatyana Parfyonova modnyy dom**, whose garments have been purchased by the Russian Museum (see pp104–7).

Locally made jewellery of semi-precious stones from the Urals and amber from the Baltic is sold in outlets such as **Kristall** and souvenir shops such as **Samotsvety** and **Yuvelirnyy**. One north-Russian speciality is niello silver jewellery, with its distinctive patterns and pictures etched in black.

The best furs come from **Fur Salon** and **Lena**, although traditional hats can be bought in the department stores.

DIRECTORY

DEPARTMENT STORES

DLT
ДЛТ
Bolshaya Konyushennaya
ulitsa 21/23. **Map** 6 E1.
w www.dlt.ru

Gostinyy dvor
Гостиный двор
Nevskiy prospekt 35.
Map 6 F2.

Moskovskiy univermag
Московский универмаг
Moskovskiy prospekt 205.

Passazh
Пассаж
Nevskiy prospekt 48.
Map 6 F1.

MARKETS AND BAZAARS

Andreevskiy rynok
Андреевский рынок
Bolshoy prospekt,
Vasilevskiy Island.
Map 5 A1.

Anna
Nevskij Palace Hotel,
Nevskiy prospekt 57.
Map 7 B2.

Apraksin dvor
Апраксин двор
Sadovaya ulitsa. **Map** 6 E2.

Kuznechnyy rynok
Кузнечный рынок
Kuznechnyy pereulok 3.
Map 7 A3.

Rynok suvenirov
Рынок сувениров
Kanal Griboedova, by
Church on Spilled Blood.
Map 2 E5.

Vernisazh
Вернисаж
Nevskiy prospekt 32–34.
Map 6 E1.

SHOPS

Anglia
Англия
Naberezhnaya reki
Fontanki 40. **Map** 7 A2.

Ananove
Ананов
(Jewellery)
Nevskiy pr 31. **Map** 6 E1.

Antikvariat
Антиквариат
(Antiques)
Nevskiy prospekt 51.
Map 7 B2.

The Art Shop
(Art Books)
Nevskiy prospekt 52.
Map 6 F1.

Borey
Борей (Art)
Liteynyy prospekt 58.
Map 7 A1.

Bourez Salon
Салон Буре (Clocks)
Nevskiy prospekt 23.
Map 6 E1.

Bukvoed
Буквоед
(Books)
Nevskiy prospekt 13.
Map 6 D1.

Dom knigi
Дом книги
(Books)
Nevskiy prospekt 28.
Map 6 E1.

Dom voyennoy knigi
Дом военной книги
(Military books, cameras
and memorabilia)
Nevskiy prospekt 20.
Map 6 E1.

Farfor
Фарфор (Porcelain)
Nevskiy prospekt 160.
Map 7 C2.

Farfor, Khrustal, Steklo
Фарфор, Хрусталь,
Стекло
(Porcelain, crystal & glass)
Nevskiy prospekt 64.
Map 7 A2.

Fur Salon
Салон меховых изделий
Bolshaya Morskaya ul 34.
Map 6 D2.
Zagorodnyy 22.
Map 7 A3.

Iskusstvo
Искусство (Art books)
Nevskiy prospekt 16.
Map 6 D1.

Khudozhestvennyye promysly
Художественные
промыслы
(Souvenirs)
Nevskiy prospekt 51.
Map 7 B2.

Knizhnaya lavka pisateley
Книжная лавка
писателей
(Books)
Nevskiy prospekt 66.
Map 7 A2.

Kristall
Кристалл
(Jewellery)
Nevskiy prospekt 34.
Map 6 E1.

Lena
Лена
(Furs)
Nevskiy prospekt 50.
Map 6 F1.
w www.lenafur.ru

Liviz (vodka outlets)
Ulitsa Plekhanova 2.
Map 6 E2.
Ulitsa Zhukovskovo 27.
Map 7 B1.
Ulitsa Belinskovo 6.
Map 7 A1.

Na Liteynom
На Литейном
(Antiques)
Liteynyy prospekt 61 (in
the yard). **Map** 7 A2.

Peterburg Antikvariat
Петербург Антиквариат
(Antiques)
Nevskiy prospekt 54.
Map 6 F1.

Rapsodiya
Рапсодия
(Antiques)
Bolshaya Konyushennaya
ulitsa 13. **Map** 2 E5.

Rossiysky Yuvelirnyy dom
Российский
Ньведирный дом
(Souvenirs & Jewellery)
Nevskiy prospekt 27.
Map 6 E1.

Russkaya Starina
Рчссдя Старина
(Antiques)
Nevskiy pr 20. **Map** 6 E1.

Ryba
Рыба
(Food)
Nevskiy prospekt 21.
Map 6 E1.

Samotsvety
Самоцветы
(Souvenirs & jewellery)
Mikhaylovskaya ulitsa 4.
Map 6 F1.

Sekunda
Секунда
(Soviet memorabilia)
Liteynyy prospekt 61 (in
the yard).
Map 7 A2.

Severnaya lira
Северная лира
(Sheet music, instruments
and books)
Nevskiy prospekt 26.
Map 6 E1.

Soyuz khudozhnikov
Союз художников
(Art)
Bolshaya Morskaya
ulitsa 38.
Map 6 D2.

Staraya kniga
Старая книга
(Second-hand books,
antiques & prints)
Nevskiy prospekt 3.
Map 6 D1.

Tatyana Parfyonova modnyy dom
Татьяна
Парфенова
модный дом
(Clothes)
Nevskiy prospekt 51.
Map 7 B2.

Tertsiya
Терция
(Antiques)
Italyanskaya ulitsa 5.
Map 6 E1.

Yeliseev's
Елисеевский гастроном
(Food)
Nevskiy prospekt 56.
Map 6 F1.

Yuvelirnyy
Ньвелирный
(Jewellery)
Nevskiy prospekt 69.
Map 7 B2.

The Arts

FOR A CITY RENOWNED WORLDWIDE for its rich tradition of ballet and classical music, it is not surprising that St Petersburg has a wide range of cultural events on offer. An evening at the Mariinskiy is an essential part of any visit to the city, but it is also worth venturing into the many other theatres, music halls and churches to absorb more of the city's cultural diversity. Classical music is vastly popular and local orchestras are much in demand the world over. In addition there are the evocative sounds of church choirs, the lively ambience of folk cabarets, and numerous festivals *(see pp50–53)* held to encourage young musicians, composers, film makers and dancers.

BALLET

SOME OF THE BEST dancers in the world have come from the **Mariinskiy Theatre** *(see p119)*. Its main company tours for much of the year, but usually gives performances in St Petersburg during the winter months. The greatest highlight of the year is the Christmas performances of *The Nutcracker*, danced largely by children from the Vaganova Ballet School *(see p110)*.

Dancers from the Mariinskiy also perform in the **Hermitage Theatre** and the **Mussorgsky Theatre of Opera and Ballet**. At the **Rimsky-Korsakov Conservatory** *(see p120)* ballet is of varied quality, but often includes dancers from abroad.

Outside the more traditional spheres, Boris Eifmann's modern ballet company is very popular, but the success of recent years has been Valery Mikhaylovskiy's entirely male Muzhskoy Ballet, performing classics such as *Swan Lake*, complete with tutus. They perform at venues like the **Great October Concert Hall**.

OPERA

TCHAIKOVSKY'S OPERA *Eugene Onegin* and Mussorgsky's *Boris Godunov* remain stalwarts in any repertory. Operas are performed (usually in their original language) at the **Mussorgsky Opera and Ballet Theatre** and the **Mariinskiy Theatre**, where Valery Gergiev's innovative artistic direction and sensitive conducting has recently attracted such world-famous performers as Placido Domingo. The more intimate 18th-century **Hermitage Theatre** and the tiny **Yusupov Theatre** stage lighter operas.

CLASSICAL MUSIC

THE COMPOSERS Tchaikovsky, Shostakovich, Mussorgsky and Rimsky-Korsakov lived in St Petersburg and their music is performed frequently.

The **Great Hall of the Philharmonia** *(see p98)*, the **Small Hall of the Philharmonia** *(see p48)* and **Academic Capella** *(see p112)*, are all historic venues for classical concerts. The former is where the renowned St Petersburg Philharmonic Orchestra plays when it is not on tour. Russian emigrés such as the violinist Gidon Kremer are frequent visitors, and foreign conductors including the late Sir Georg Solti have also performed here.

The Hermitage has its own orchestra which has a highly active independent life, with concerts in the **Hermitage Theatre** *(see p84)* and international tours. The **Menshikov Palace** *(see p62)* has some excellent original restored keyboard instruments, including an 18th-century English organ.

CHURCH MUSIC

THE MUSIC OF an Orthodox choir resounding over the priest's intoning is perhaps one of the most evocative sounds in Russia. Professional singers from the Capella and elsewhere often sing in church choirs. The best can be heard on Saturday evening and Sunday morning services at the Holy Trinity Cathedral in Alexander Nevsky Monastery *(see p130)* and at the **Cathedral of the Transfiguration** *(see p127)*. The services in the **Kazan Cathedral** *(see p111)* are also of a high standard. More formal religious music can be heard in the **Smolnyy Cathedral** *(see p128)*.

FOLK MUSIC

THE LOCAL tourist industry encourages visits to concerts of Russian folk music and dancing. The ensembles can be very good, with balalaikas and *bayans* or accordions, girls with red kerchiefs and whirling Cossack dancers. Some of the best performances are found at the **Beloselskiy-Belozerskiy Palace** and the **Nikolaevskiy Palace**.

Many restaurants include a folk cabaret, though these tend to be kitsch and fairly raucous. For authentic Russian folk songs, Podvorye restaurant *(see p184)* in Pavlovsk has an excellent small ensemble.

STREET MUSIC

DEMOCRACY had the unexpected effect of allowing many informal activities such as busking, which brought some highly talented musicians on to the streets. As skilled players stake their pitches, the sounds of music fill the city's streets. The two underpasses beneath Nevskiy prospekt are busy busking spots, while other metro stations are popular sites for old ladies singing Russian romances, rather like ballads.

THEATRE

SINCE THE DAYS of the Soviet Union, the leading light in the drama world has been the **Bolshoy Dramatic Theatre** (BDT), which remains the city's main traditional theatre. The **Alexandriinskiy Theatre** *(see p110)*, whose company is the oldest in Russia, offers a wider repertoire than the BDT.

In recent years, Lev Dodin's direction of the **Malyy Drama Theatre** has brought it international fame, even though all performances are in Russian.

Productions of well-known plays, such as the *Cherry Orchard*, may be interesting to experience, but other theatres, staging modern plays, are likely to be less accessible to non-Russian speakers. The **Kommissarzhevskaya, Liteynyy** and **Akimov** theatres also have good reputations.

CINEMA

MOST CINEMAS now show Hollywood blockbusters but the majority of foreign films are dubbed into Russian rather than subtitled. However, there are some cinemas, such as the **Dom Kino**, that do occasionally show undubbed English language films.

A large number of film festivals are held every year, often including films in the original language. *The St Petersburg Times* gives full coverage of all festivals including the main Festival of Festivals *(see p51)*.

DIRECTORY

TICKETS

Tickets are sold in city kiosks and individual theatres unless otherwise stated.

BALLET AND OPERA

Hermitage Theatre
Эрмитажный театр
Ermitazhnyy teatr
Dvortsovaya nab 34.
Map 2 E5. 279 0226.
(Tickets from city kiosks and hotels only.)

Mussorgsky Opera and Ballet Theatre
Театр оперы и балета имени Мусоргского
Teatr opery i baleta imeni Musorgskovo
Pl Iskusstv 1. **Map** 6 E1.
318 1978.
late Jul–Aug. www.mussorgsky.narod.ru

Mariinskiy Theatre
Мариинский театр
Mariinskiy teatr
Teatralnaya pl 1. **Map** 5 B3.
114 5264.
late Jul–Aug.
www.mariinsky.ru

Great October Concert Hall
Большой концертный зал Октябрьский
Bolshoy kontsertnyy zal Oktyabrskiy
Ligovskiy pr 6. **Map** 7 C1.
275 1300.

Rimsky-Korsakov Conservatory
Консерватория имени Римского-Корсакова
Konservatoriya imeni Rimskovo-Korsakova
Teatralnaya pl 3.
Map 5 C3. 312 2519.

Yusupov Theatre
Юсуповский театр
Yusupovskiy teatr
Yusupovskiy dvorets, nab reki Moyki 94. **Map** 5 B3.
314 9883.

CLASSICAL MUSIC

Academic Capella
Академическая Капелла
Akademicheskaya Kapella
Nab reki Moyki 20.
Map 2 E5. 314 1058.

Menshikov Palace
Меньшиковский дворец
Menshikovskiy dvorets
Universitetskaya nab 15.
Map 1 B5. 323 1112.

Great Hall of the Philharmonia (Shostakovich Hall)
Большой зал филармонии имени Шостаковича
Bolshoy zal Filarmonii imeni Shostakovicha
Mikhaylovskaya ulitsa 2.
Map 6 F1 110 4257.

Small Hall of the Philharmonia (Glinka Hall)
Малый зал филармонии имени Глинки
Malyy zal Filarmonii imeni Glinki
Nevskiy pr 30. **Map** 6 F1.
311 8333.

CHURCH MUSIC

Cathedral of the Transfiguration
Спасо-Преображенский собор
Spaso-Preobrazhenskiy sobor
Preobrazhenska pl 1.
Map 3 B5.
10am & 6pm daily.

Holy Trinity Cathedral
Свято-Троицкий собор
Svyato-Troitskiy sobor
Alexander Nevsky Monastery, pl Aleksandra-Nevskovo. **Map** 8 E4.
10am & 6pm daily.

Cathedral of Our Lady of Kazan
Собор Казанский Богоматери
Sobor Kazanskoy Bogomateri
Kazanskaya ploshchad 2.
Map 6 E1.
9am & 7:30pm daily.

Smolnyy Cathedral
Смольный собор
Smolnyy sobor
Ploshchad Rastrelli 3.
Map 4 F4. 278 5596.

FOLK MUSIC

Beloselskiy-Belozerskiy Palace
Дворец Белосельских-Белозерских
Dvorets Beloselskikh-Belozerskikh
Nevskiy pr 41. **Map** 7 A2.
315 5236.

Nikolaevskiy Palace
Николаевский дворец
Nikolaevskiy dvorets
Pl Truda 4. **Map** 5 B2.
312 5500.

THEATRE

Akimov Comedy Theatre
Театр комедии имени Акимова
Teatr komedii imeni Akimova
Nevskiy pr 56. **Map** 6 F1.
312 4555.

Alexandriinskiy Theatre
Александринский театр
Aleksandriinskiy teatr
Ploshchad Ostrovskovo 2.

Map 6 F2.
312 1545.

Bolshoy Drama Theatre (BDT)
Большой драматический театр
Bolshoy dramaticheskiy teatr
Nab reki Fontanki 65.
Map 6 F2. 310 9242.

Komissarzhevskaya Drama Theatre
Театр им. Комиссаржевской
Teatr im Komissarzhevskoy.
Italyanskaya ulitsa 19.
Map 6 F1. 311 3102.

Liteyniy Theatre
Театр на Литейном
Teatr na Liteynom
Liteynyy pr 51.
Map 7 A1. 273 5335.

Malyy Drama Theatre
Малый драматический театр
Malyy dramaticheskiy teatr
Ulitsa Rubinshteyna 18.
Map 7 A2. 113 2078.

Molodyozhnyy Theatre
Молодёжный театр
Molodyozhnyy teatr
Nab reki Fontanki 114.
Map 3 A5. 316 6564.

CINEMA

Aurora Cinema
Аврора
Nevskiy pr 60.
Map 7 A2. 327 0770.

Crystal Palace
Кристалл–Палас
Kristal-Palace
Nevskiy pr 72.
Map 7 A2. 272 2382.

Dom Kino
Дом Кино
Ul Karavannaya 12. **Map** 7 A1. 314 0638.

Live Music and Nightlife

ST PETERSBURG was at the heart of the underground Soviet rock scene and some of the best new Russian sounds still originate here. Rock, rockabilly and jazz clubs have sprung up in abandoned bomb shelters and cinemas all over the city, and most feature an eclectic mix, with live music one night and alternative fashion shows or avant-garde films the next. The nightclub scene, offering mostly techno music and mainstream pop, is moving out of the bunkers and into vast halls with strobe lights that attract the nouveaux riches. Only the larger clubs and casinos will accept credit cards.

ROCK VENUES

UNDER THE Soviet regime, Leningrad rock was rebellious without being overtly political. Though there is now more emphasis on the lyrics, Russian rock still owes much to the past, while also managing to incorporate the latest in Western music trends.

There is a wide variety of styles on offer, from pop to hard rock. **Moloko** and **Manhattan** are cheap venues offering live rock and a good atmosphere. **Polygon** is popular with fans of hard rock.

Rockabilly gave birth to **Money Honey Saloon**, which in turn led to an explosion of rockabilly groups in the city. **Jimi Hendrix** is another rock venue. Open around the clock, the name speaks for itself.

Mass rock and pop concerts are held in the **Oktyabrskiy kontsertnyy zal**, **Yubileynyy dvorets sporta** and **SKK**.

JAZZ VENUES

FOR MANY YEARS the jazz scene was dominated by David Goloshchokin who set up the **Jazz Philharmonic Hall** where, as its name suggests, dancing or talking are often prohibited. As young musicians emerged, the resulting competition on the jazz scene led Goloshchokin to open the **Ellington Hall** which is more like a relaxed Western jazz club. For improvisation and innovative jazz, **JFC Jazz Club** leads the way, with a variety of acid-jazz and blues. The musicians who make the club such a success also perform on a guest basis elsewhere. During the summer, the city's best swing band can be seen free of charge on the corner of Nevskiy prospekt and Mikhaylovskaya ulitsa.

BARS

A NUMBER OF BARS, such as **Shamrock**, the Mexican **La Cucaracha**, **Mollie's Irish Bar** or the **Manhattan**, have live music. **Bistro Sadko**, in the Grand Hotel Europe, was one of the few official bars where new bands used to play. It has recently been left behind by the appearance of numerous rock clubs, but maintains the tradition by putting on occasional live music.

Liverpool is an all-round Beatles experience, hosting live bands playing nothing but Beatles cover versions.

Two venues occupy a special place on the city's entertainment scene, neither of them exactly bars or art clubs. **Fish Fabrique**, hidden away in the artists' colony dubbed "Pushkinskaya desyat", is a drinking club, occasional concert venue, film club and favourite hangout for punks, rock 'n' rollers, advanced youth and, more and more, the "yuppies" of the Petersburg art scene. The **Idiot**, named after Dostoevsky's novel (see p123), has rapidly become one of the city's most popular bars for young intellectuals and artistic foreigners. Scatter cushions, vegetarian food and stacks of books make it an ideal place to relax in the daytime, or to attend a poetry reading in the evening. **Korsar** and **Tschaika** both have regular jazz evenings, while the noisy **Tribunal**, always filled with a young crowd, has occasional discos.

NIGHTCLUBS AND DISCOS

SMALLER, MORE DIVERSE clubs, such as the underground **Griboedov**, are still very much of the alternative culture trend, playing a variety of the latest hits from Europe, and hosting fashion shows and other cultural events. **Port Club** goes one step further, providing video halls and an art gallery.

Nevsky Melody is a vast entertainment complex, with casinos, restaurants and nightclubs. **La Plage** (La Plyazh) is a huge disco and dance hall located on the outskirts of town in the high-rise heartland. One of the most respectable clubs, **Hollywood Nites**, invites more serious acts and has one of the city's best casinos. **Metro**, mainly for the young and upwardly mobile, plays house, techno and Russian dance music. **Mama** is best known for its drum 'n' base and house, while **Havana Club** has Latin evenings, when all Latinos can enter for free. **Saigon** trades on its romantic history as a 1970s hang-out for dissident musicians, and often has performances of modern and progressive music. Closed in 1988, the club reopened here in 1999. The "erotic" **Monroe Club** has video screens and peepshows.

On the gay scene, **69 Club** is constantly popular, while other venues tend to come and go. Gay culture in the city is very much involved in the art world, and events are advertised at Saturday exhibitions in the New Academy of Fine Arts at Pushkinskaya ulitsa 10.

CASINOS

DESPITE a bad reputation as the haunt of a selection of the city's lowlifes, the larger casinos are now respectable and safe. **Premier**, in the Titan Cinema, has roulette and cards and is a trouble-free option as are **Olympia**, **Astoria Club** and **Hollywood Nites**. All are top of the list for quality and style. **Premier** and **Olympia** both have excellent restaurants, and, in fact, it is worth bearing in mind that all St Petersburg's casinos offer good food.

DIRECTORY

ROCK VENUES

Jimi Hendrix
Liteynyy prospekt 33.
Map 3 A5.
279 8813.
24 hours daily.

Moloko
Молоко
Perekupnoy pereulok 12.
Map 8 D3.
274 9467.
7–11:30pm Wed–Sun.

Money Honey Saloon
Apraksin dvor 14.
Map 6 E2.
310 0549.
10am–5am. Shows:
7:30pm–midnight daily.

Oktyabrskiy kontsertnyy zal
Октябрьский
концертный зал
Ligovskiy prospekt 6.
Map 7 C1. 275 1273.

Polygon
Полигон
Poligon
Lesnoy prospekt 65.
245 2720.

SKK
СКК
Prospekt Yuriya Gagarina 8.
378 1710.

Yubileynyy dvorets sporta
Юбилейный дворец
спорта
Prospekt Dobrolyubova 18.
Map 1 B3. 119 5615.

JAZZ VENUES

Ellington Hall
Эллингтоновский зал
Ellingtonovskiy zal
Zagorodnyy prospekt 27.
Map 6 F3.
164 8565.
7–11pm Tue–Sun.

Jazz Philharmonic Hall
Джаз-Филармоник холл
Dzhaz-filarmonik kholl
Zagorodnyy prospekt 27.
Map 6 F3. 164 8565.
7–11pm Wed–Sun.

JFC Jazz Club
Shpalernaya ulitsa 33.
Map 3 C4. 272 9850.
7–11pm daily.

Red Chub
Рыжий Чуб
Ryzhiy Chub
Ul Nekrasova 37.
Map 7 B1. 279 1852.
noon–5pm.

BARS

Manhattan
Маихеттен
Nab reki Fontanki 90.
Map 6 E3. 113 1945.
noon–5am daily.

Bistro Sadko
Grand Hotel Europe,
Mikhaylovskaya ulitsa 1/7.
Map 6 F1. 329 6000.
noon–1am daily.

La Cucaracha
Nab reki Fontanki 39.
Map 7 A2.
110 4006.
noon–1am Sun–Thu,
noon–5am Fri & Sat.

Fish Fabrique
Pushkinskaya ulitsa 10,
5th floor (entrance via
Ligorskiy 53). **Map** 7 B2.
164 4857.
3pm–2am daily.

Idiot
Nab reki Moyki 82.
Map 5 C2. 315 1675.
11am–1am.

James Cook
Shvedskiy per 2.
Map 6 E1. 312 3200.

Korsar
Корсар
Bolshaya Morskaya
ulitsa 14. **Map** 6 D1.
318 4181.
1pm–3am.

Liverpool
Ливерпуль
Ulitsa Mayakovskovo 16.
Map 7 B1. 279 2054.
11am–2am Sun–Thu;
11am–5am Fri & Sat.

Mollie's Irish Bar
Ulitsa Rubinshteyna 30.
Map 7 A3. 319 9768.
11am–2am daily.
(Live music Tue–Thu & Sun).

Shamrock
Ulitsa Dekabristov 27.
Map 5 B3.
318 4625.
noon–2am daily.
(Live music Mon, Thu, Sat.)

Tribunal
Corner of Angliyskaya nab
& proezd Dekabristov.
Map 5 C1.
311 1690.
4pm–6am daily.

Tschaika
Чайка
Naberezhnaya kanala
Griboedova 14.
Map 6 E1.
312 4631.
11am–3am daily.

NIGHTCLUBS AND DISCOS

69 Club
Клуб 69
Klub 69
2-ya Krasnoarmeyskaya
ulitsa 6.
Map 6 D5.
259 5163.
1pm–6am Tue–Sun.

Griboedov
Грибоедов
Voronezhskaya ulitsa 2A.
Map 7 B4.
164 4355.
6pm–6am Wed–Mon.

Havana Club
Гавана Клуб
Moskovskiy pr 21.
Map 6 D5.
259 1155.
9pm–6am.

Hollywood Nites
Nevskiy prospekt 46.
Map 6 F1.
325 7474.
10pm–6am daily.

La Plage
Ля Пляж
La Plyazh
Prospekt Kosygina 17.
525 6313.
10pm–6am Wed–Sun.

M 111
Moskovskiy prospekt 111.
Map 6 D3. 320 4400.
10pm–6am.

Mama
Malaya Monetnaya ul. 3b.
Map 2 E2.
232 3137.

Metro
Метро
Ligovskiy prospekt 174.
166 0204.
10pm–6am daily.

Monroe Club
Клуб Монро
Klub Monro
Nab kanala Griboedova 8.
Map 6 E1.
312 1331.
noon–11pm Tue–Sun,
5–11pm Mon.

Nevsky Melody
Невские Мелодии
Nevskie Melodii
Sverdlovskaya nab 62.
227 1596.
10pm–6am daily.

Port
Порт
Klub Port
Pereulok Antonenko 2
(in yard).
Map 6 D2.
314 2609.
3pm–6am daily.

Saigon
Nevskiy prospekt 7–9.
Map 6 D1.
314 7377.

CASINOS

Astoria Club
Клуб Астория
Klub Astoriya
Malaya Morskaya ul 20.
Map 6 D1.
313 5020.
4pm–6am daily.

Olympia Club
Клуб Олимпия
Klub Olympiya
Liteynyy prospekt 14.
Map 7 A1.
327 6700.
noon–8am daily.

Premier
Премьер
Nevskiy prospekt 47.
Map 7 A2.
103 5370.
24 hours daily.

SURVIVAL
GUIDE

PRACTICAL INFORMATION

THE STREET SIGNS and maps of St Petersburg are not as difficult to negotiate as it may first appear when confronted with daunting Cyrillic letters. Not only do hotels, restaurants and all service sectors attempt to compensate by being helpful to foreigners, but in recent times the city has started putting up English signs pointing out major sights and shops.

Conventional tourist offices do not exist in the city and information points, along with services such as foreign

Sign advertising the Mir Travel Company

exchange offices, are often concentrated in hotels and other areas frequented by foreigners. Once out on the street, things will seem unfamiliar, but with patience and determination everything is possible, from making international telephone calls and exchanging money to finding emergency medical treatment.

Telecommunications are rapidly gaining ground but, as quality improves, prices come closer to, and occasionally outstrip, Western equivalents.

TOURIST INFORMATION

HOTELS ARE the main source of tourist information. In the Europe and the Sheraton Nevskij Palace the concierge will provide travel and booking services and general assistance. Other, Russian-run, hotels have a Service Bureau offering similar services, but advice can be indifferent. **Cosmos** and the **MIR Travel Company** run reliable, tourist information services as well as booking accommodation and entertainment. Also try www.petersburgcity.com which is a useful English-language website.

English-language newspapers *(see p209)* give up-to-the-minute useful information.

Grand Hotel Europe concierge

The logo of Cosmos

EXCURSIONS

HOTELS CAN BOOK guided group tours and day trips in several languages. In addition to city tours and canal cruises, there are day trips to the suburban palaces and

Novgorod *(see pp144–63)*. Both **Cosmos** and the **MIR Travel Company** offer several excellent tours. City-run excursions, which gather tourists on Palace Square *(see p83)* and the Portik Rusca on Nevskiy prospekt *(see p48)*, tend to be in Russian, as do ordinary river cruises *(see p218)*.

On summer weekends there are helicopter tours operating on a turn-up basis from the Peter and Paul Fortress *(see pp66–7)*. Groups of 20 can book through **Baltic Airlines**.

ADMISSION CHARGES

MANY MUSEUMS and theatres, notably the Hermitage *(see pp84–93)*, the Russian Museum *(see pp104–107)* and the Mariinskiy *(see p119)* charge foreigners more than Russians, although prices are still within European and American norms. Students and schoolchildren are entitled to discounts. Credit cards are usually accepted at any sights.

The ticket office or *kassa* is often far from the entrance, so look for the KACCA sign.

Tour helicopter picking up tourists by the Peter and Paul Fortress

OPENING HOURS

MOST SIGHTS open standard hours, 10 or 10:30am to 6pm, with no break for lunch, and close one day a week. They also close one day each month for cleaning; this date varies, so phone to check. Last tickets are sold about one hour before closing. Parks are usually open from 8am to 8pm, later during White Nights.

ОТКРЫТО

Sign for open (*otkryto*)

ЗАКРЫТО

Sign for closed (*zakryto*)

VISITING CHURCHES

ATTENDING an Orthodox service is a fascinating experience. Since services tend to run for several hours, it is generally fine simply to drop in. It is polite to make a donation and certain dress codes must be observed: no shorts; men should remove hats; ladies should cover their shoulders and chest and preferably wear a hat or headscarf. Women in trousers are accepted in town churches, but all monasteries will strictly enforce the no trousers rule. The most important services are on Saturday evening, Sunday morning and on church holidays.

Most major faiths are represented in the city. Churches tend to be open all day from early morning till late. Church service times are published in Friday's *St Petersburg Times (see p209)*.

Friends greeting with a handshake

LANGUAGE

CYRILLIC, the alphabet used in the Russian language, is named after the 9th-century monk Cyril who invented it. The apparent similarity between Cyrillic and roman letters can be misleading. Some letters are common to both alphabets, others look similar but represent totally different sounds. Various systems of transliteration are in usage, but they do not differ enough to cause serious confusion.

Most people who come into contact with tourists speak some English and passers-by on the street will do their best if asked directions. Knowledge of a few Russian words *(see pp252–6)* will be appreciated and taken as a sign of respect.

ETIQUETTE

DESPITE AN ever increasing Westernization of manners and language, the use is still strictly in force of the formal you (*vy*) and the informal (*ty*).

On public transport, it is accepted that young men should relinquish their seats to children or the elderly.

Smoking is prohibited in cinemas, museums, theatres and on public transport. Special areas are usually allocated for smoking in these places.

Russians take great pleasure in smoking and drinking and frequent toasts are required to justify the filling and draining of glasses. At a private home you should always toast to the hostess (*za khozyayku*) or the host (*za khozyayina*). Greetings amongst friends involve a handshake or kiss, or a simply saying *privet* (Hi).

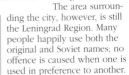
House number and Cyrillic street name

PAYING AND TIPPING

ROUBLES ARE the sole valid currency in Russia *(see p207)*. Some large shops and hotels give prices in US dollars or "y.e." (units), but all cash payments must be in roubles only. Credit cards are accepted in some restaurants and most hotels, and larger shops, mainly those selling expensive imported goods. Tipping is a matter of choice, but baggage

handlers at the airport and the train station may ask for or expect exorbitant sums. Simply pay what you feel is right; less than a dollar is usually quite sufficient.

ADDRESSES

RUSSIAN ADDRESSES are given in reverse order: index/zip code, city, street name, house number, apartment number and finally name of person.

After 1917, many streets and sights were renamed to avoid imperial connotations or in order to commemorate new Soviet heroes. Since the city itself resumed its original name after a referendum in 1991, most streets in the centre have officially reverted to their pre-1917 names, while others are still being discussed.

The area surrounding the city, however, is still the Leningrad Region. Many people happily use both the original and Soviet names; no offence is caused when one is used in preference to another.

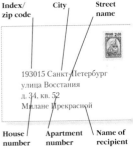

Index/zip code	City	Street name

193015 Санкт-Петербург
улица Восстания
д. 34, кв. 52
Милане Прекрасной

House number	Apartment number	Name of recipient

BRIDGE OPENING TIMES

Dvortsovyy most (leading to Vasilevskiy Island), raised to allow ships access along the Neva

From early April until mid-November, when navigation is possible on the Neva river, all its bridges are raised between approximately 2am and 5am. This timetable is a guide, but variations do occur. Make sure you are on the right side of the river.
Dvortsovyy most: 1:35–2:55am & 3:15–4:50am.
Troitskiy most: 1:50–4:50am.
Most Leytenanta Shmidta: 1:40–4:55am.
Liteynyy most: 1:50–4:40am.
Birzhevoy most: 2:10–4:50am.
Tuchkov most: 2:10–3:05am & 3:35–4:55am.
Bolsheokhtinskiy most: 2:00–5:00am.
Most Aleksandra Nevskovo: 2:30–4:55am.
Volodarskiy most: 2:10–3:45am & 4:15–5:45am.

Information office, offering free advice and literature to visitors

REGISTRATION

ALL FOREIGNERS must register with **OVIR** within three days of arrival, and obtain a stamp of registration on their visa. Hotels do this for their guests (as do **Cosmos** and **MIR**), but those staying in private accommodation must register at the branch of **OVIR** where their invitation was issued. For an extended visa an application must be made at the same branch. Visitors who forget to register can be fined and prevented from leaving Russia until all the necessary paperwork is in order.

EMBASSIES AND CONSULATES

ANYONE INTENDING to reside in Russia for longer than three months is advised to register with their consulate or embassy. If visitors are hospitalized, robbed, imprisoned or otherwise rendered helpless, consular officials will help make arrangements, find an interpreter, or at least offer advice. They can reissue passports and in some emergency cases provide money to get visitors home.

Great Britain, USA, Canada and South Africa have consulates in St Petersburg. Visitors from New Zealand, Australia or Ireland, however, have to contact their embassies in Moscow.

DISABLED TRAVELLERS

ST PETERSBURG has almost no facilities for the disabled. Transport is inaccessible, entrances have steps and narrow doors and there are rarely public lifts. It takes real determination for disabled travellers to get around.

VISAS

VISAS ARE REQUIRED by all visitors to Russia. Package tour companies will organize visas for you, but independent travellers need to arrange their own. This can be a complex, time-consuming process. Document requirements change regularly and it is essential to check these in advance. You will need to show proof of either pre-booked accommodation or an invitation (visa support) from a tour company, business or private individual in Russia. **Cosmos** and the **MIR Travel Company** can fax express invitations directly. Private invitations cannot be faxed and the process of issuing them takes at least one month through **OVIR** (Visa Registration Dept). The easiest option is to pay your travel agency to process the visa for you. The alternative is to go along in person to the Russian Embassy where visas are issued.

The cost of a visa ranges from around £30 for a short-term, single entry visa to about £100 for multiple entry business visas. A visa usually takes ten days, but for an extra fee can be arranged in one day.

Inside Russia, visa extensions can only be granted by the organization which issued the initial invitation. If you overstay, expect to be stopped at the airport and turned back until you have either obtained the necessary extension visa or paid a considerable fine.

CUSTOMS AND IMMIGRATION

PASSPORTS AND VISAS are checked thoroughly at immigration. All visitors must fill out a customs declaration form, which is available in several languages. These completed forms are returned to customs, together with a new form, on departure. Essentially there are no limitations on the amount of money people are allowed to bring into Russia, however, visitors should have less hard currency on departure and Russian money cannot be exported. Any items of considerable value, such as diamond jewellery and computers, should be noted on the customs form on entry. All such valuables must be re-exported, or import duty will be charged. You should be aware that on arrival and also on departure, all items of luggage will be put through X-ray machines.

Departure customs are extremely thorough and strict, particularly when it comes to dealing with works of art and antiques (*see p186*), however, there should be no problem at all with modest quantities of ordinary, everyday consumer goods.

STUDENT TRAVELLERS

AN INTERNATIONAL student card entitles its holder to discounts in museums, and on rail and air travel if it is booked through Sinbad Travel at the **St Petersburg International Youth Hostel** (*see p168*).

HOSTELLING RUSSIA

Sign for the St Petersburg International Youth Hostel

TRAVELLING WITH CHILDREN

RUSSIANS adore children, and travellers in the company of under-tens are likely to attract a good deal of attention and many compliments. Russian *babushki* (grannies) also think nothing of telling parents of their failings.

The city has many play parks and during school holidays temporary playgrounds are sometimes set up around town.

Museums and public transport are free for under-fives. Schoolchildren pay the full price on transport but pay a reduced price at museums.

Men's toilet sign

Women's toilet sign

Children playing on temporary bouncy castle in Palace Square

PUBLIC TOILETS

MANY CAFÉS and bars have no toilet facilities and in general the rather unhygienic public toilets are best avoided. It is much better to go to the nearest hotel or, if lacking an alternative, to use the pay toilets in department stores, for example. The person who takes the money hands out toilet paper rations.

PHOTOGRAPHY

PHOTOGRAPHIC restrictions have more or less disappeared. In museums expect to purchase a ticket for the right to photograph or use a video camera – tripods and flashes are prohibited.

ELECTRICAL APPLIANCES

THE ELECTRICAL CURRENT IS 220 V. Two-pin plugs are required, but some of the old Soviet two-pin sockets do not take modern European plugs which have slightly thicker pins. American appliances require a 220:110 current adaptor. Adaptors are widely available in St Petersburg.

TIME DIFFERENCE

ST PETERSBURG follows Moscow time, which is three hours ahead of Greenwich Mean Time (GMT), and eight hours ahead of Eastern Standard Time. In line with the rest of Europe, Russia puts its clocks forward one hour at the end of March and back one hour at the end of October.

CONVERSION TABLE

Imperial to Metric
1 inch = 2.54 centimetres
1 foot = 30 centimetres
1 mile = 1.6 kilometres
1 ounce = 28 grams
1 pound = 454 grams
1 pint = 0.6 litres
1 gallon = 4.6 litres

Metric to Imperial
1 centimetre = 0.4 inches
1 metre = 3 feet, 3 inches
1 kilometre = 0.6 miles
1 gram = 0.04 ounces
1 kilogram = 2.2 pounds
1 litre = 1.8 pints

Personal Security and Health

DESPITE LURID media reports worldwide about the mafia, St Petersburg is still a relatively safe city. Petty crime should be the only concern for tourists, and even this is generally avoided if the usual precautions are taken. Make copies of your passport and visa, note traveller's cheque and credit card numbers and, for language reasons, keep a card with your Russian address on it.

Medical insurance is essential, as local healthcare compares poorly with Western standards, and English-speaking services or medical evacuation via Finland are very expensive. Many medicines are readily available, but it is best to bring specific medicines needed.

Traffic policeman checking papers

PROTECTING YOUR PROPERTY

EVERY VISITOR to Russia is seriously advised to take out travel insurance. Once in St Petersburg, simple rules should be observed, such as not displaying large sums of money; carrying cash in a concealed money belt, and keeping passports, tickets and all valuables in the hotel safe whenever possible. Security in Western-run hotels is very high, but in all hotels it is advisable to place valuables in the safe. Traveller's cheques (see p206) may have an insurance policy but are expensive to use and are easily laundered in Russia.

Avoid the gypsies who occasionally group on Nevskiy prospekt, apparently begging. If they do approach, do not stop for them and keep a firm hold of your possessions.

If you have property stolen, report it to the local police station for insurance purposes. They are unlikely to have an interpreter, so you should ask your hotel for assistance.

PERSONAL SAFETY

THE GREATEST danger faced by foreigners is that posed by pickpockets and petty thieves who might use violence if they meet with resistance. As in any country, it is advisable to hand over belongings that are demanded with menace.

The mafia, an organization largely overrated by the media nowadays, has almost no contact with tourists, who are generally much less wealthy than Russian businessmen.

Women on their own are unlikely to encounter sexual harrassment, though they should ignore kerbcrawlers and avoid taking a cab alone at night. Of course, there is no such thing as a completely safe place, so always be alert and make sure that you take responsibility for your own safety. The main threats on the streets come from local drivers, who see all pedestrians as a nuisance, and from manhole covers, which

tend to rock or even collapse under your feet. This can be hilarious on a movie screen, but is not so funny in real life.

POLICE

SEVERAL KINDS of police operate on St Petersburg's streets. Their uniforms change according to the weather, with the very neccessary addition of fur hats and big overcoats in the winter.

The street officers or militia (militsya) wear dark blue-grey combat-style uniforms

Free, state-run ambulance service

New-look police fleet as Volvos (top) replace Ladas (below)   Fire engine in central St Petersburg

Militsya **policeman**

and many carry guns. Their uniform is very similar to that worn by the riot police or OMON, the only obvious difference being in the badges.

Separate from both these are the traffic police, whose uniforms carry the logo ДПС (DPS) on the chest and shoulder. They have the authority to stop any vehicle to check documents.

Both the militia and traffic police supplement their low income by fining people for minor infringements of the law, notably for crossing Nevskiy prospekt between signals. It is best to pay the moderate "fine" imposed – from 50 to 100 roubles.

PHARMACIES

THE BEST PHARMACIES (*apteka*), are located along Nevskiy prospekt. These sell many imported medicines, some with Russian instructions, others in their original language. Strong medications can be bought over the counter, so prescriptions are not necessary. Every assistant is a trained pharmacist and can advise alternative drugs. If you have very specific requirements, particularly insulin, you should bring a sufficient supply for your stay.

MEDICAL TREATMENT

IF YOU FALL ILL, seek advice at your hotel, which should have its own doctor. Several companies, notably **Emergency Medical Consulting** and **American Medical Center**, specialize in dealing with foreigners. They cover everything from dental care, X-rays and pre-natal care to medical evacuation. Their charges are fairly high, but they are used to dealing with foreign insurance policies. Slightly cheaper is the **Clinic Complex** which has English-speaking Russian doctors and can deal competently with minor emergencies.

For those in need of immediate attention, the casualty department of the **Trauma Clinic of the Central District** is just off Nevskiy prospekt. English is not spoken here, but basic care involving stitches or injections can be administered.

If you are taken to a local hospital and require further treatment, it is best to contact either your consulate or one of the above medical centres. They can either have you moved or they can oversee your treatment in the hospital.

A good dentist can be fiendishly expensive in St Petersburg. The American Medical Center is good, and is covered by insurance policies. Others such as the **Dental Palace** are also good, but costs will not be reimbursed.

Pharmacy in a Nevskiy underpass

HEALTH PRECAUTIONS

NEITHER VISITORS nor residents should drink tap water, which contains heavy metals and *giardia*, a parasite causing stomach problems. To be safe drink bottled water only. If you do pick up *giardia*, it can be treated with metronidazole.

Russian food on the other hand is unlikely to do much harm. Avoid raw fruit and vegetables that may have been washed in tap water, and the meat pies sold on the streets.

Diphtheria is now becoming prevalent, and inoculation is advisable. Also on the rise are syphilis, HIV and other sexually transmitted diseases.

MOSQUITOES

MOSQUITOES (*komari*) are rife between June and late September. Repellents are available locally but not all are very effective and it is best to come well equipped. Burning oils, sprays or plugs which heat chemical tablets are recommended at night time, particularly out on the Gulf of Finland or in the woods.

АПТЕКА

Sign for pharmacy or *apteka*

Banking and Local Currency

ST PETERSBURG IS MOVING into the credit card age and major European debit and credit cards can now be used in hotels and some restaurants and shops. Everywhere else, however, cash is the norm, and roubles are the only legal currency. The city is well provided with exchange points where you can turn your currency (US dollars still being the most popular), travellers' cheques or credit cards into roubles, at varying rates of commission. Since bank rates are so good, money should never be changed on the streets. What appear to be higher offers from individuals will lead to visitors being cheated.

CHANGING MONEY

ROUBLES CANNOT be obtained outside Russia, but there are numerous exchange offices throughout St Petersburg, including at the airport. Some offices open 24 hours a day. A passport has to be shown when changing money. Any visible defect on foreign bank notes, especially vertical tears or ink or water stains, makes them extremely difficult to exchange. Make sure that all the bank notes you bring into Russia are in good condition, and that any US dollars were issued after 1990.

On completion of an exchange transaction, a receipt slip is issued. Keep these slips safe as they will need to be attached to the customs declaration form filled in on arrival in Russia (*see p202*), and returned to customs on departure.

A sign for a currency exchange office (*obmen valyuty*)

Official currency exchange slip

BANKS AND EXCHANGE OFFICES

NONE OF THE foreign banks in Russia offers over-the-counter services. The most reliable Russian banks are **Sberbank** and **Promstroybank**. Exchange offices are plentiful in St Petersburg. They are often branches of banks, offering both cash currency exchange and cash advances on credit or debit cards. Larger branches also cash travellers' cheques. Exchange offices often work long hours: those at the Europe and the Corinthia Nevskij Palace hotels are open 24 hours. Sberbank exchange rates are not particularly high, but there are branches conveniently located all over the city.

A fast and safe, but expensive, way of transferring cash to Russia is by Western Union, available at Promstroybank, Most-bank and the **American Express** office.

CREDIT CARDS

IT IS POSSIBLE to obtain both roubles and US dollars, with a credit card through the larger banks and from automatic cash dispensers which are springing up all over town. The local commission is between 2 and 5 per cent, plus whatever the card company charges. The

Automatic cash dispenser

most commonly accepted card is VISA, with MasterCard, Eurocard, Diners Club and American Express much less widely recognized. Cash dispensers at **Alfabank** are the best, offering more cash per transaction than others. Less commission is charged if you take out cash in roubles.

Lost or stolen credit cards should be reported immediately to the credit card company back home as no local security service is offered.

TRAVELLERS' CHEQUES

BANKS CHARGE at least 3 per cent to cash travellers' cheques. However, only large banks, such as **Alfa-Bank** and **Sberbank**, offer this service. The cheapest alternative is American Express cheques, with a 2 per cent commission if cashed at the **American Express** office. Travellers' cheques can only be used as payment for goods or services in a few large hotels, and are acceptable only in US dollars and euros. In most cases euro cheques are generally preferred.

LOCAL CURRENCY

THE RUSSIAN currency is the rouble (or ruble), written рубль or abbreviated to p or руб. The higher denominations of roubles are currently available in banknotes, which all bear images of well-known Russian cities, the lower denominations in coins. The kopek, of which there are 100 in a rouble, is issued in coins.

In 1998 the rouble was re-valued owing to its stronger value and lower inflation rate. Values were divided by 1,000 (with 1,000 roubles becoming 1 rouble).

Banknotes
There are five denominations of banknote, with face values of 10, 50, 100, 500 and 1,000 roubles, and they have the same designs as their pre-revaluation equivalents. When changing money check that the notes correspond to those shown here.

10 roubles

50 roubles

100 roubles

500 roubles

1,000 roubles

Coins
The revaluation of the Russian rouble in 1998 led to the revival of the long-redundant but much-loved kopek. Traditionally, the rouble had always consisted of 100 kopeks. As well as coins for 1, 2 and 5 roubles, there are now coins for 1, 5, 10 and 50 kopeks. Any coins which were issued before 1997, prior to revaluation, are essentially valueless and you are perfectly within your rights to refuse to accept them if they are given to you in your change.

1 rouble

2 roubles

5 roubles

1 kopek

5 kopeks

10 kopeks

50 kopeks

GETTING TO ST PETERSBURG

ST PETERSBURG IS SLOWLY regaining its popularity as a tourist destination, after the severe drop in numbers during the early 1990s. Now, as the number of businessmen regularly travelling in and out is also rising, the number of flights and alternative means of transport is on the increase. Flying remains the most popular way of travelling to St Petersburg, both for individuals and groups, with the train from Moscow or Helsinki a close second.

Aeroflot plane landing in St Petersburg

Independent travel in Russia is difficult as well as costly and for this reason it is worth considering a package tour. British companies run a variety of tours with specialist guides, which often incorporate St Petersburg and Moscow. Since overall tourist numbers are still fairly limited, package tours are not among the cheapest. Shopping around can uncover some good deals, particularly on flights with stopovers in Europe or low-season packages.

Stalinist architecture at Pulkovo 2, St Petersburg's international airport

ARRIVING BY AIR

DIRECT FLIGHTS from the UK to St Petersburg run five days a week on British Airways and three days on Aeroflot. There are connecting flights on other airlines every day and these are often a much cheaper option. **Scott's Tours** in London are particularly good for budget fares. The plane journey from London takes around three-and-a-half hours, or about six hours with a stopover in a European city.

Direct flights to St Petersburg from Ireland, US, Canada, South Africa and Australasia are either extremely limited or simply do not exist. The usual route from these destinations is to fly via a European city or via Moscow from where you can transfer to another flight or continue by road or rail.

The only direct flight to St Petersburg from Ireland is a weekly Aeroflot service from Shannon on the west coast. From the US, Aeroflot operates

a direct flight from New York to St Petersburg three times a week. From Canada and South Africa, direct flights, also on Aeroflot, only go to Moscow. Travelling from Australasia can be fairly complicated. The most usual route is to pick up a European carrier in Singapore, with a stopover in Europe.

On landing, passengers are sometimes required to confirm onward flights. You can do this through the airline you are travelling with or the **Central Air Communication Agency** on Nevskiy prospekt.

ST PETERSBURG AIRPORTS

INTERNATIONAL FLIGHTS arrive at **Pulkovo 2** which, although recently modernized, is still small and relatively primitive. Its separate arrival and departure buildings each have a small duty-free shop. Arrivals also has a

foreign exchange office. On arrival, the longest wait is likely to be for baggage, while departures on the weekend can be hectic and it is best to arrive at least 90 minutes before a flight in high season.

Pulkovo 1 is for domestic flights only. The 1970s building is cramped and dark, but foreigners and those using commercial flights to and from Moscow have a separate arrivals and departure lounge. Located on the first floor, this has its own entrance which cannot be reached from inside the main terminal building.

GETTING INTO THE CITY

BOTH AIRPORTS are located 17 km (11 miles) south of the city centre. The major hotels operate cars to pick up individual tourists for a cost of around $45. The service, which can be charged to

Limousine transfer service from the Grand Hotel Europe (see p181)

Ordinary yellow taxi waiting outside the domestic airport, Pulkovo 1

No. 13 bus from Pulkovo 2 to Moskovskaya metro station

Minibus or *marshrutnoye taksi*

metro station. Minibuses, known as *marshrutnoye taksi* or route taxi, travel the same route and charge a minimally higher fare *(see p219)*.

TRAVELLING BY TRAIN

RAIL IS a relatively cheap way to travel from Finland, Moscow and within Russia in general, although European student discount passes provide little or no reduction in fares.

Eleven trains a day run in each direction between Moscow and **Moscow Station** and two between Helsinki and **Finland Station** *(see p126)*. For those with time and some sense of adventure, it is possible to

Ticket office or *kassa* at Central Train Ticket Office

travel by train between London and St Petersburg via Central Europe (Warsaw, Prague, Berlin). It takes about three days and is generally more costly than flying. The trains are comfortable and usually run on time, but carriages can be overcrowded and thefts are common. Transit visas may also be necessary for countries such as Ukraine. The simplest and most reliable route is via Belarus (Belorussia) which accepts a Russian visa for transit passengers. (All visitors to Russia need a visa and obtaining one can be a complicated procedure. For information on visa acquisition see page 202.)

Trains travelling from Eastern Europe arrive and depart from **Vitebsk** or **Warsaw Station**. Tickets for train journeys from St Petersburg should be bought from the upstairs booking hall at the **Central Train Ticket Office**.

Taxis from stations can be overpriced, but all train stations have efficient transport connections.

the hotel bill, should always be requested when making a hotel booking. The luxury taxis waiting at the airport only tend to undercut hotel cars by about $5 while ordinary yellow cabs, rarely found at the international airport, are a great deal cheaper, charging around $10–15 in roubles. Official yellow cabs are usually plentiful at the domestic airport.

Anyone on a more limited budget, and who has already changed money at the airport, can take the No. 13 bus (from Pulkovo 2) and No. 39 (from Pulkovo 1) to Moskovskaya

Exterior of Finland Station, the point of arrival for daily trains from Helsinki in Finland

---

TRAVELLING BETWEEN MOSCOW AND ST PETERSBURG

Many visitors fly in to Moscow and out of St Petersburg, or vice versa. The most popular form of transport between the two cities is the train, of which there are ten a day. Daytime trains take about ten hours, while faster night-time trains take eight and a half hours. Prices vary according to the class of the train – the Red Arrow being most expensive – and the choice of seat. All trains have a choice of *SV* (two-person compartment), *coupé* (four-person), *platzkarte* (open seating), or *sidyashchyy* (open seating). All except *sidyashchyy* are sleepers.

For daytime travelling *sidyashchyy* is more comfortable and cheaper than *platzkarte*. One-way prices range from the equivalent in roubles of around $70 for *SV* to $11.50 for *sidyachyy*. Prices do not always include bed linen, for which there is an additional charge when you purchase your ticket. On cheaper trains, the *provodnik*, or carriage attendant, will issue and charge for bed linen. Food may be available but it is best to travel with your own supplies.

Regular commercial flights connecting the two cities take about 50 minutes. These are run by Aeroflot and independent companies such as Pulkovo and Transaero. Prices are modest, at around $65 for an economy class one way ticket, and $122 for business class. Tickets are sold at the airport, or at the **Central Air Communication Agency**. Travelling by boat to and from Moscow is also possible *(see p212)*.

St Petersburg – Moscow sign in train carriage

SV compartment on the luxurious Red Arrow train from Moscow

One of Finnord's coaches

TRAVELLING BY COACH

COMFORTABLE coaches run to and from Helsinki in Finland, offering a cheaper alternative to the train. **Finnord** runs one daytime coach and one overnight in each direction; the journey takes around eight hours. Coach companies do not always use the city's inconvenient coach stations but will drop off instead at various locations in St Petersburg. Finnord's final stop is by the Pulkovskaya Hotel. Advance booking is advised with this company as many Russians take advantage of these coaches to go shopping in Lappeenranta, just over the border, or in Helsinki itself.

TRAVELLING BY BOAT

ARRIVING by boat can be one of the most exciting and novel ways to approach St Petersburg. However, ferries and cruises operate irregularly and it is best to check with a travel agent for details.

Ferries from Scandinavia usually dock at the **Maritime Passenger Terminal**, on the west side of Vasilevsky Island. Trolleybus No. 10 and bus No. 7 run from here to the centre or, heading in the other direction, to Primorskaya metro station.

In summer, river cruises between Moscow and St Petersburg are run along the Volga and across Lake Ladoga. The trips last about two weeks and make a very pleasurable way to see more of Russia. The cruises are bookable in the UK through **Noble Caledonia** or **Voyages Jules Verne**, and in the US through **Panorama Travel Ltd**. Ships dock at St Petersburg's **River Terminal**, ten minutes' walk from Proletarskaya metro. Cruise companies run buses to and from the city centre.

Luxury cruise ships from London, the US and elsewhere arrive at the city's cargo port, 5 km (3 miles) southwest of the centre. Access to the port is restricted, so the ships have their own coaches to carry tourists into town and back.

Ferry moored at Maritime Passenger Terminal on western edge of Vasilevsky Island

---

DIRECTORY

UK AND US TOUR COMPANIES

Panorama Travel Ltd
156 Fifth Ave, Suite 1019,
New York, NY 10010.
[(212) 741 0033.
FAX (212) 645 6276.

Scott's Tours
141 Whitfield Street,
London W1P 5RY.
[0171 383 5353.
FAX 0171 383 3709.

Voyages Jules Verne
21 Dorset Square,
London NW1 6QG.
[0171 616 1000.
FAX 0171 723 8629.

Noble Caledonia
11 Charles Street,
London W1X 8LE.
[0171 409 0376.

AIRPORT INFORMATION

Pulkovo 1
Пулково 1 [104 3822.
Pulkovo 2
Пулково 2 [104 3444.

AIRLINE OFFICES

Austrian Airlines
Nevskiy pr 57. **Map** 7 B2.
[325 3260.
[346 8100 (Pulkovo 2).

British Airways
Malaya konyushennaya
ulitsa 1/3. **Map** 6 E1.
[329 2565.
[346 8146 (Pulkovo 2).

Central Air Communication Agency
Nevskiy pr 7/9. **Map** 6 D1.
[315 0072 (inter).
[311 8093 (dom & CIS).

Delta Airlines
Bolshaya Morskaya 36.
Map 5 C2.
[311 5819.

Finnair
Kazanskaya ul. 44.
Map 6 D2. [326 1870.
[324 3249 (Pulkovo 2).

KLM
Zagorodnyy prospekt 5.
Map 7 A3. [325 8989.

Lufthansa
Voznesenskyy pr. 7.
Map 5 C2. [314 4979.
[324 3244 (Pulkovo 2).

Malev Hungarian Airlines
Voznesenskyy pr. 7.
Map 5 C2. [315 5455.
[324 3243 (Pulkovo 2).

SAS
[325 3255.
[324 3244 (Pulkovo 2).

Transaero
Liteynyy pr 48. **Map** 7 A1.
[279 6463/1974.

TRAINS

All Train Enquiries
[055.

Central Train Ticket Office
Центральные железно-
дорожные кассы
*Tsentralnye zhelezno-
dorozhnye kassy*
Nab kanala Griboedova 24
(upstairs for foreigners).
Map 6 E2. [162 3344.

Finland Station
Финляндский вокзал
Finlyandskiy vokzal
Pl Lenina 6. **Map** 3 B3.

Moscow Station
Московский вокзал
Moskovskiy vokzal
Pl Vosstaniya. **Map** 7 C2.

Vitebsk Station
Витебский вокзал
Vitebskiy vokzal
Zagorodnyy prospekt 52.
Map 6 E4.

Warsaw Station
Варшавский вокзал
Varshavskiy vokzal
Nab Obvodnovo kanala 118.

COACHES

Finnord
Italyanskaya ulitsa 37.
Map 6 F1.
[314 8951.

BOATS

Maritime Passenger Terminal
Морской пассажирский
вокзал
*Morskoy passazhirskiy
vokzal*
Pl Morskoy Slavy.
[322 6052.

River Terminal
Речной вокзал
Rechnoy vokzal
Prospekt Obukhovskoy
Oborony 195.
[262 0239/8994.

GETTING AROUND ST PETERSBURG

A LTHOUGH PUBLIC transport in the city is abundant, efficient and very cheap, the most enjoyable way to get around and fully appreciate St Petersburg is on foot. A glance at a map reveals that some attempt was made to bestow the city with a rational, organized layout, which makes it considerably easier to negotiate. When exhaustion sets in, however, a boat cruise along the waterways can be a wonderful way to become acquainted with the city.

Sign indicating pedestrian crossing

Nevskiy prospekt is where many of the city's transport routes and main roads meet. Metro lines, tram, bus and trolleybus routes radiate out from here, criss-crossing the city with a network of rail tracks and overhead wires. It is possible to travel without too much difficulty to almost anywhere in town from this main avenue.

Driving is not recommended due to the combination of poor road conditions, aggressive Russian driving and over-efficient traffic police.

WALKING

I N SOME AREAS, particularly around Palace Embankment, sights are situated so close together that using public transport from place to place is pointless. A few of the more scattered sights are at some distance (20 mins on foot) from the nearest transport and walking the last stretch is

Street sign for Nevskiy prospekt

often the most practical option. Apart from the ease, getting around on foot can be a most rewarding way to explore the city, allowing you to soak up the atmosphere and appreciate the fascinating architectural and sculptural detail on many of St Petersburg's buildings.

As soon as the sun appears, in winter as well as in summer, people of all ages emerge onto the streets and into the

parks. Locals are very fond of walking, whether it be promenading up and down Nevskiy prospekt, or ambling around the Neva at 2am during the White Nights (see p51). The Summer Gardens (see p95) and Mikhaylovskiy Gardens have long been popular with Petersburgers. For longer walks mixed with some architectural interest, two good areas to try are Kamenniy and Yelagin islands (see pp136–7), with their official residences and dachas, many dating from the early years of the 20th century.

For a romantic stroll around the city away from the traffic, walk along the Moyka or Griboedov canals (see pp134–5). To the south of Nevskiy prospekt, majestic buildings gradually give way to smaller, 19th-century residential blocks, complete with rows of trees by the waterside and leafy squares and courtyards.

Drivers have little respect for pedestrians and traffic is the main hindrance to walking. Cars drive on the right-hand side, so look left first when crossing the road. If there is an underpass, use it and, if not, look for a light-controlled crossing with red and green figures indicating pedestrian right of way. Crossings without lights are marked by a blue sign showing a pedestrian, but

Sign showing a pedestrian underpass

these are simply recommended crossing sites and drivers are not obliged to stop. Be warned that if you are caught crossing a road where there are no marked crossings, you are liable to be fined by a traffic policeman (see p205).

There are few bicycles on the roads, but cyclists tend to ignore traffic lights and signs of all descriptions, causing an additional hazard for the unwary pedestrian.

On the main city streets, dark blue sponsored nameplates give street names in Russian and English. Elsewhere, black-on-white street names are in Cyrillic only. Many maps, like the free pull-out in Neva News (see p209), give the main street names in Cyrillic and in transliteration. If you get lost, a dual-language map can be helpful when asking passersby for assistance.

Excellent walking tours in English, both general and on specialized topics, can be booked through **Cosmos** and the **MIR Travel Company** (see p203).

Mikhaylovskiy Gardens, behind the Russian Museum (see pp104–107)

Street signs indicating street directions and major shops

Travelling by Metro

Blue neon metro sign

SINCE OVERLAND TRANSPORT is the most efficient means of getting around the city centre, the metro is used mainly to get to and from the outskirts of the city. As a tourist attraction, however, the metro's stunning stations, intended by Stalin to be "palaces for the people", should be high on your itinerary. The metro is extremely safe and runs a full service until after midnight. Travelling in the late evening will avoid most of the two million people estimated to use the metro each day. The main setback is that signs are only in Cyrillic but, with just four lines, negotiating the network is still fairly straightforward.

Steep escalators to platforms

Exterior of Ploshchad Vosstaniya metro station

The metro now has 59 stations, ranging in style and ambience from the dim lighting and memorial atmosphere of Ploshchad Muzhestva (Courage Square, 1975) near Piskarovskoe Memorial Cemetery *(see p126)*, to the 1980s vulgarity of Udelnaya and the crisp, clean coldness of Sadovaya (1992).

is no rush hour as such but the metro tends to be full at most times of day which makes it very safe. Platforms are not staffed, but there is an attendant in a booth at the bottom of each escalator who can call for assistance.

Because of the many waterways in the city, stations are buried deep underground and long escalators lead down to the platforms. Stand on the right, leaving the left side free for those walking.

New stations are still being added, the latest ones being Krestovskiy Ostrov and Staraya Derevnya on the yellow line. Structural problems on the red line have resulted in its closure between Lesnaya and Ploshchad Muzhestva. A courtesy bus service runs between these stations.

THE METRO AS A TOURIST ATTRACTION

THE SOVIET UNION's best architects were employed to design St Petersburg's metro stations. Thousands of tonnes of marble, granite and limestone were used to face the walls, and sculptures, mosaics and chandeliers were commissioned from leading artists. The first line opened in 1955, its eight stations connecting ploshchad Vosstaniya with the new Stalinist blocks of flats in the southwest and the city's largest factory, the Kirov Factory. This line is one of the most fascinating, being the supreme embodiment of Stalinist style and ideals. The station at Kirovskiy Zavod is a fine example, a vast basilica, a temple to the factory workers. The line's crowning glory has to be Avtovo, incorporating a wealth of style and detail, even down to the moulded glass columns.

THE NETWORK

THE METRO is vital for getting to and from the further afield hotels and the airport. The four lines run from the outskirts through the centre, where they intersect at one of six main stations. Trains run every few minutes during the day and every five minutes late at night and, although doors into stations close at midnight, the last trains leave the centre ten minutes after this. There

Directional sign listing all stops on this line in Cyrillic

Interchange sign listing all stations on the other line

FINDING YOUR WAY

BEFORE setting foot in St Petersburg's metro, ensure you have a network map with the Cyrillic and transliterated names to hand. All signs inside the metro are in Cyrillic only and wall maps have become rare in station ticket halls and on the trains. Inside a station, the name is only written on the far wall of the platform which means that, if the train is in the station, or if you are on the train itself, it is not possible to see the sign.

Mosaics and unusual glass columns at richly decorated Avtovo metro station

Metro platform sign showing stations and interchanges

Busy stations in the city centre have a central concourse with safety doors between this and the trains. When the train stops, these doors open, and only then do the train doors open. At these stations, a map of the line you are on is to be found on the concourse. Other stations have platforms and the map of the line is on the wall on the far side of the tracks.

Before the train doors close, the driver will announce, "*Ostorozhno. Dveri zakryvayutsya*" (Be careful. The doors are closing). As the train approaches a stop, he will say the name of the station and mention if you need to change here for another line, followed by the name of the next station. It is always best to keep count of the stops, in case you do not catch the announcements.

To change to another line, follow the interchange signs for переход (*perekhod* – crossing). The exception is at Tekhnologicheskiy Institut, where the two southbound lines are on parallel platforms, as are the two northbound lines: thus to continue in the same direction on another line you simply cross the central concourse.

Exits are marked выход (*vykhod*). Some stations, such as of the Moskovskaya (for the airport) and Gostinyy Dvor, have two or more exits.

TICKETS AND TRAVEL CARDS

THE MOST COMMON means of paying for the metro is the token (*zheton*), purchasable only from metro stations, but also usable in some public phones (*see p208*). Magnetic cards, valid for ten or more trips, are also available. When travelling on the red line, due to the line closure between Lesnaya and Ploshchad Muz-

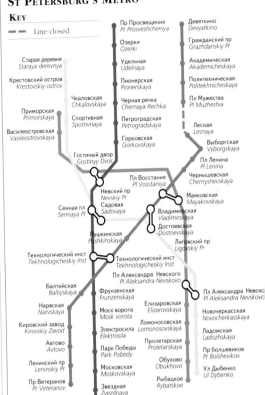

ST PETERSBURG'S METRO

KEY

- - - Line closed

Пр Просвещения / Pr Prosveshcheniya	Девяткино / Devyatkino
Озерки / Ozerki	Гражданский пр / Grazhdanskiy Pr
Старая деревня / Staraya derevnya	Академическая / Akademicheskaya
Удельная / Udelnaya	Политехническая / Politekhnicheskaya
Крестовский остров / Krestovskiy ostrov	Пионерская / Pionerskaya	Пл Мужества / Pl Muzhestva
Чкаловская / Chkalovskaya	Черная речка / Chernaya Rechka	Лесная / Lesnaya
Приморская / Primorskaya	Спортивная / Sportivnaya	Петроградская / Petrogradskaya	Выборгская / Vyborgskaya
Василеостровская / Vasileostrovskaya	Горьковская / Gorkovskaya	Пл Ленина / Pl Lenina
Гостиный двор / Gostinyy Dvor	Чернышевская / Chernyshevskaya
Невский пр / Nevskiy Pr	Пл Восстания / Pl Vosstaniya	Маяковская / Mayakovskaya
Сенная пл / Sennaya Pl	Садовая / Sadovaya	Владимирская / Vladimirskaya
Пушкинская / Pushkinskaya	Достоевская / Dostoevskaya
Технологический инст / Tekhnologicheskiy Inst	Лиговский пр / Ligovskiy Pr
	Технологический инст / Tekhnologicheskiy Inst
Балтийская / Baltiyskaya	Пл Александра Невского / Pl Aleksandra Nevskovo	Пл Александра Невск / Pl Aleksandra Nevskovo
Нарвская / Narvskaya	Фрунзенская / Frunzenskaya	
Кировский завод / Kirovskiy Zavod	Моск ворота / Mosk vorota	Елизаровская / Elizarovskaya	Новочеркасская / Novocherkasskaya
Автово / Avtovo	Электросила / Elektrosila	Ломоносовская / Lomonosovskaya	Ладожская / Ladozhskaya
Ленинский пр / Leninskiy Pr	Парк Победы / Park Pobedy	Пролетарская / Proletarskaya	Пр болшевиков / Pr Bolshevikov
Пр Ветеранов / Pr Veteranov	Московская / Moskovskaya	Обухово / Obukhovo	Ул Дыбенко / Ul Dybenko
	Звездная / Zvezdnaya	Рыбацкое / Rybatskoe
	Купчино / Kupchino	

hestva, you will have to take the courtesy bus part of the way so, for convenience, it is best to buy a single-journey magnetic transit (*tranzitnyy*) card, valid on all forms of public transport. The ticket can be reused when you continue your journey on the metro.

Barrier machines are installed at the top of the escalators; most take both cards and tokens. Cards must be inserted with the magnetic strip facing up. If you try to go through a machine without paying, an automatic barrier closes in front of you. At the far right an attendant checks passes and allows you to put your token in a machine which does not have automatic barriers. Those with magnetic cards cannot

Metro token

pass through this machine.

Monthly magnetic passes for the metro or for all forms of public transport are valid for 70 metro journeys and an infinite number of journeys on overground transport during a calendar month. They can only be purchased from the 10th to the 20th of the current month, and are valid until the 15th of the next month. There are no ticket checks once you are past the barriers inside the station.

Monthly travel cards, valid on all forms of city transport

Travelling by Tram, Bus and Trolleybus

Tram-stop sign, seen hanging over the rails

OVERGROUND TRANSPORT is crowded during the day, particularly at rush hour, but it is still the best way to make short trips around the city or simply to sightsee. In the centre of town, an array of tramline tracks and overhead tram and trolleybus cables crisscross many roads. Each form of transport has its advantages and disadvantages. Trolleybuses are frequent and conveniently routed but overcrowded; trams run on a less main-line route across town and are less busy but noisy; buses are usually sporadic. The newer outlying areas, however, are often accessible only by bus. On all forms of public transport you are unlikely to get a seat during the day; more frequent and comfortable, but more expensive, are the commercial bus and minibus routes.

People getting on a tram

TRAMS

TRAMS OFFER a marvellous way to see St Petersburg and are less crowded than trolleybuses. Tram stops are marked by red and white signs suspended on wires above the tram rails. Separate islands for people to embark are found only on wide roads outside the centre; elsewhere passengers wait on the pavement. When the tram doors open, the oncoming traffic is obliged to wait and let passengers cross to and from the pavement. In practice, there is always one car which cannot wait, so take care before stepping out.

At various crossroads along the route, the driver may need to change points on the rails. He will open his door or the front passenger door to do this. Do not attempt to board or exit a tram when it has stopped for this purpose.

Tram at a stop in front of the Mariinskiy Theatre

GENERAL INFORMATION

TRAMS, BUSES and trolleybuses start at around 5:30am, and a little later along the middle of the routes. The services operate with rather arbitrary frequency during the day and very infrequently after 11pm, grinding more or less to a halt around midnight. Only a few of the city bus routes display timetables. Each form of overground transport has its own separate stops, and distances between them can be great.

Queueing is not standard practice, so be prepared for an unruly rush to get on first. Trams, buses and trolleybuses can be boarded at the front, middle or back. The front eight seats are reserved for the disabled, the elderly and people with children, all of whom have precedence getting on and off at the front. On board, a conductor collects the fares.

As a stop approaches, people near an exit may be asked *Vy vykhodite?* ("are you getting out?"), which really means "could you move aside?". At busy times, head for the exit well before your stop, or prepare to do some pushing.

Good for sightseeing is the No. 10 trolleybus, which runs from ploshchad Vosstaniya through the centre and across Vasilevskiy Island (*see pp56–63*) to Primorskaya metro station. Other scenic routes are the No. 28 tram from the Field of Mars (*see p94*) to the Chern-aya Rechka metro station, the No. 22 bus from the Smolnyy Institute (*see p128*) via St Isaac's Square (*see p79*) and the Mariinskiy Theatre (*see p119*) towards the Stalinist architecture in the southwest, and the No. 46 bus from the Field of Mars up Kamennoostrovskiy prospekt (*see p70*) and onto Kamenniy Island (*see pp136–7*).

Sign for a bus stop, showing name of stop and bus numbers

BUSES AND MINIBUSES

BUSES OPERATE mostly on the outskirts of the city. All services run about every 20 minutes, sometimes less often. Bus stops in the city centre are marked by white signs with a red letter "A" for *autobus*, placed by the side of the road or attached to building walls. These are slowly replacing the old-style yellow signs.

Side view of a single section tram

City trolleybus on Nevskiy prospekt

A commercial bus on Vasilevskiy Island

Many routes are now duplicated by commercial buses or minibuses, marked with a "T" before the route number or with a "K". Fares on these buses are two to three times those on non-commercial equivalents, and are paid to the driver when getting on or off – just follow what other passengers do. These buses can be hailed or requested to stop anywhere along the route.

TROLLEYBUSES

TROLLEYBUSES ARE the most frequent form of transport along the city's main artery, Nevskiy prospekt. They offer convenient routes and stops around the city but are nearly always overcrowded. Ticket inspectors are most often on patrol on trolleybuses.

Trolleybus stops are marked by small blue and white signs suspended from wires, indicating the trolleybus numbers. On main roads, stops are also marked by other signs on building walls. These show what seems to be a flat-topped blue "M", but is in fact a Cyrillic "T" for *trolleybus*, on a white background.

The power rods on the roofs of the trolleybuses are known familiarly as "horns" (*roga*) or "little whiskers" (*usiki*). Occasionally these become detached from the overhead cables and the trolleybus lurches to a halt. It is the driver's responsibility to reattach them, causing a slight but generally negligible delay.

Trolleybus-stop sign on building wall

TICKETS AND TRAVEL CARDS

A FLAT FARE is payable on all forms of transport, whatever the length of the journey. Tickets are purchased from the conductor (who wears a red armband saying "Кондуктор") or, on commercial transport, from the driver. The ticket must be bought before the next stop after you got on, and large items of baggage must be paid for separately. Fines for non-payment can be imposed on the spot by plain-clothes inspectors. Check the inspector's identity document. Fines should not come to more than 100 roubles.

The cheapest way to travel in St Petersburg, if you are staying a few weeks or more, is to buy a monthly or half-monthly card for all forms of transport, including the metro (*see pp214–15*). The magnetic monthly card, or *yedinyy bilet*, is valid from the 16th of the current month until the 15th of the next, and can be bought from the 10th to the 20th of the current month. Half-monthly *yedinyy bilety* run from the 1st until the 15th of the month, and can be purchased from the last day of the current month to the 5th of the next month. Separate monthly cards are also sold for each form of transport. Travel cards are valid for trips to Tsarskoe Selo and Pavlovsk, but not Peterhof, Gatchina or Oranienbaum (*see pp220–21*).

Waiting at a trolleybus stop on Nevskiy prospekt, near ploshchad Vosstaniya

Canal and River Cruises

Sign for water taxi

ST PETERSBURG'S NUMEROUS natural waterways were adapted and added to, to make it resemble Peter the Great's beloved Amsterdam (see pp20–21). Indeed, it would be true to say the city vies with Amsterdam for the title "Venice of the North".

A wide selection of cruises, for small and large groups, in open and closed boats, depart from bridges along Nevskiy prospekt. They offer marvellous opportunities to see more of the city, especially for those unable to walk long distances. Forming part of any cruise are the broad Fontanka river with its Neo-Classical palaces, the leafy Moyka river with its ironwork bridges, and the Griboedov canal which twists and turns its way through southwest St Petersburg. Bring a bottle of champagne, a picnic and a warm jumper and just relax.

NEVA CRUISES

A VARIETY OF BOATS cruise up and down the Neva between the Gulf of Finland and the River Station (Rechnoy vokzal) to the southeast. The trips, operating hourly between 10am and 10pm, last an hour. Foreigners pay more than the locals, but the tickets are not expensive and can be bought on the landing stage or on the boat. The boats leave from the landing stage opposite the Bronze Horseman on Decembrists' Square, and from the one near the main entrance of the Hermitage (see p75).

These boat trips are a pleasant way of passing the time rather than a serious sightseeing opportunity. Food and drink are usually served and, in the evenings, alcohol is available on some of the boats.

Luxury catered cruises can be booked in advance. **MIR** and **Russkiye Kruizy** offer a variety of routes along the Neva and along a number of the city's many canals.

Canal cruise on the Moyka

GENERAL INFORMATION

THE WEATHER plays a vital role in determining the exact time of year canal cruises start and finish. Most boats operate daily from mid-May to late September. Their routes also vary because regular construction work, reinforcing the granite embankments, sometimes prevents movement along small parts of the canals.

The Gulf of Finland is tidal and this affects the Neva and inland waterways. Strong winds can cause the water level to rise significantly and all boat trips may then be cancelled.

GUIDED CANAL TRIPS

LARGE, COVERED cruise boats depart every 30 minutes, between 11:30am and 8pm, from the Anichkov Bridge on Nevskiy prospekt (see p49).

Tickets for the next available boat should be purchased from the kiosk on the embankment, although, if the queues are long, tickets may be sold in advance for later cruises on the same day. The trip lasts 70 minutes and takes in the Moyka, Griboedov and Fontanka. Weather permitting, the boats usually go out onto the Neva, from where there are superb views of the whole city.

Ticket kiosk for canal trip, Anichkov Bridge

Foreigners pay around $5 in roubles for these trips, slightly more than the Russians. The guided tour is in Russian only. Large groups are advised to book in advance, through the kiosk or by phone, especially during school holidays. Boat trips providing guided tours in English can be booked through any of the major hotels.

During hot weather, it can get very stuffy and confined inside the boats. The visibility through the scratched perspex windows can also be less than perfect at times. If you wish to stand outside to see more, there is a platform at the back of the boat for which there may be an extra charge. Take your own soft drinks and sandwiches, as these are rarely available on board these cruises.

Cruise boat on the Neva with the Hermitage and Palace Embankment in the background

Water taxis moored on Griboedov canal near Kazanskiy most by Nevskiy prospekt

WATER TAXIS

WATER TAXIS are similar to private motorboats, carrying anything from 4 to 20 people. During White Nights, boats run late into the night.

For a small boat, wait at the landing stage on the north side of Politseyskiy most where Nevskiy prospekt *(see pp46–9)* crosses the Moyka, or alongside the Gostinyy Dvor metro station on the Griboedov canal close to Kazanskiy most. Larger boats may need to be negotiated at least a couple of hours in advance to ensure their availability.

Prices are negotiable, but generally range from about $30 to $50 an hour, depending on the size of the boat and the route you decide to follow. One hour takes you along the inland waterways, but an extra half hour includes the Neva, crossing over to go round the Peter and Paul Fortress *(see pp66–7)* and giving a good view of all the

Water taxis on the Moyka by Politseyskiy most

waterfronts. Most drivers can at least point out major sights in English, others can give you a basic guided tour. If you ask in advance, it may be possible to find an English-speaking guide. Boats can be booked in advance on payment of a small deposit, but are generally plentiful and are best picked up spontaneously.

Since the boats are open and it can be cold on the waterways, particularly at night, warm clothing is necessary, even during the summer months. There is usually at least one blanket on board for anyone who is unequipped. Pilots allow you to do more or less as you like on board the boat as long as it is safe, and tend to be undisturbed by the noise of popping champagne corks or other sounds of merrymaking.

Taxis

ST PETERSBURG's official yellow taxis are gradually being replaced by unmetered private cabs. Most locals, however, use the cheaper alternative of catching a *chastnik*, effectively hitching a ride in any passing vehicle.

St Petersburg's bright yellow taxi

OFFICIAL TAXIS

THE CITY'S DISTINCTIVE yellow official taxi fleet has in recent years faced tough competition from expensive private taxi firms which run imported modern cars. The private taxis, which usually charge a flat fare agreed in àdvance, tend to monopolize certain areas near many major hotels, restaurants, bars and the airport. In order to save money, try hailing a yellow cab a short distance away from such places.

Whatever type of taxi you choose to take, always name your destination before getting in. Taxis are not obliged to take you, and they may well refuse, or simply drive away if they do not wish to go in the same direction as you. Taxi fares are relatively cheap. Newer yellow cabs are fitted with modern meters, which indicate the sum to be paid, but meters in the older taxis are unreliable or simply switched off. For this reason it is wise to agree on a price before starting out on the journey to avoid unnecessary confusion. If you feel you have been over-charged however, it is worth disputing the matter.

In some areas, official taxis are not readily available, and you must either book one by phone or hope for a *chastnik*.

CHASTNIKI

FOR MANY YEARS Russians have been used to flagging down the drivers of private cars, which are easier to locate and often cheaper to use than official taxis. Thus, as soon as you stick your hand out to hail a taxi, as likely as not, a private car will stop. Some of the cars are not overly salubrious, but the driver is likely to be more willing with baggage than official taxi drivers, and the fares are often considerably cheaper. Exercise reasonable caution by not getting into any car with more than the driver already in it. Neither private cars or taxis are particularly recommended if you are travelling alone at night.

As with ordinary taxis, name your destination and, if the driver agrees, be sure to settle a price before setting off.

St Petersburgers flagging down a *chastnik*, or private car

Travelling out of St Petersburg

Every weekend during the summer, and even in winter, a large proportion of locals leave the city. They head for their *dacha* or for the woods, to gather seasonal fruits and vegetables, go cross-country skiing or visit one of the former imperial summer residences. Buses and suburban trains operate frequently throughout the year and are the usual means of transport to access sites out of town. Peterhof is a unique exception in being accessible by hydrofoil across the Gulf of Finland. Foreigners tend to take coach excursions out of town but, with a bit of planning, travelling independently can be part of the fun.

Passengers boarding suburban train at Vitebsk Station

Interior view of one of St Petersburg's suburban trains

SUBURBAN TRAINS

These are the most convenient way to visit most of the outlying sights. Tickets can be bought from the local cash desks *(prigorodnyye kassy)* at each station, where a timetable is displayed. Return tickets are no cheaper than two singles. Note that smoking is prohibited and that, between the hours of 10am and midday, there is often a break in the timetable.

Style-Moderne architecture in Vitebsk station restaurant

GETTING TO TSARSKOE SELO AND PAVLOVSK

Trains for Tsarskoe Selo *(see pp150–53)* and Pavlovsk *(see pp156–9)* depart every 20 minutes from **Vitebsk Station**. The line was originally built for the royal family to reach their summer residences and the station is a marvellous example of Style-Moderne architecture. The ticket office is on the right of the main building. All local trains take about 25 minutes, stopping first at Tsarskoe Selo (Detskoe Selo), then Pavlovsk.

At Detskoe Selo station, the 382 and 371 buses go to Tsarskoe Selo, stopping near the palace. At Pavlovsk, the train station is opposite the entrance to the park, through which it is a pleasant half-hour walk to the palace, or you can catch bus No. 370, 383 or 493. The 370, 383 and 545 buses also run between Pavlovsk palace and Detskoe Selo station. City bus tickets and monthly passes continue to be valid here.

The No. 287 bus and a host of minibuses run to Tsarskoe Selo from Moskovskaya metro.

GETTING TO PETERHOF AND ORANIENBAUM

There are suburban trains for Peterhof *(see pp146–9)* and Oranienbaum *(see pp144–5)* departing every 20 minutes from **Baltic Station**. The trains that reach Oranienbaum are those destined for Kalishche, or Oranienbaum itself.

For Peterhof, get off the train at Novyy Petergof (40 minutes from town), from where it is ten minutes to the palace on bus 348, 350, 351, 352 or 356.

By far the easiest and most pleasant way to get to Peterhof during the summer months is by hydrofoil, which costs about $12 in roubles each way.

Oranienbaum is the first stop after the Gulf of Finland comes into view an hour into the journey. Turn right out of the station and walk about 200 m (650 ft) to the main road. Almost directly opposite is the entrance to the park, and from here it is only a five minute walk to the Great Palace or into the heart of the park.

GETTING TO GATCHINA

Trains run approximately every half hour from **Baltic Station** to Gatchina *(see p145)* and the journey takes an hour. Opposite Gatchina train station is a short road leading directly to the square in front of the palace. Trains also run from **Warsaw Station**, arriving at a different station in the town, further from the palace.

Alternatively, there is a bus No. 431 as well as regular, fast minibuses running from Moskovskaya metro station. On this particular suburban route, city bus tickets and monthly passes are not valid.

GETTING TO REPINO AND THE GULF OF FINLAND

For Repino (*see p144*) and the Gulf of Finland, trains depart every 20 minutes or so from **Finland Station**. Tickets should be bought at cash desks within the main building. Avoid any train marked Beloostrov or Krugovoy.

At Repino, cross the main road, head down the hill towards the Gulf of Finland and turn left onto the asphalt road until you reach Penaty.

Bus No. 411 also runs to Repino and stops right outside Penaty. The bus leaves from Chernaya Rechka metro.

Coach No. 948 to Novgorod

GETTING TO NOVGOROD

Coach No. 948 leaves for Novgorod (*see pp160–63*) every two hours from **Coach Station**. A quicker alternative to the four-hour coach journey is to travel on the weekend by train. The weekend train sets off from **Moscow Station** at 5:20pm and takes two-and-a-half hours. It returns to St Petersburg around 11am.

DRIVING IN ST PETERSBURG

Car hire is still not widely available in Russia and, at present, cars and minibuses in St Petersburg can usually be hired only with company drivers, for example, from a company such as **Cosmos**. **Hertz** are the only exception, and their prices are much higher than in Europe.

For the few who do find themselves at the wheel, there are a number of things to bear in mind. An international licence is obligatory, as well as international insurance and documents proving you have the right to be driving the car, eg registration documents or a hire agreement bearing your name, failing that a witnessed power of attorney in Russian from the registered owner. Traffic policemen (*see p205*) have the right to stop you and check your documents. They can also fine you on the spot for minor infringements, such as having a dirty number plate, not having a first-aid kit, or more serious offences such as drink-driving. Drivers are not allowed to drink any alcohol whatsoever. The traffic police are highly active as they regard fining drivers as a means to increasing their income.

Local drivers tend to ignore rules of the road and do more or less as they like, so be on your guard. Drive on the right and make no left turns on any main roads unless a road sign indicates that it is permitted.

In winter conditions, driving requires studded tyres as chains can be damaged on tram lines and vice versa. It is also advisable not to use your handbrake in cold weather as it has a tendency to freeze.

Unleaded petrol is rarely available and you should use nothing lower than grade 98 petrol. There is a charge for parking in most parts of the city centre. The Nevskij Palace and Europe hotels (*see p173*) have 24-hour security parking which is recommended since car theft is a fairly popular business in St Petersburg.

СТОП

Road sign in Russian indicating driver must stop

THE HYDROFOIL TO PETERHOF

Hydrofoil arriving at the Hermitage landing stage

The most enjoyable and by far the most scenic way to reach the imperial summer palace of Peterhof is the 45-minute trip across the Gulf of Finland by hydrofoil. The service runs from early June until early October and sets off from the second landing stage outside the Hermitage (*see p75*) where a weekly timetable is posted. Generally hydrofoils operate every hour from 9:30am with the last boat returning at 6pm. Buy your return ticket on arrival at Peterhof. A fee is charged to enter the lower park and this ticket is needed to get back into the park to return by hydrofoil.

ST PETERSBURG STREET FINDER

THE KEY MAP below shows the areas of St Petersburg covered by the *Street Finder*. The map references given throughout the guide for sights, restaurants, hotels, shops or entertainment venues refer to the maps in this section. All the major sights have been clearly marked so they are easy to locate. The key below shows other features marked on the

Pausing on the steps of Kazan Cathedral

maps, such as post offices, metro stations, ferry stops and churches. The *Street Finder* index lists street names in transliteration, followed by Cyrillics (on the maps, Cyrillics are only given for major roads). This guide uses the now reinstated old Russian street names, rather than the Soviet versions *(see p201)*. Places of interest are listed by their English name.

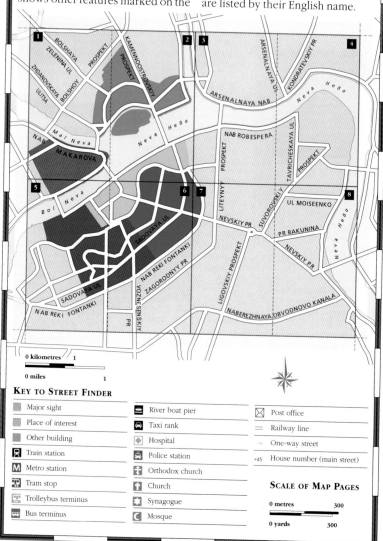

0 kilometres 1

0 miles 1

KEY TO STREET FINDER

Major sight	River boat pier	Post office
Place of interest	Taxi rank	Railway line
Other building	Hospital	One-way street
Train station	Police station	«45 House number (main street)
Metro station	Orthodox church	
Tram stop	Church	**SCALE OF MAP PAGES**
Trolleybus terminus	Synagogue	0 metres 300
Bus terminus	Mosque	0 yards 300

Street Finder Index

ABBREVIATIONS & USEFUL WORDS

ul	ulitsa	street
pl	ploshchad	square
pr	prospekt	avenue
per	pereulok	lane
	most	bridge
	sad	garden
	shosse	road

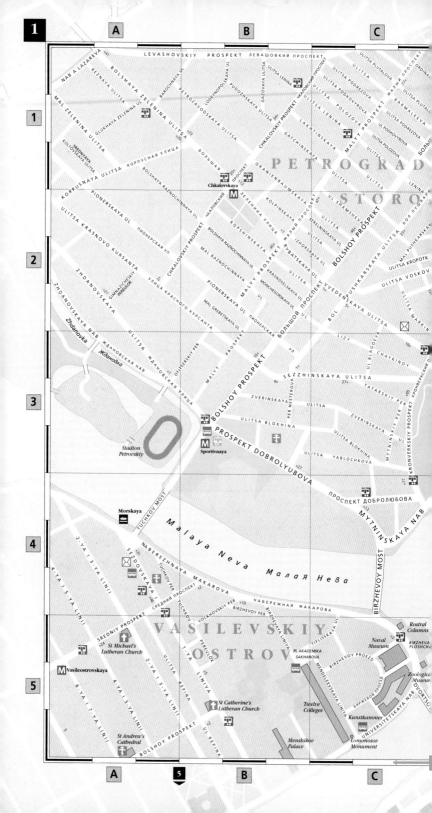